Crisis and Challenge in the Roman Catholic Church

Crisis and Challenge in the Roman Catholic Church

Perspectives on Decline and Reformation

Edited by
Debra Meyers and Mary Sue Barnett

LEXINGTON BOOKS
Lanham • Boulder • New York • London

Published by Lexington Books
An imprint of The Rowman & Littlefield Publishing Group, Inc.
4501 Forbes Boulevard, Suite 200, Lanham, Maryland 20706
www.rowman.com

6 Tinworth Street, London SE11 5AL, United Kingdom

British Library Cataloguing in Publication Information Available

Library of Congress Cataloging-in-Publication Data Available

ISBN 978-1-7936-0491-0 (cloth : alk. paper)
ISBN 978-1-7936-0492-7 (electronic)

∞™ The paper used in this publication meets the minimum requirements of American National Standard for Information Sciences—Permanence of Paper for Printed Library Materials, ANSI/NISO Z39.48-1992.

Contents

Introduction

Crisis and Challenge in the Roman Catholic Church: Perspectives on Decline and Reformation

Debra Meyers

When the iconic symbol of European Roman Catholicism—Notre Dame Cathedral in Paris—burned on April 15, 2019, the entire world seemed to stop and watch the riveting footage of the implosion of the steeple and roof. Many believed that the building's collapse mirrored the current collapse of the institutional church's power and authority. Thomas Reese noted that "the building is as much a symbol of the recent history of the Catholic Church in Europe as it once was a symbol of the Church's power and cultural supremacy. The church had been in disrepair for decades." He notes that in recent years, "Notre Dame was more a tourist destination than a place of pilgrimage or a seat of Catholic potency. . . . This spiritual emptiness didn't come overnight." Reese suggests that the decay of the church began as early as the eighteenth century when the hierarchy joined forces with the European nobility to ward off the omnipresent waves of modernization. The church opposed freedoms of the press, free speech, as well as religious liberty. "By opposing political freedoms and unions in the nineteenth century, the church lost European men. In its opposition to feminism, it lost women" in the twentieth century.[1]

Despite this massive exodus from the church pews, Auxiliary Bishop Robert Barron of Los Angeles urges Catholics to remain in the pews and work for a better church as the sexual abuse allegations and their subsequent cover-up by the church hierarchy keep pouring in from every corner of the United States and many other nations as well. Barron refers to the current situation as "choppy waters" that make it difficult for Catholics to navigate.[2] More than 5,000 clerics in the United States alone have been credibly accused of sexual abuse, with few sanctions by religious authorities or civil law enforcement despite mountains of indictments. "Before 2018's landmark Pennsylvania grand jury report, which named more than 300 predator priests accused of abusing more than 1,000 children in six dioceses, the official lists of credibly accused priests added up to fewer than 1,500 names nationwide. Now, within the span of a little more than a year, more than 100 dioceses and religious orders have come forward with *thousands of names*—but often little other information that can be used to alert the public."[3] In fact, many defrocked priests now hold positions of trust as foster parents, counselors, educators, social workers, and medical personnel.[4] They live near schools and they volunteer at churches—they avoid being identified in formal background checks because they have not been prosecuted in secular courts for their crimes.

In an effort to keep people from fleeing the church amid the gross mismanagement of the abuse scandal, Bishop Barron argues that the church has *always* been "marked to varying degrees by sin, scandal, stupidity, misbehavior, misfortune, and wickedness" and the current sexual abuse crisis is merely a continuation of this "darkness."[5] He is correct in his assertion that the church has seen its share of corruption and scandal. Certainly, the Inquisition and the subsequent torture and killing of thousands of innocent men and women left its unmistakable mark on the church. Yet, the list of church "darkness" is much longer and more corrosive. This long list includes the selling of indulgences to get into heaven that led to the Protestant movement, murderous popes like John XII (d. 964), rapist popes like Benedict IX (d. 1056c.), the selling of high offices—including the papacy—to wealthy families like the Borgias, popes who waged wars and sometimes fought in them like Julius II (d. 1513), and the Great Schism when three popes ruled Christendom at the same time. These are only some highlights of this long list of "darkness."[6]

However, viewing the current "darkness" from a historical continuum is neither helpful nor instructive and it certainly does not offer Catholics a way forward. The current crisis is deeply rooted in a dysfunctional clericalism whose hierarchical structure is anachronistic to most Catholics' lives in the twenty-first century.[7] In addition to the horrific global sexual abuse crisis and subsequent ecclesiastic cover-up that includes the Vatican, the church is dealing with numerous deeply rooted issues that could ultimately lead to its demise. The following chapters help us to uncover a limited number of these potentially fatal problems while offering some possible alternatives to the current state of the church.

The chapters in this volume address institutional dysfunctions in the Roman Catholic Church today, with a particular emphasis on misogyny and sex abuse in the church, as well as women's inequality more generally. The first five chapters provide us with wide-ranging examinations of some of the struggles the current church hierarchy faces grounded in comprehensive contexts. In outlining feminist theology and practice, Mary Hunt's chapter, "After the Smoke Clears," provides us a solid survey of the contributions Catholic feminism can make as we address the institutional dysfunctions discussed in later chapters. Paul Tenkotte, in chapter 2 "Cleaning the Church Attic," clearly articulates the interaction of eternal truths and the imperative of embracing change if the church is to continue. In chapter 3, Pierre Hegy, in "Crisis and Opportunities Since Vatican II," suggests ways in which *Humanae Vitae* on birth control, liberation theology, and the 1983 Code of Canon Law addressing clerical sex abuse, continue to impact the church today. Miriam Duignan's "Grave Injustice and Great Deception" outlines the flawed arguments behind the official church ban on women's ordination and the fertile ground on which Catholic women can recover the true mission of the Catholic Church. In chapter 5 "The Deconstruction of Clerical Hegemony," Sylvia Hübel fleshes out the connections between clericalism, censorship, and institutional misogyny more broadly.

Chapters 6–10 focus more narrowly on the direct impact church doctrine and practice have had on the people in the pews. Siobhan Fleming sheds light on the Archdiocese of Galveston–Houston, Texas, in chapter 6 to uncover explicit episcopal mismanagement of clerical pedophiles. In chapter 7, Tara Tuttle describes the MeToo movement's influence on the media's interest in the hidden sexual violence perpetrated by clergy on women religious. Jo Scott-Coe's "The Perfect Victim" in chapter 8 describes the interaction of childhood sexual trauma with Catholic misogyny, catechism, and the practice of confession. Mary Sue Barnett creates a pathway to reconnect with divine feminism as a means to rise above institutional misogyny in chapter 9. And we end this investigation into the current institutional malaise with an essay on the connections between Catholic teaching and the proliferation of domestic abuse in Catholic homes in chapter 10, "I Am Heartily Sorry."

This collection of chapters makes a valuable contribution to current discussions focused on institutional reform with every new report on clerical sexual abuse, its institutional cover-up, and the deliberate abdication of responsibility for their victims. Many of the topics included in this book have been largely neglected in previous publications focused on church reform; namely, clerical abuse of women religious, in-depth investigations into handling of abuse allegations in a specific archdiocese, as well as the inadequacy of the church's response to any allegations that threaten the preeminence of the male hierarchy. This unique collection of chapters centers on the dominance of inequality in the church as the predicate for much of the institution's malaise today.

NOTES

1. Thomas Reese, "Notre Dame, Long a Symbol of Catholicism in Europe, Becomes a Picture of Its Collapse," *National Catholic Reporter*, April 16, 2019, https://www.ncronline.org/news/opinion/signs-times/notre-dame-long-symbol-catholicism-europe-becomes-picture-its-collapse.

2. Bishop Robert Barron, *Letter to a Suffering Church: A Bishop Speaks on the Sexual Abuse Crisis* (Park Ridge, IL: Word on Fire Catholic Ministries, 2019) preface.

3. Emphasis added. [Claudia Lauer and Meghan Hoyer, "Without Oversight, Scores of Accused Priests Commit Crimes," *The Salt Lake Tribune*, October 7, 2019, https://www.sltrib.com/religion/2019/10/07/without-oversight-scores/.]

4. Defrocking, commonly referred to as laicization, is a formal removal from ordination responsibilities by the Church.

5. Barron, *Letter to a Suffering Church,* 41.

6. See, for instance, John Carr, *The Pope's Army: The Papacy in Diplomacy and War* (Pen and Sword Military, 2019); Eamon Duffy, *Saints and Sinners: A History of the Popes* (Yale Nota Bene, 2006); and John Norman Davidson Kelly, *The Oxford Dictionary of Popes* (Oxford University Press, 1986).

7. See, for instance, James Carroll, "Abolish the Priesthood," *The Atlantic*, June 2019, https://www.theatlantic.com/magazine/archive/2019/06/to-save-the-church-dismantle-the-priesthood/588073/.

BIBLIOGRAPHY

Barron, Robert. *Letter to a Suffering Church: A Bishop Speaks On the Sexual Abuse Crisis.* Park Ridge, Illinois: Word on Fire Catholic Ministries, 2019.

Carr, John. *The Pope's Army: The Papacy in Diplomacy and War.* Pen and Sword Military, 2019.

Carroll, James. "Abolish the Priesthood." *The Atlantic*, June 2019, https://www.theatlantic.com/magazine/archive/2019/06/to-save-the-church-dismantle-the-priesthood/588073/.

Duffy, Eamon. *Saints and Sinners: A History of the Popes.* Yale Nota Bene, 2006.

Kelly, John Norman Davidson. *The Oxford Dictionary of Popes.* Oxford University Press, 1986.

Lauer, Claudia and Hoyer, Meghan. "Without Oversight, Scores of Accused Priests Commit Crimes." *The Salt Lake Tribune*, October 7, 2019, https://www.sltrib.com/religion/2019/10/07/without-oversight-scores/.

Reese, Thomas. "Notre Dame, Long a Symbol of Catholicism in Europe, Becomes a Picture of Its Collapse." *National Catholic Reporter*, April 16, 2019, https://www.ncronline.org/news/opinion/signs-times/notre-dame-long-symbol-catholicism-europe-becomes-picture-its-collapse.

Chapter 1

After the Smoke Clears

Insights and Challenges from Feminist Catholicism

Mary E. Hunt

When altar candles are blown out after Mass, some smoke remains. Eventually that smoke dissipates revealing a new reality. People trickle out of the church, much as they arrived, going their separate ways, hopefully to love and do justice. The Roman Catholic Church as an institution is in an analogous situation. It is imploding; people are leaving. As the smoke left behind begins to give way, clearer paths forward come into view. To that end, I offer insights and challenges from a feminist perspective about what comes next.

I think of this feminist approach as a kind of speculative ecclesiology grounded in deep respect for the Catholic tradition and high hopes for its potential to be part of the creation of a just and fruitful world. I lay out some of the contours of the context in which the implosion is happening. Then I offer some analytic observations of how and why things have played out as they have, combined with some possible ways forward. I limit my perspective largely to the western sector which I know best, cognizant of the complexity of a global church. I conclude with my underlying commitment, namely, that the needs of the world and not the failings of the church should set the agenda at this liminal time.

Astonishing changes have transformed Catholicism in the seventy years from 1950 to 2020. Beginning with the achievements of Vatican II, first under the leadership of Pope John XXIII to bring about significant cultural if not structural changes, new articulations of an ancient faith tradition emerged. The impact was to open the church in ways that included encouraging religious communities to shape their own styles of life according to their individual charismas; shifting to the vernacular for sacraments, especially Eucharist, to foster greater inclusion and participation; openness to the wisdom of other world religions; and eventually (1983) a revision of Canon Law which reflected some of the spirit, if not the letter, of the conciliar era in the church's legal structure. There was a sense that a medieval church was coming into the modern age though postmodernity was dawning quickly.

New ideas surfaced, especially in moral theology. For example, birth control and abortion became topics of public conversation though not agreed upon consensus. Just as swiftly, the doors and windows of Catholicism were slammed shut a few years later. Catholicism would never be the same again. Once Catholics tasted the nectar of inclusion, participation, and equality, in however abstemious sips, many were hooked. Simultaneously, many Protestant denominations were moving forward with women clergy, struggles over the participation of LGBTIQ people, and the like while Catholics were still adjusting to a priest who presided looking at the congregation instead of with his back to the people. Catholics had a long way to go.

An important reason for the insistence on more inclusive, participatory, and egalitarian forms of church was because women joined the theological fray and brought with us a focus on gender in a church characterized by gender apartheid. We joined liberation theologians who were doing similar work, albeit from economic and racial starting points. Just as women were asking questions about the gender of God and the hegemony of males in clergy and family life, Latin American liberationists were exploring a role for Marxist economic theory and other social scientific tools in theological reflection. African American theologians insisted that Jesus always favored the oppressed, including people of color. People from economically marginalized countries and from oppressed racial/ethnic groups, mainly people of African descent and Latinx folks, entered successfully, although still in small numbers, into the idea making process that we call theology. They, like women, wanted to be agents of their own theologies, not subjects of religious colonialism.

The entrance of women in large numbers into the study and practice of religion, virtually all religions, was one of the most significant changes in modern religious history. So when Latin American women, women of African descent, Asian, and indigenous women started to do theology, things really began to change. They challenged white western women as much as they challenged men of color to hear their voices, take seriously their ways of being religious, and pave the way for more variety and diversity than most people dreamed possible. This means that there are now a wide range of feminist approaches, complicating the work in a positive and authentic way among Catholics.

In the subsequent pontificates of Popes John Paul II and Benedict XVII, the same doors and windows that had been flung open were closed in desperate attempts to return the institution to its pre-Vatican theological and ecclesiastical ways. Those efforts were quite effective given the top-down power of the papacy. The placement of conservative clerics in both the dicasteries in Rome and in episcopal and diplomatic postings around the world added weight to conservatizing forces. Tensions emerged and persist between the so-called conservative and so-called liberal Catholics (the terms are contested but roughly descriptive of the reality) with conservatives wielding far greater economic clout and media attention.

Catholic feminists have long rejected what theologian Elisabeth Schüssler Fiorenza helpfully defined as the "kyriarchal" church.[1] "Kyriarchy" or structures of lordship is the inter-structured forms of oppression that create conditions for injustice. The institutional Roman Catholic Church is set up that way with literal lords: clergy over laity, men over women, religious over secular, and so forth. Feminists in religion have joined Professor Schüssler Fiorenza for decades in creating bountiful research and resources, journals, blogs, and publishing projects, all alternative ways of thinking, structuring and acting that are inclusive, participatory, and egalitarian. We were ahead of the curve on intersectionality, critically analyzing and linking race, sex, gender, class, nationality, age, ability, and so forth in trying to do justice.

What sticks in the craw of traditionalists is that progressive religious women—like women rabbis, or even the new Roman Catholic women priests who are ordained variously outside of the institutional structures—do not back off of the identity from which women are supposedly excluded. Women rabbis are Jews, after all, and Catholic women priests are Catholic women priests even if the institutional church does not recognize them and tries to excommunicate them. These are not matters simply of semantics, but of how real people live their lives and go about their ministry.

Women around the world have created small base communities as well as theological, ethical, and spiritual resources to thwart kyriarchy and construct viable new forms of being religious. With formerly Catholic philosopher Mary Daly, feminists have left aside "God the Father" and the trappings of a patriarchal church.[2] Many call ourselves "Catholic," claiming the tradition as our birth or baptismal right, and calling out the institutional church that has so studiously insisted on male-only leadership, a male gaze at scripture, and a deeply misogynist worldview with disastrous results. We assert that we, too, are what "Catholic" looks like, refusing to grant the institution the power that belongs to all. Moreover, we see that the everyday ministerial needs of people—for pastoral care and education, for sacraments and solidarity—do not change in the face of gender discrimination. That is the impetus to act as church for social justice as well as for the sake of coherence with the Gospel message.

Catholic women's history includes monasteries and religious congregations, women's work as theologians and liturgists, as medical and educational professionals, as founders and heads of hospitals, schools, and universities. Catholic women are currently serving at the U.S. southern border welcoming immigrants and refugees. Some lead the way against sex trafficking. Others, including those at NETWORK, the Catholic social justice lobby known for the Nuns on the Bus, are involved in politics. They insist on a national budget centered on the common good with a preferential option for those made poor by an unjust economic system. Still others are working to end the death penalty like Sr. Helen Prejean of *Dead Man Walking* fame.

Fast forward to the pontificate of Francis (2013). There were both high expectations engendered by his personal simplicity and the deep backlash he experienced from those who saw his election as an affront to orthodoxy. The first six years have been largely mixed with a clear trajectory toward attention to ecological and economic questions that have global impact, concrete actions for refugees and against war, some small changes in ecclesial functioning especially in the area of finances, and a tiny opening on same-sex questions. But he has, albeit with a smile, maintained the same postures as his predecessors on women in leadership. Save for a few committee appointments, contested issues—including reproductive justice, women in priesthood and diaconate, in essence, those Catholic brand issues that reinforce traditionalist identity—marginalize half of the membership, reduce the community's people power, and function as a bulwark for mistreatment of women in other areas of life remain as before. A strong group of nuns from India recently issued a call for "due process" in their ecclesial setting, condemning "toxic masculinity and femininity."[3] Their insistence on rights shows how widespread this movement has become.

Ironically, the rest of the world is now catching up with Catholic feminists as the Catholic institution stands in global disrepute and soon in financial ruin. Recent reports of Catholic clergy's criminal conduct and its cover-up by church officials at the highest levels signal an end to the Roman Catholic Church as we knew it in the United States and in many other parts of the world.[4] Damage is just coming to the fore in countries like India where the patterns of abuse of power replicate those in the West.

Catholics were 20 percent of the U.S. population in 2018, 51 million adults which is roughly 3 million fewer than in 2007. The percentage of U.S. Catholics who attend weekly Mass dropped by 6 percent from 2014 to 2017 with current figures well under 40 percent.[5] Scholars report that Catholic remain the single largest denomination in this country with former Catholics making up the second largest.

American Catholics are very similar to those in many European countries like Spain and formerly Catholic Ireland where the church's market share has shrunk. In Chile, where a major scandal unfolded such that all of the bishops were forced to tender their resignations, the numbers are plummeting.

Ten years ago, 73 percent of Chileans called themselves Catholic. The current percentage is 45 and dropping. There are reports that in Latin America as a whole numbers are down 20 percent in the same period.[6] Those are noticeable drops that make a difference in revenues and culture.

Clergy sexual abuse and its cover-up is a powerful engine for the implosion of the institution. The movie *Spotlight* (2015) highlighted the problem in the Archdiocese of Boston focusing on the first decade or so of the twenty-first century though the problem goes back many decades. Through dogged reporting, *The Boston Globe* chronicled myriad cases of abuse and consistent efforts on the part of local church officials, including now disgraced Cardinal Bernard Law, to stonewall legal actions to bring the guilty to justice.

In 2018, a Pennsylvania Grand Jury Report documented over 1,000 children raped and abused by more than 300 priests in just that one state.[7] There are forty-nine more states where similar investigations need to be done with some already in process.[8] Officials give every assurance that the real numbers of victims/survivors are many times higher than reported. The Pennsylvania report revealed that bishops routinely reassigned criminal clergy rather than prohibit them from ministry much less prosecute them. Some religious orders have made public their lists of abusers as well though statutes of limitations in many states keep perpetrators from the law.

This is a national problem as clergy and religious have been moved around as if on a giant chessboard from parish to parish within a diocese, or from diocese to diocese across the country. While I used to think there were ideological differences between Catholic feminists and hierarchical church leaders, now I realize we were also up against a criminal element. The same is true of many religious orders whose leaders often protected their members instead of victims.

The stories are numerous and consistent in pattern: a patriarchal, hierarchical church with all-male, allegedly celibate leadership replete with an unwritten policy of "don't ask, don't tell" on sex in general; clergy with unfettered access to young people and publicly unaccountable relationships with adults; and attempts at monetary settlements to silence victims and hide the problems. These add up to a convergence of dangerous and finally destructive factors leading to crimes and abuse. The net result is a crisis of confidence that has led millions of Catholics to leave their faith of origin or choice, many with no plans to return.

For example, former Washington DC cardinal Theodore McCarrick is now Mr. McCarrick, living in exile in a Kansas monastery. His successor, Cardinal Donald Wuerl, had his mandatory (at age seventy-five) resignation accepted quickly. He left under a cloud with more than 600 mentions of him in the Pennsylvania Grand Jury Report for his handling of abuse allegations against priests when he was bishop of Pittsburgh and his apparent lying about what he knew and when he knew about then cardinal McCarrick's activities.

West Virginia Bishop Michael Bransford is currently under investigation for spending millions of dollars from one of the poorest states in the union on lavish air and limousine travel, hotels, and housing for himself. Then there are the gifts he gave to his friends, including the Bishop of Baltimore, William Lori, who was put in charge of investigating him. Bishop Lori conveniently left out of his investigation report the names of the priests to whom the offending bishop had given money, including his own name. Both men are still in office at this writing. The sheer volume, scope, and audacity of these cases is cause of scandal, not to mention the crimes themselves, even though they have not yet been adjudicated.

Another nail in the institutional Catholic coffin is the recognition that some clergy have perpetrated sexual abuse against women, in particular against Catholic nuns to whom priests have had access without accountability in sacramental situations including in the sacrament of confession. Reports of clergymen raping women, paying for abortions of pregnancies they caused despite the institutional church's ban on abortion, coercing young women to have sex with them because the women were assumed to be virgins and therefore not HIV-infected, are just some of the terrible stories beginning to surface around the world.[9] The Catholic institution is in shambles, opening a new era for many new forms of Catholicism to be taken seriously.

Catholic feminists have known these problems for decades. The very religious tradition that gave us our deepest values is completely unreliable in its institutional form. That is why the Women-Church Convergence, the umbrella organization of Catholic-rooted feminist groups, has not tried to reform or restructure the church, rather, to let the needs of the world not the failings of the church set the activist agenda.[10] Catholics read familiar stories of clergy sexual abuse in some Protestant churches such as the Southern Baptist Convention and in some Buddhist communities, so there is no way we are alone in all of this. But it is small consolation in the face of large damages.

The moral urgency of ecological destruction, nuclear threats, and wars making any future at all for the world doubtful, has a way of dwarfing internal religious matters. So, the very raising of the issues of sex, gender, race, class, and more within denominations can seem churlish. But a major religious organization, in this case the institutional Roman Catholic Church, is loose from its moorings. Many of its teachings and practices are greeted with skepticism and outright rejection at a time when reliable moral compasses are scarce. Thus, it is ironic that feminists and other practitioners of liberation persevere, insisting on certain moral imperatives, albeit with new parameters including gender and sexual diversity, reproductive health options, and empowerment of people, especially women on the margins who are explicitly rejected by the kyriarchal institution. This is all part of the new day for Catholicism as the smoke clears.

Catholic moral theologian Daniel C. Maguire describes this dynamic with his felicitous phrase, "the renewable moral energy of religion."[11] Religious traditions are dynamic, with each generation and local community adding their unique stamp as its needs and insights determine. This amounts to taking seriously those who have suffered at the hands of the tradition, especially those who were abused or left aside. Likewise, a class analysis and an anti-racism lens are necessary to clarify just what comes next as diversity of gender, nationality, age, ability, and so forth is woven into the new Catholic fabric.

The worst outcome of the demise of the Catholic institutional church would be to throw the baby out with the baptismal water, as it were, for people to leave aside that tradition's powerful message of love and justice, sacrament and solidarity. Confusing those grounding concepts with an institution that has proven itself incapable of carrying the weight of its own message would be a serious error. Rather, there are multiple ways in which the Catholic tradition is being expressed in the world which provide clues for what will come into view as the smoke clears.

This context admits of several observations that point to the ways ahead. First, progressive Catholic groups have been at work for decades despite the virulent and sometime vicious reactions of the hierarchy. Groups like Women's Ordination Conference, DignityUSA, Catholics for Choice, Call to Action, and many more in the United States, and groups like We Are Church, Women's Ordination Worldwide, and the Global Network of Rainbow Catholics around the world make it obvious that such work is not new.[12] Colleagues in India and the Philippines, for example, are stepping up their public efforts, branching into LGBTIQ advocacy as well as dealing with sexism. The trend is picking up in Latin America and even in parts of Africa. Australia has felt the impact of the conviction for sexual abuse of its Cardinal George Pell with serious loss of membership and credibility.

In many developing countries, most notably in the Amazon Region of Latin America about which a synod was convened in 2019 to address what appears to be a deep crisis caused by the strictures imposed by the institutional church, the picture is mixed. In that area, the lack of priests due to the celibacy requirement for clergy, blatant disregard for women's shouldering of a great deal of the pastoral responsibilities, and the resultant faltering of a vibrant sacramental life have precipitated what can only be called a pastoral emergency. A physicalist theology results in the gender of persons and their public marital status trumping the pastoral needs of people who understand physical bodies and human relationships in quite different ways.

It remains to be seen at this writing how proposals for an Amazonian Rite with certain specific changes will fare in a global church. For example, if indigenous married men are ordainable why not other men, indeed women? If women deacons are apt for the Amazon, why are they not also apt for Brooklyn? As that smoke clears from the fires both physical and ideological in the Amazon, the Catholic Church in the region will change or die. Protestant churches growing in the area offer far more reasonable and attractive terms so market share is in the balance.

A second observation concerns the limited and inadequate resources available to ecclesial change groups. Most have small budgets, limited staff, local and for the most part countrywide (rather than global) reach. For example, the member groups of the Women-Church Convergence include a few national organizations that have ties with sister groups in other parts of the world (Women's Ordination Conference with Women's Ordination Worldwide, for instance), but several of the roughly twenty member groups are local base communities. It is remarkable that the ideas of these groups have spread as far and as fast as they have. Scholarship, networking, and the sheer sense these people make over against the kind of tradeoff described earlier in the Amazon are influential, but it is David and Goliath when it comes to having sufficient resources to move a message and create a new consensus.

That is beginning to change with the infusion of cash and access from the Fidel Götz Foundation, a Lichtenstein-based charitable trust.[13] Their project, Voices of Faith, began to hold a series of meetings in the Vatican in 2014 to amplify the voices of Catholic women. Leaders began with ample money and personal and professional connections with Vatican staff. They started with fairly traditional voices, proving that the expectations of change come not simply from elite, theologically educated feminists in the West, but also from the rank and file of the church. I suspect that they have learned by doing that no matter how many resources they can muster or how many family and professional friends they have inside the Vatican, the walls are thick, not porous, and off limits to women who raise hard questions.

One of their annual International Women's Day events (2018) planned to be held on Vatican property was moved because of a conflict. Cardinal Kevin Farrell objected to some of the proposed speakers, including Mary McAleese, the former President of his home country, Ireland. She is a proponent of women's equality and LGBTIQ inclusion. He also objected to Ugandan Catholic LGBTIQ rights advocate Ssenfuka Joanita Warry and to British theologian Tina Beattie on the grounds that their views did not conform with church teaching. Voices of Faith leaders changed the venue rather than capitulate to such a non-dialogic and territorial demand. So the women's trajectory has become increasingly daring, and therefore, in my view, more realistic and useful given the intransigence of the Vatican's opposition to inclusivity, participation, and equality.

A third observation centers on the role of women religious in the work of ecclesial change. The active, public participation of women members of religious congregations is another marker of a new moment in the struggle. While there are many conservative orders in the world, with some in developing countries growing more rapidly than their progressive counterparts, women religious in general are taking the matters of church leadership and participation seriously. This is based in the main on their concrete pastoral insertion in the lives and struggles of people around the world in increasingly unjust circumstances. They know the needs and would be remiss not to meet them when they can.

The Vatican attempted to thwart women's agency by mounting an Apostolic Visitation of active U.S. women's religious communities in 2009 that culminated in a final report in 2014.[14] Vatican-approved teams visited many of the groups to ascertain something about their lifestyles, employment, prayer patterns, and the like. Some observers speculated that the Vatican wanted to get a handle on (if not a hand in) the women's communities' finances as settlements from sex abuse cases drained diocesan coffers.

The nuns reacted variously, but a common feeling was that both within and among communities the sisters became more deeply tied to one another. In response to a request for documentation from the committee, a number of communities simply sent in their own already approved constitutions to refresh the Vatican officials' memories, thinking nothing further was needed nor warranted. Nonetheless, the intrusion left many women religious with a sense that they were not immune from Vatican pressures.

Likewise, the Vatican launched a Doctrinal Investigation of the Leadership Conference of Women Religious in 2012 to evaluate its positions, plans, and certain programs.[15] LCWR is the more progressive of two such groups that represent the U.S. leadership of women's religious communities. The presumption of the investigation was that LCWR was not in the public arena sufficiently vocal about its fealty to the institutional church's positions on question such as women's ordination and the notion that only Catholics can be saved (*Dominus Iesus*).

The investigation was perceived by many other lay people (sisters being lay, after all, since they are not clergy) to be unacceptable interference into the life and work of some of the church's most tireless justice advocates and exemplary minsters. The median age of U.S. nuns is upwards of eighty with no replacement cohort in sight but their legacy is powerful in the people and institutions they have created. Such a waste of the women's time and resources was inexcusable. In 2015, when the final report emerged, it was clear that a diplomatic solution had been reached to save face on both sides, probably due in part to the common sense of Pope Francis. But both instances of Vatican interference were seen as cautionary tales for women religious in other countries to heed. Clearly the tactic did not work.

The Götz Foundation's Voices of Faith project focused on the experiences of women religious in an October 3, 2019, day-long symposium in Rome entitled "And Sister . . . What Do You Say?"[16] In a series of short talks, women religious made their collective voices heard. U.S. sister Simone Campbell, executive director of the social justice lobby NETWORK, led off. She asserted that silence would not be an option. It went from there.

A Swedish Dominican nun, Sister Madeleine Fredell, made a compelling case for women's right to preach homilies. She argued that there are no doctrinal reasons, no valid theological arguments to prohibit women from preaching. Her cogent and easily understood presentation, her Swedish sense of humor and irony, and her deep pastoral commitment added up to as good an ad for women preachers as Madison Avenue could create.

A Spanish Benedictine from Montserrat, Teresa Forcades (who is not only a theologian, but also a medical doctor, and a Green Party politician involved in the Catalonian succession movement), offered a brilliant analysis. She laid out how thirteenth-century abbesses were forbidden to hear confessions, breaking a long custom in women's monasteries. But St. Gertrude the Great insisted that they could and would hear confessions. Gertrude was canonized after all, meaning that she was lauded by the same institution that she opposed on confession. Dr. Forcades concluded that the Roman Catholic Church has always had a variety of approaches to issues. She observed that the church has to run to catch up with society that has been far more welcoming of women. But she said it is not just to be up-to-date that the church must change; it is to be coherent with its own message.

A German Cistercian sister working in Bolivia, Sister Maria Johanna Lauterbach, made a strong case against the Vatican Congregation for Institutes of Consecrated Life and Societies of Apostolic Life's (CICLSAL) May 2018 attempt to direct the lives and administration of women religious especially in congregations that are declining in numbers. The document, *Cor Orans* (Praying Heart), dictates that if a women's congregation gets too small it must end or federate with other such groups. If it has fewer than five women, it must disband. There are other stipulations too, some of them practical. But what the women found unacceptable was that the institutional church, and not the sisters, decreed the policies. No such provisions exist for men's religious groups no matter how small they become. Sister Lauterbach signaled that the days of nuns being told what to do by the Vatican are numbered, if not over completely.

There were more such speeches, including one by an Australian nun, Sister Chris Burke, who made clear that the use of terms like God as Father, Lord,

Ruler, King was unacceptable without other options for more inclusive forms. She reported that the image of a white male God has devastating effects on colonized people such as indigenous people in Australia. Many young people have already left Catholicism there, she said.

It went on like that all day. But it is not the usual people at work, feminist theologians, and our colleagues who are seeking inclusive forms of Catholicism. It was Catholic sisters who continue to be part of the institution's life but are now calling foul on the hierarchy. It is safe to say that change is nigh.

Many more observations emerge. Among them are the unjust treatment of married LGBTIQ people who have been fired from U.S. Catholic educational institutions. More than 100 cases have been documented with some court battles ahead.[17] Even if the cases are not successful, the mere fact of shining light on the institution's treatment of its own people is devastating to its claims to be about love and justice. In some cases, popular teachers and counselors are being fired after more than a decade of service simply because their marital status is public. In one instance, the father of a fired faculty member was put out of his volunteer work with youth because he supported his daughter in her love relationship. Fair-minded people, even if they are not LGBTIQ supportive, recoil at such treatment. It is hard to fathom what is "Catholic" about it.

There are other factors in the U.S. religious landscape that make change in Catholicism inevitable. One is the historical fact of religious pluralism, one of the most consequential developments in American religion in the past fifty years. Harvard scholar Diana Eck captured the essence in 2002 in her groundbreaking book *A New Religious America: How a "Christian Country" Has Become the World's Most Religiously Diverse Nation.*[18] It has taken twenty years for most people to experience the impact of her research. But the decline of mainline Protestant denominations—both numbers and budgets—is evidence that the religious marketplace is wide open with not just Catholics feeling the loss.

Another major trend in recent years is the rise of those who are called "spiritual but not religious." According to a 2017 Pew Foundation study, more and more people are inclined to define themselves as spiritual but not religious. This means that they are interested in and intent upon learning about, perhaps developing a spiritual life, but they do not want to do so within a religious tradition: "About a quarter of U.S. adults (27 percent) now say they think of themselves as spiritual but not religious, up 8 percentage points in five years, according to a Pew Research Center survey conducted between April 25 and June 4 of this year (2017). This growth has been broad-based: It has occurred among men and women; whites, blacks and Hispanics; people of many different ages and education levels; and among Republicans and Democrats. For instance, the share of whites who identify as spiritual but not religious has grown by 8 percentage points in the past five years. . . . The growth of 'spiritual but not religious' Americans has come mainly at the expense of those who say they are religious *and* spiritual. Indeed, the percentage of U.S. adults in this latter group has fallen by 11 points between 2012 and 2017."[19]

Age is a huge factor in all of this. A 2018 Pew Research Center study reports that:

> In the U.S., the age gap is considerable: 43% of people under age 40 say religion is very important to them, compared with 60% of adults ages 40 and over. Age gaps also are especially common in Latin America, with gaps appearing in 14 out of 19 countries. In the average country in the region, 63% of young adults consider religion to be very important, compared with 73% of their elders. In Europe, an age gap appears in 18 out of 35 countries, with 19% of young adults in the average country and 26% of their elders saying religion is very important in their lives.[20]

These are the numbers to watch in terms of the ways forward.

A fascinating new project that is emerging called "Nuns & Nones" reflects the age question. It is self-described as "an alliance of spiritually diverse millennials, women religious, and key partners working to create a more just, equitable and loving world. Together, we are envisioning and creating new futures for the legacies and sacred spaces of religious and monastic life, in response to the social and environmental needs of our times."[21] The median age of U.S. nuns is above eighty, and millennials were born between 1981 and 1996 so they are twenty-three to thirty-eight. This combination portends challenging but exciting prospects for this intergenerational project. Some of these folks have lived together; others eat and pray together, all in an effort to learn from one another what it means to be a nun, a sister in a Catholic religious community with views of poverty, chastity, and obedience, and to be a None, as in none of the above when it comes to religious persuasion.

There are also those known as religious Never Agains, people who are not simply None of the Above (Nones), but want nothing more to do with religion in organized terms ever. They are not religion shopping; many have no interest in spirituality. They remind us secularism is a potent force in the world, and that religious freedom implies the freedom not to be religious. Many feminists fit into the group, having lost respect for and patience with outmoded religious offerings.

These changes—religious pluralism, the spiritual but not religious, and the never agains—lay the groundwork for a Pew study's 2010–2050 projections: "The religious profile of the world is rapidly changing, driven primarily by differences in fertility rates and the size of youth populations among the world's major religions, as well as by people switching faiths. Over the next four decades, Christians will remain the largest religious group, but Islam will grow faster than any other major religion. If current trends continue, by 2050 . . . The number of Muslims will nearly equal the number of Christians around the world. . . . In the United States, Christians will decline from more than three-quarters of the population in 2010 to two-thirds in 2050, and Judaism will no longer be the largest non-Christian religion. Muslims will be more numerous in the U.S. than people who identify as Jewish on the basis of religion."[22] All of these and more are shaping forces for the future of Catholicism.

A major issue at hand for Catholics is simply whether women are full, equal members of the Catholic community or not. The short, honest answer is that we are not. Ordination, which confers sacramental/ministerial responsibilities and the right to jurisdiction or decision-making is reserved to male (in Latin, *vir*) persons. Until and unless women as well as men are eligible for ordination, this asymmetrical power model renders Catholicism impotent in its claims to Gospel values. It also leaves more than a billion people in the spiritual lurch as more inclusive and welcoming, egalitarian faith options are emerging. A better alternative in my view would be a wholesale overhaul of Catholic theology, especially ecclesiology. It would eliminate levels of clergy and laity, erase barriers to priestly responsibilities that are conferred to all with baptism, and create networks of interlocking local communities that make their own decisions as appropriate and collaborate as necessary to be justice-seeking forces in the world. Alas, that approach is still in the distance.

On a contemporary practical level, the current gender-rooted disparities result in Catholic women engaged in many forms of church service, but without decision-making power. Even the most mundane local things, for example, what groups can use a parish hall, how money donated to the community will be spent, who will preside at the sacraments, and so forth, are totally out of women's hands. For instance, it is common for women to prepare children for First Communion and then stand idly by while a male priest leads the celebration.

In Catholicism, sexism is raised to an ontological level. Priests are seen as ontologically different, read: better than lay people. Even the best educated, most skilled woman minister has no ecclesial standing next to the most minimally prepared man. Those who oppose this model of priesthood have no interest in replicating it so that a few women can be ontologically better than the rest of humankind. But it is important to recognize that this theological teaching is at the heart of the Catholic experience. It is not outdated, outmoded, or old fashioned. Rather, it is today's reality in many places, fifty years of feminist theology later.

While women's priestly ordination is off the table, Pope Francis was cornered into considering the matter of the diaconate for women three years ago. He had the temerity to joke, "when you want something to remain unresolved, set up a commission." So he did, and the group was composed of scholars who saw the issue quite differently among themselves. There appears to be consensus among them that there were women deacons in the early church who tended to the needs of the women and children. They handled women's baptism by immersion; they examined beaten women for bruises so that marriages could be dissolved (no word on what happened to the abusers). In short, women deacons were engaged in service, which is what today's women want to do as well.

The glitch is that along the long historical road, the male way of being a deacon was split in two—one way being an early stage of ordination after which one would transition to being a priest; the other way being a permanent status in the church, the so-called transitional and permanent diaconates respectively. Deacons are clergy though not with the same jurisdiction or decision-making power as presbyters. For example, priests have certain forms of inherent juridical authority while deacons have only the juridical authority delegated to them by bishops.

Progressives feared that the commission would urge a second class diaconate, namely, deaconesses, in which women would not be eligible for future ordination to the priesthood. Nor would they engage in the common diaconal tasks of preaching, presiding at weddings, and more. Instead, they would be commissioned to handle what amounts to "women's work," freeing up priests and male deacons for more substantive matters.

However, in a press conference at 35,000 feet returning from Bulgaria on May 7, 2019, Pope Francis explained that the commission could not come to a common conclusion so there will be no women deacons on his watch. Apart from the absurdity of expecting or inferring that any such commission would come to unanimity on such a sticky question, the Pope could not resist saying that pagan groups had women priests, and, well, Catholics are not pagans. Aside from casting aspersions on pagans, the Pope did not even accord the question of women deacons the dignity of a proper document or press statement, reflecting centuries of mistreatment of women and ecclesial recalcitrance when it comes to rejecting women's good faith offers of service. Even theologians who counsel against the diaconate for women as an obvious trap to further women's subordination in the Roman Catholic Church (my position) sympathize with women who feel called to this work and now have had cold, unholy water tossed in their faces one more time.

Meanwhile, lots of Catholic women have made their own ways out of no way. Some have left the institution and now worship and/or minister in other traditions, Christian or not. In the United States, Buddhism has seen an influx of Catholics as have the United Church of Christ and the Unitarian Universalists. Other women have got ordained in groups like Roman Catholic WomenPriests, the Ecumenical Catholic Communion, the Association of Roman Catholic Women Priests, and other groups that model themselves on some aspects of Catholicism and reject others, but at least ordain women. Still other Catholic-by-tradition women are without any religious affiliation or practice, and seem to be doing just fine.

The real impact of the church's implosion is on those I think of as people on the edge of the pews. They are people who go to Mass for Christmas and Easter, perhaps a few other Sundays when time allows, but who expect that their family baptisms, weddings, and funerals will be held in Catholic spaces in Catholic ways. They do not belong to small house churches or intentional eucharistic communities; they are not up on the latest internal wrangling, nor are they interested. But they are deeply scandalized by the growing reputation of the Roman Catholic Church as a haven for sexual perpetrators and those who cover-up criminal activity. They want no part of it anymore.

Lay people, women and men, have no agency when it comes to decision-making, virtually no synods to attend to vote their views, no annual meetings to decide on a parish budget, no search committee to find a new bishop. Most of them are busy working to feed and educate their families such that these kinds of ecclesial concerns are far down their list of priorities. They want their religion crafted for them, all the more reason to encourage inclusion, participation, and equality, to change the consumer model to a cooperative.

Many ecumenical colleagues wonder why any Catholic women bother any more. How many ways do we have to be told "no" before we decide to move on to more fruitful fields? As ways forward begin to emerge from the wafting smoke, two reasons for even raising these issues become obvious. First, injustice is injustice, made all the more egregious when it is perpetrated in the name of the Divine. Deeply formative, spiritually rooted values are violated when exclusive, elitist, and unequal ways of being church reign. Another generation of girls need not imbibe the lies previous generations received. Many women know better and are implementing different theologies regardless of the institution's reception of them.

The biggest mistake women can make is not demanding enough justice. Such partial strategies as calling for women deacons along with ordained married men in the Amazonian synod discussion are flawed. Similarly, demanding that religious sisters along with religious brothers be among the voters at the synod was an attempt to gain rights for some women when all women and men deserve them. It was a shortsighted goal in the service of incremental progress. When justice does not come to all, when it comes in small doses to a few more it is hardly worthy of the name.

The most telling damage wrought by dualistic, hierarchical thinking is incalculable. The roots of climate change, for example, are deep in the top-down, over-against, we-they, male-female ways of thinking that encourage human exceptionalism and discourage cosmic community. Scriptural interpretations that privilege humans over animals, that reinforce our dominion over Earth rather than our sharing of it are dangerous. Subsequent generations of people will likely reject such ideology as its results become chokingly clear.

Likewise, a world in which the winners and losers of wars, the privileged and oppressed of racism, the citizens and immigrants who compete for belonging and power, is modeled on the same top-down ways of thinking. This top-down approach results in terrible consequences making Catholicism complicit in global problems. It provides, baptizes, confirms, and replicates the theoretical frameworks of kyriarchy that hold sway worldwide, and it claims to do so in the name of the Divine.

To stop this because we know the language and the culture is why Catholic feminists bother at all to dismantle the ecclesial apparatus that is already collapsing of its own dead weight. The fallout along the way, the bodies and spirits strewn in its path, are too damaging to ignore. It is the needs of the world and not the failings of the church that set the agenda. Creating a just, sustainable, and inviting world is a huge challenge as the smoke clears. Then, perhaps, a more just world can mirror back to the Catholic community what it means to be inclusive, participatory, and egalitarian.

NOTES

1. Elisabeth Schüssler Fiorenza defines kyriarchy as "constituted by intersecting multiplicative structures of oppression." Fiorenza, *Wisdom Ways: Introducing Feminist Biblical Interpretation* (Maryknoll, NY: Orbis Books, 2001) 118.

2. Mary Daly, *Beyond God the Father: Toward a Philosophy of Women's Liberation* (Boston: Beacon Press, 1973).

3. Matters of India Reporter, "Indian Nuns Call for Women's 'Due Place' in Church Leadership," *Matters India*, October 18, 2019, http://mattersindia.com/2019/10/indian-nuns-call-for-womens-due-place-in-church-leadership/?fbclid=IwAR3lwaVbYJdDO-vdYRpqU84JiLXlXqte8t75FUrVf0SpMAWM8-tzAJQLiTI.

4. See Mary E. Hunt, "Rome Has Spoken and Rome Is Finished: The Vatican's Sexual Abuse Summit 'Failed Miserably,'" *Religion Dispatches*, February 27, 2019, https://rewire.news/religion-dispatches/2019/02/27/rome-has-spoken-and-rome-is-finished-the-vaticans-sexual-abuse-summit-failed-miserably/.

5. Lydia Saad, "Catholics' Church Attendance Resumes Downward Slide," *Gallup*, April 9, 2018, https://news.gallup.com/poll/232226/church-attendance-among-catholics-resumes-downward-slide.aspx.

6. "Papa Francisco en Chile," *24 Horas*, December 1, 2018, https://www.24horas.cl/papafranciscoenchile/cifra-de-chilenos-que-se-declaran-catolicos-bajo-desde-73-a-45-en-la-ultima-decada-2612241.

7. Pennsylvania Grand Jury, "Pennsylvania Diocese Victims Report," Pennsylvania Attorney General Website, August 2018, https://www.attorneygeneral.gov/report/.

8. "Report on Pennsylvania Church Sex Abuse," *Washington Post*, August 2018, http://apps.washingtonpost.com/g/page/local/report-on-pennsylvania-church-sex-abuse/2319/.

9. Jason Horowitz, "Sexual Abuse of Nuns: Longstanding Church Scandal Emerges from Shadows," *New York Times*, February 6, 2019, https://www.nytimes.com/2019/02/06/world/europe/pope-francis-sexual-abuse-nuns.html.

10. Women-Church Convergence, 2018, https://www.women-churchconvergence.org/.

11. Daniel C. Maguire on "renewable moral energy of religion," *Sacred Energies: When the World's Religions Sit Down to Talk about the Future of Human Life and the Plight of This Planet* (Minneapolis, MN: Fortress Press, 2000) 10.

12. Marianne Duddy-Burke, "An Open Letter to Catholics: The Church You Long for Already Exists," DignityUSA Website, September 2019, https://www.dignityusa.org/article/open-letter-catholics-church-you-long-already-exists.

13. Fidel Gotz Foundation Website, 2019, http://fidelgoetzstiftung.com/?page=5&lan=en.

14. Margaret Cain McCarthy and Mary Ann Zollman, *Power of Sisterhood: Women Religious Tell the Story of the Apostolic Visitation* (Lanham, MD: University Press of America, 2014).

15. Annemarie Sanders, ed., *However Long the Night: Making Meaning in a Time of Crisis* (Silver Spring, MD: LCWR, 2018).

16. Voices of Faith Website, 2019, https://voicesoffaith.org/event201.

17. New Ways Ministry keeps a growing list of these incidents. Francis DeBernardo, *New Ways Ministry*, 2019, https://www.newwaysministry.org/issues/employment/employment-disputes/.

18. Diana L. Eck, *A New Religious America: How a "Christian Country" Has Become the World's Most Religiously Diverse Nation* (San Francisco: HarperSanFrancisco, 2001).

19. Michael Lipka and Claire Gecewicz, "More Americans Now Say They're Spiritual But Not Religious," Pew Research Center Website, September 6, 2017, https://www.pewresearch.org/fact-tank/2017/09/06/more-americans-now-say-theyre-spiritual-but-not-religious/.

20. Stephanie Kramer and Dalia Fahmy, "Younger People Are Less Religious than Older Ones in Many Countries, Especially in the U.S. and Europe," Pew Research Center Website, June 13, 2018, https://www.pewresearch.org/fact-tank/2018/06/13/younger-people-are-less-religious-than-older-ones-in-many-countries-especially-in-the-u-s-and-europe/.

21. Nuns and Nones Website, 2018, https://www.nunsandnones.org/.

22. Pew Research, "The Future of World Religions: Population Growth Projections, 2010–2050," Pew Research Center Website, April 2, 2015, https://www.pewforum.org/2015/04/02/religious-projections-2010-2050/.

BIBLIOGRAPHY

Daly, Mary. *Beyond God the Father: Toward a Philosophy of Women's Liberation.* Boston: Beacon Press, 1973.

DeBernardo, Francis. New Ways Ministry, 2019. https://www.newwaysministry.org/issues/employment/employment-disputes/

Duddy-Burke, Marianne. "An Open Letter to Catholics: The Church You Long For Already Exists." DignityUSA Website, September 2019. https://www.dignityusa.org/article/open-letter-catholics-church-you-long-already-exists.

Eck, Diana L. *A New Religious America: How a "Christian Country" Has Become the World's Most Religiously Diverse Nation.* San Francisco, HarperSanFrancisco, 2001.

Fidel Gotz Foundation Website. 2019. http://fidelgoetzstiftung.com/?page=5&lan=en.

Fiorenza, Elisabeth Schüssler. *Wisdom Ways: Introducing Feminist Biblical Interpretation.* Maryknoll, NY: Orbis Books, 2001.

Horowitz, Jason. "Sexual Abuse of Nuns: Longstanding Church Scandal Emerges from Shadows." *New York Times.* February 6, 2019. https://www.nytimes.com/2019/02/06/world/europe/pope-francis-sexual-abuse-nuns.html.

Hunt, Mary E. "Rome Has Spoken and Rome Is Finished: The Vatican's Sexual Abuse Summit 'Failed Miserably.'" *Religion Dispatches*, February 27, 2019, https://rewire.news/religion-dispatches/2019/02/27/rome-has-spoken-and-rome-is-finished-the-vaticans-sexual-abuse-summit-failed-miserably/.

Kramer, Stephanie and Fahmy, Dalia. "Younger People Are Less Religious than Older Ones in Many Countries, Especially in the U.S. and Europe." Pew Research Center Website, June 13, 2018. https://www.pewresearch.org/fact-tank/2018/06/13/younger-people-are-less-religious-than-older-ones-in-many-countries-especially-in-the-u-s-and-europe/.

Lipka, Michael and Gecewicz, Claire. "More Americans Now Say they're Spiritual But Not Religious." Pew Research Center Website, September 6, 2017. https://www.pewresearch.org/fact-tank/2017/09/06/more-americans-now-say-theyre-spiritual-but-not-religious/.

Maguire, Daniel C. *Sacred Energies: When the World's Religions Sit Down to Talk about the Future of Human Life and the Plight of this Planet.* Minneapolis, MN: Fortress Press, 2000.

Matters of India Reporter. "Indian Nuns Call for Women's 'due place' in Church Leadership." *Matters India*, October 18, 2019. http://mattersindia.com/2019/10/indian-nuns-call-for-womens-due-place-in-church-leadership/?fbclid=IwAR31waVbYJdDO-vdYRpqU84JiLXlXqte8t75FUrVf0SpMAWM8-tzAJQLiTI.

McCarthy, Margaret Cain and Zollman, Mary Ann. *Power of Sisterhood: Women Religious Tell the Story of the Apostolic Visitation.* Lanham, MD: University Press of America, 2014.

Nuns and Nones Website. 2018. https://www.nunsandnones.org/.

"Papa Francisco en Chile." *24 Horas*, December 1, 2018. https://www.24horas.cl/papafranciscoenchile/cifra-de-chilenos-que-se-declaran-catolicos-bajo-desde-73-a-45-en-la-ultima-decada-2612241.

Pennsylvania Grand Jury. "Pennsylvania Diocese Victims Report." Pennsylvania Attorney General Website. August 2018. https://www.attorneygeneral.gov/report/.

Pew Research. "The Future of World Religions: Population Growth Projections, 2010–2050." Pew Research Center Website, April 2, 2015. https://www.pewforum.org/2015/04/02/religious-projections-2010-2050/.

"Report on Pennsylvania Church Sex Abuse." *Washington Post*. August 2018. http://apps.washingtonpost.com/g/page/local/report-on-pennsylvania-church-sex-abuse/2319/.

Saad, Lydia. "Catholics' Church Attendance Resumes Downward Slide." *Gallup*, April 9, 2018. https://news.gallup.com/poll/232226/church-attendance-among-catholics-resumes-downward-slide.aspx.

Sanders, Annemarie (ed.). *However Long the Night: Making Meaning in a Time of Crisis*. Silver Spring, MD: LCWR, 2018.

Voices of Faith Website. 2019. https://voicesoffaith.org/event201.

Women-Church Convergence. 2018. https://www.women-churchconvergence.org/.

Chapter 2

Cleaning the Church Attic

Discarding "Uniformity and Division" for "Unity in Diversity"

Paul Tenkotte

A couple of years ago, my spouse and I transitioned from a 3,000-square-foot suburban house to a 990-square-foot urban condominium. We divested ourselves of decades of furniture, dozens of file cabinets filled with research, and thousands of books. Libraries, archives, family members, friends, and charities were the recipients of our years of amassing way more material possessions than we needed. We wanted to see others enjoy our gifts. Further, we desired to simplify our lives in order to focus more time on assisting family and friends, as well as helping our community. With the exception of an occasional book every now and then, we actually miss very little.

Like people, institutions—including the Roman Catholic Church—have a tendency to collect unnecessary things. In the church's case, this includes traditions and philosophical arguments that no longer relate to new scientific findings nor to significant cultural changes. Some may argue that change is basically antithetical to eternal truths. However, without touching the heart and soul of Christian doctrine as contained in the Apostles' or Nicene Creed,[1] this chapter will argue that much of the remainder has been added during the centuries, and hence, can and should be changed.

A CHANGEABLE CHALLENGE

A former newspaper editor, once stated to his staff at a now-defunct newspaper, "If you don't like change, you'll like irrelevance even less." In many respects, the Roman Catholic Church is already well advanced along the path to irrelevance in the United States. In the respected Pew Research Center's

(Pew Charitable Trusts established by the Pew family) 2014 U.S. Religious Landscape Study, 39 percent of Catholics reported attending religious services "at least once a week," 40 percent "once or twice a month/a few times a year," and 20 percent "seldom/never."[2] Likewise, a 2018 Gallup poll reported similar numbers. Overall, an average of 39 percent of Catholics "over the past ten years" attended weekly liturgies, down significantly from 75 percent in 1955. Further, congregations are also aging: "The age group with the highest number of weekly attendance was the 60 and above demographic, with 49 percent. That number dropped from 59 percent over the past decade."[3] What explanations can be offered for this decline in church attendance, a phenomenon also affecting many Protestant mainline denominations in the United States? Has science displaced God? Are mindfulness (attempting to be truly mindful of the present moment) and other forms of meditation supplanting organized religion? Are people discouraged by church scandals? Has American individualism overtaken our need for collective identities?

Truly, all of these—and many more explanations—play some role in the decline of mainline organized religions in the United States. However, these are merely symptoms of a larger and quite changeable challenge—the need to clean out the church's attic, and to use newly available scientific evidence to tie the eternal truth of "unity in diversity" with Jesus Christ's command to love, forgive, and heal.

As Jesus often taught in parables (stories that illustrate a moral teaching), today we tend to encapsulate our thoughts in short quotes and slogans. Undoubtedly, we are products of our age, the so-called Information Revolution of the late twentieth and early twenty-first centuries. Like all revolutions—technological and otherwise—change is pervasive, rapid, and sometimes unsettling. Old answers to eternal problems may seem to fall short, while new explanations may appear both promising and challenging.

Crane Brinton (1898–1968) was a well-known American historian who studied the cycle of political change, particularly as expressed in the French and American Revolutions. In his book entitled *The Anatomy of Revolution*, he painted a simple yet eloquent picture of the beginnings of the French Revolution that speaks volumes about change itself: "France in 1789," he claimed, "was like an attic stuffed full of all kinds of old furniture . . . that just wouldn't fit in the living room."[4] Of course, the Roman Catholic Church has accumulated lots of old furniture itself in an attempt to answer some of the eternal questions of humankind. For instance, why does the world seem so broken? Why do bad things sometimes happen to good people? Are we the victims of fate, or do we exercise free will? Is there an afterlife? Why is hate sometimes so easy, and forgiveness so difficult? These and many other questions are common to human experience and to all world religions and philosophies.

CHANGE: ANCIENT EUROPE AND THE IDEA OF "UNITY IN OPPOSITES"

Change is all around us. Indeed, the only thing that sometimes seems certain in our life is change. To some, change is to be feared; to others, embraced. There is yet another certainty, however. If we fail to respond to change, it will happen anyway. As the Chinese Daoists used to state, in a famous double-negative: Do nothing, and nothing will not be done. In other words, if you do nothing, something will happen anyway.

The ancient Greek philosopher Heraclitus (ca. 500 BCE) is generally associated with a philosophy of flux, or change. In other words, you cannot step into the same river twice. Yet, at the same time, Heraclitus asserted that there was a universal *Logos*, which he called "Word," that underlay the rationality of the world. Further, Heraclitus believed in the "unity of opposites," providing a number of examples, including: "Collections: wholes and not wholes; brought together, pulled apart; sung in unison, sung in conflict; from all things one and from one all things."[5]

CHANGE: EUROPE AND LINEAR DUALISM

Greek philosophers of the Classical Period (also called the Golden Age), Plato (ca. 429–347 BCE) and Aristotle (384–322 BCE), changed the direction of the discussion significantly. To Plato, this world was only a pale shadow of reality. Ideal forms, or universals, such as beauty, truth, and justice, existed somewhere and were knowable in fragments by our human souls from a former existence. Somewhere, out there—the universe—things were perfect and were governed by a different set of laws than here on earth, where change evidenced imperfection. This philosophical Dualism—the theory of opposites somehow in opposition, rather than in unity—became enmeshed in Western civilization.

Later, Aristotle also struggled with change, including that of the physical world. His answer was what he called Hylomorphism, that is, that everything is composed of matter and form. For example, if a sculptor took marble and chiseled a statue, the marble was the matter, and the statue was the form. Similar matter was attracted to each other. Objects fell because they were of the earth and wanted to return to it. Air rose because that's where it belonged. Starting with general assumptions and proceeding to more and more detailed specifics, this kind of deductive reasoning would hold sway in Western civilization until the Scientific Revolution. To modern eyes, the basic disadvantage of deductive reasoning is obvious. If the original premise is wrong, everything else that follows is potentially flawed.[6]

In medieval Europe, St. Thomas Aquinas (1225–1274) and others immersed themselves in the rediscovery of ancient philosophical works, like those of Plato and Aristotle. Using philosophy to help explain theology, they liberally borrowed and applied ancient themes to newer Christian doctrines. The results were sometimes forced and obtuse. On the other hand, Thomas Aquinas's use of Aristotle's teleology (the study of the purpose of material things) of "final causes" has become one of Christianity's well-known explanations for the existence of God. To Aquinas, God made humans in the image and likeness of God and implanted within them their essence ("forms/ universals"). Humans had free will, and through original sin, brokenness entered human history. Jesus Christ became incarnate in human form to bring redemption. Hence, Christianity was inherently linear in perspective, a cause-and-effect chronology of our individual lives from birth to death to an afterlife.[7]

Medieval Christian theology also borrowed extensively from natural law, which dated back to the time of the ancient Greeks and Romans and which "was regarded as consistent with reason and as universally applicable."[8] Christian thinkers especially applied natural law to matters of sexuality. For example, sexual intercourse between married couples in the missionary position, with the intention of producing children, was regarded as natural. On the other hand, sexual outlets not capable of procreation were viewed as unnatural, including cunnilingus, fellatio, masturbation, mutual masturbation, and sodomy.

CHANGE: ASIA AND CYCLICAL UNITY IN HARMONY

In contrast to Christianity, Eastern (i.e., Asian) religions and philosophies have tended to view the world in a cyclical manner. Asian philosophies and religions, including Buddhism, Confucianism, Daoism, Shintoism, and other Eastern worldviews, have long emphasized the importance of groups over individuals. Shaming one's group is to be avoided. Similarly, the world and all of its creation are seen as intimately connected—mountains, humans, trees, and everything in-between. Cycles are important too. What goes around eventually comes around. Harmony is always to be maintained. Bad and good karma of past lives have consequences, but there are many gray areas of life too. Reincarnation is possible, but so is nirvana, the merger of the individual with the universal soul. In Eastern philosophy, time repeats in cycles, and harmony maintains unity.

CHANGE AND PEASANTS

Our generalizations about Eastern and Western religions and worldviews require a basic disclaimer. Before 1500, the vast majority of the population of human civilizations was composed of peasant farmers, often 90 percent or more. Peasants were intimately tied to nature. Their lives literally revolved around the seasons, resulting in a cyclical outlook on life. For example, in Europe the Catholic liturgical year reflected the seasons. To largely uneducated, and often illiterate peasants, the deeper philosophical underpinnings of Christian theology were unknown and unknowable. The Roman Catholic Church provided answers to the eternal questions. In a society where almost everyone worked on the land, harmony was a priority. Diversity was a novelty. Unity in harmony was the basic way of life.

The same was true of Eastern society, although Asian answers to the eternal questions of life tended to be more flexible than in the West. In China, for instance, the Chinese emperor, ruling by the so-called Mandate of Heaven, assured the peasants continued harmony between the heavens and the earth. If harmony were disrupted, the peasants could rebel and seat a new emperor. On the other hand, in Europe, it was believed that kings and queens ruled by divine right. Rebellion was generally not considered an option. And yet, all of the world's major religions, whether monotheistic (belief in one god), polytheistic (belief in multiple gods), or pantheistic (the universe and the divine as basic equivalents), underscored the beauty of creation, and the immense capacity of humans to love. More often than not, they celebrated unity in diversity. Then how did many of the world's religions become so complex over the centuries? In particular, we will examine the evolution of Christianity, and how it eventually encompassed a series of doctrines and policies, some of which have become outdated and counterproductive.

THE SCIENTIFIC REVOLUTION OF THE 1500s AND 1600s

Today, we take the scientific method for granted. In primary and secondary school science classes, we learn that scientists conduct experiments under controlled circumstances before they arrive at new theories. The scientific method is an example of inductive reasoning, which proceeds from very specific evidence to general theories. However, before the time of Francis Bacon (1561–1626), author of the 1620 work *Novum Organum* (*New Method* or *New Logic*), induction (i.e., the scientific method) was not as respected as it is presently. The inductive, experimental model of the European Scientific Revolution of the 1500s and 1600s set the stage for the modern world. Increasingly, nature began to be viewed as a machine, and the world as a sum of its parts. Individual objects, experiments, and people assumed new importance.

Already by Bacon's time, the emphasis was moving from theology to the science of astronomy. Just before he died in 1543, Nicolaus Copernicus (1473–1543) published *On the Revolution of the Heavenly Orbs* (1543), which argued for the heliocentric model of the universe (i.e., that the earth and planets revolved around the sun, not the sun and planets around the earth). Soon after, Galileo Galilei (1564–1642) took what had been a toy, a spyglass, perfected it into a telescope, pointed it toward the heavens and saw imperfections (e.g., the moon was pitted with craters and defaced by mountains). He also saw that four moons orbited Jupiter, proving the heliocentric model since Jupiter's moons were not revolving around the earth. Further, Johannes Kepler (1571–1630) theorized that the planets moved not in perfect circles, but in imperfect ellipses.

What Galileo and Kepler did was essentially two things: (1) they claimed that both the heavens and the earth were subject to the same laws of nature; (2) they stated that these laws of nature were regulated by time. Kepler had noted, for instance, that the planets moved more quickly in their orbits as they neared the sun. The mathematics of time, or calculus (called fluxions by Newton) was developed separately by two figures: Isaac Newton (1642–1729) and Wilhelm Gottfried Leibniz (1646–1716). Newton was further known for his discovery of gravity (the Universal Law of Gravitation).

THE EVOLUTION OF THE ROMAN CATHOLIC CHURCH

Of course, the Roman Catholic Church was slow to accept some of the new scientific theories. In 1633, the church's Inquisition found Galileo guilty of heresy and placed him under house arrest for the remainder of his life. Through the centuries, the church has evolved from small, scattered Christian communities into a large centralized bureaucracy. From a purely objective, historic standpoint, this development of church doctrine, rituals, and hierarchy has included syncretism, that is, the adoption of practices from other religious traditions. In the great age of Scholasticism (a form of medieval European philosophy that included Thomas Aquinas), it further attempted to clarify theological beliefs through the use of philosophical tools, including ancient Greek sources like Plato and Aristotle.

By the time of the 1500s, and of the great reformer, Martin Luther (1483–1546), the Roman Catholic Church was unfortunately tethered to the politics of its age. It seems safe to conclude that the marriage of church and state did not produce—in the end—favorable consequences for the church's role in spreading the Good News of salvation. Instead, the church became embroiled in politics and imperialism, that is, the growth of colonial empires. Luther and other leaders of the Protestant Reformation tried to steer the church back to the basic principles of Christianity. However, they too became embroiled with politics, as the Protestant Reformation in the Holy Roman Empire (now Germany and parts of Central, Eastern, and Southern Europe) began to resemble a patchwork quilt of different religious sects forged by petty princes, warfare, and the terms of the Peace of Westphalia of 1648.

THE PROTESTANT REFORMATION AND FRAGMENTATION

Martin Luther was certainly not the first Protestant reformer. The Moravian Church (sometimes called the Unity of the Brethren, *Unitas Fratrum*), founded in 1457, is the "oldest international Protestant church in the world," preceding Luther's nailing of his Ninety-Five Theses on the door of Wittenberg church in 1517 by more than half a century. The Unity of the Brethren originated in Bohemia and Moravia (both regions in the current Czech Republic). John Huss (ca.1373–1415), one of its founders, was burned at the stake for his beliefs. His followers, and those of other similarly based religious groups, faced intense periods of persecution, especially when the Roman Catholic Habsburg dynasty began to rule Bohemia and Moravia in 1526.[9]

By the 1600s, Germany was a patchwork quilt of hundreds of kingdoms, duchies, principalities, archdioceses, dioceses, counties, and free imperial cities. The umbrella over all of them was the Holy Roman Empire, and more specifically, the Holy Roman Empire of the German Nation (*Heiliges Römisches Reich Deutscher Nation*), a linguistic formula then used to describe the German-speaking territory of the Reich (Empire). Each political division of the Reich largely governed its own affairs, on paper, but bowed to the Holy Roman Emperor in foreign affairs. Since 1452, the Holy Roman Emperor had been a member of the powerful Habsburg family, whose holdings eventually extended into Italy, Spain, and to the Spanish New World in North and South America.[10]

Staunchly Roman Catholic, the Habsburg family found its dominions in the Holy Roman Empire increasingly splintered by the Protestant Reformation. The religious Schmalkaldic War, resulting in the Peace of Augsburg of 1555, had achieved recognition of the existence of the Lutheran Church in the Reich, but no other form of Protestantism. The principle of *cuius regio, eius religio* held sway, whereby each ruler of each petty principality, duchy, and so forth could choose the official religion of his domain, Catholic or

Lutheran. As German historian Heinrich August Winkler has noted, however, Augsburg "did not consider the individual believer; only the prince had the right to decide between the old and new faiths. Dissidents had only the right to leave the country."[11]

Religious fragmentation continued to grow in the Reich, and in fact, deepened, as dissident Calvinists, adhering to the doctrine of predestination (the belief that God knew whom would be saved and whom would not) and called the Reformed Church in Germany, steadily increased in number in the German-speaking states. Religious struggles, often with imperial and political overtones, scarred the physical, political, and psychological landscape. The Thirty Years' War (1618–1648) led to immense devastation of lives and property in the German territories. Peace treaties at Osnabrück and Münster, collectively known as the Peace of Westphalia (1648), ended the war. By their terms, only three religions—Catholicism, Lutheranism, and Reformed—were permitted in the Holy Roman Empire.

UNIFORMITY AND DIVISION

For Winkler and countless other historians of Germany, the Thirty Years' War marked a massive setback for the formation of a sense of nationalism and of modern institutions of representative democracy in Germany. The irony of the situation was clear. Individual conscience had been a hallmark of Lutherans and of other German Protestants, but it was subjected to authoritarian princely power. Political fragmentation and absolutism became the chains that bound the empire to antiquated governmental forms that were incapable of embracing the new spirit of capitalism. While representative democracy would forge ahead in England, the Netherlands, and eventually France, Germany became a political backwater, and a social aberration.

The Roman Catholic and the Protestant churches drew new lines in the sand. Diversity within a territory was not an option. The Holy Roman Empire was divided into Protestant and Catholic areas. Within each division, uniformity was expected. Meanwhile, in France, England, and other nations, the Protestant Reformation spread. The Christian world experienced the largest division since the Great Schism of 1054 had ruptured Christianity into Roman Catholic and Eastern Orthodox branches.

COUNTERCULTURAL PIETISTS

Beginning as a movement in the Lutheran Church in the late 1600s led by Philipp Jakob Spener (1635–1705) of Alsace, Pietism sought to personalize

Christianity by emphasizing a conversion of the heart, and to avoid contentious debates over trivial theological differences. In America, Pietism fed a Great Awakening, leading people to experience conversion in an individualistic, even emotional manner. In addition, Pietists valued charity and education. It had far-reaching effects on both shores of the Atlantic.[12]

The Moravian Brethren's principles of "In essentials, unity; in nonessentials, liberty; in all things, charity" were decidedly countercultural.[13] The Brethren's concern for the well-being of American Indians and slaves underscored just how revolutionary their doctrines must have appeared. Its outreach to African slaves impressed the British abolitionist William Wilberforce (1759–1833), while the church's theological stances influenced John Wesley, the founder of Methodism. In America, members of the Moravian Church settled in Pennsylvania, founding Bethlehem and Nazareth, and in South Carolina, establishing Salem (now Winston-Salem). In what later became Ohio, they established Moravian settlements for Christianized Delaware Indians, including Schönbrunn, Gnadenhutten, and Lichtenau along the Tuscarawas River.

ROMAN CATHOLICS IN THE UNITED STATES

The Catholic-Protestant divide traveled with immigrants to North and South America. In the United States, the Roman Catholic Church faced an uphill battle. Anti-Catholicism had deep roots in the Protestant Reformation in England. Further, England's imperial competition with the Catholic powers of France and Spain in North America had long depicted their enemies as mindless papists. The Catholic Church then, as now, was not a democracy. America was a democratic republic. In Protestant minds, perhaps Catholics would not be able to separate church and state. The foreignness of the Catholic Church—seen in immigrant Catholics and in the ritualism and hierarchy of the church itself—led to a sense of paranoia. Were the Pope and Catholic monarchs encouraging poor Catholics to leave Europe for America? Were they planning a Catholic takeover of the United States? While these fears seem somewhat incredulous by today's standards, they were nonetheless real at the time.

Of course, Catholic immigrants proved just as able as other religious groups to embrace American democracy. In fact, Catholic parishes in the United States helped immigrants in assimilating to American life. They offered English classes for adults, primary and secondary education for immigrant children, and a vast array of clubs and social groups where immigrants could learn the essentials of both their faith and of organizing and leading groups. In addition, some parishes actually operated savings organizations, and Catholic fraternal organizations, like the Knights of Columbus offered insurance programs.

Until 1908, the Catholic Church in the United States was literally considered mission territory, under the direct administration of the Sacred Congregation for the Propagation of the Faith in Rome. It lacked the financial resources and personnel to operate a growing network of parishes, schools, colleges, hospitals, orphanages, and other facilities. Lay women and men proved instrumental in the late nineteenth and early twentieth centuries in establishing and funding the many activities and institutions of the church, as well as recruiting religious orders of sisters, priests, and brothers to immigrate to the United States.[14]

At least until the time of the Second Vatican Council (1962–1965), ecumenical dialogue was discouraged. Then, everything changed. I remember the reforms of Vatican II vividly as a child. Mass in English replaced the liturgy in Latin. The priest now faced the congregation during Mass, rather than stand with his back to them. Eucharist in the hand became common, as well as reception of the wine by the chalice. New hymns became popular, and Martin Luther was no longer regarded as an anathema. Parishes began to elect parish councils, and bishops asked parish leaders to meet with diocesan officials when pastoral vacancies occurred to help discern future leadership.

In the twenty-first century, however, there appears to have been a reversal of these progressive reforms in the United States. Today elected parish councils are largely a thing of the past, replaced by pastor-appointed (and in some cases, diocesan-approved) members. Archdioceses and dioceses have employees who have assumed the many volunteer tasks of parish councils, committees, subcommittees, and other organizations. Diocesan annual appeals have replaced many fundraisers. Festivals, picnics, and other events designed to connect parishes with their communities are disappearing. Not surprisingly, many of my fellow Catholics feel that their time and talents are no longer valued.

THE TWENTY-FIRST CENTURY: UNITY IN DIVERSITY

Scientists can only estimate the number of species in the world. There could be as many as 8.7 million, according to a 2011 study. Of these, only "about 1.2 million species have been formally described, the vast majority from the land rather than the oceans."[15] The diversity of animal, plant, and other species is so vast, in fact, that many may become extinct before humans have the opportunity to discover and catalog them.

Human beings are themselves a very diverse species. As of 2019, human population stands at 7.7 billion,[16] growing at the rate of about "82 million people per year," and set to reach 10 billion by 2057.[17] However, despite the uniqueness and individuality among the billions of us, we are surprisingly similar. Genetically, "All humans are 99.9 percent identical, and, of that tiny 0.1 per cent difference, 94 per cent of the variation is among individuals from the same populations and only six per cent between individuals from different populations."[18] At the same time, human personalities, talents, traits, and physical attributes are extraordinarily diverse, evidence of unity in diversity.

The scientific evidence leads to the only logical conclusion possible for those of faith—God loves diversity. Further, God sees unity in diversity. Despite our far-ranging differences, God has connected all humans together in a common bond of DNA. In fact, the Big Bang theory of the origins of the universe would extend this theory even further. All of us are literally related to everyone *and* everything in the universe.

Further, the universe is constantly expanding and evolving. Some stars are fading, while others are being formed. Our old conceptions of time and space have been turned upside down. Albert Einstein (1879–1955) described the relativity of time, and Werner Heisenberg (1901–1976) opened our eyes to the Uncertainty Principle of quantum mechanics. Scientists have mapped the human genome, and others have described the continual process of human cells disassembling and reformulating. It is mind-boggling to consider what keeps all of us intact and not merely molecular matter floating off elsewhere.

The universe of the ancient and medieval philosophers was simply wrong—everything in the universe is changing, not just our imperfect world. There are unifying theories behind all change, not all of which humans yet understand. The scientific evidence is again clear for those of faith—God loves change. Change is merely another facet of the overwhelming diversity of the universe that God created.

POLARIZATION AND COGNITIVE DISSONANCE

Our current world—whether in its theology, philosophy, politics, or culture—is witnessing a vast polarization. On any issue, the spectrum varies from the reactionary to the radical. Our logical abilities seem to be failing us. For example, scientists warn us about climate change, and that a mere 1.5°C change in our global temperatures will produce catastrophic consequences for our world.[19] People have responded in vastly different ways. Some are climate change deniers, others are believers, and some are sort of relativists, believing that change is occurring but that the mechanisms behind it are uncertain.

Likewise, as humans, some of us are intensely rational, others irrational, and many in-between these two poles. To some extent, however, we all experience cognitive dissonance. Cognitive dissonance describes how we, as humans, process what happens when a disconnect occurs between what we believe and some new information that we encounter. How we respond to that new information can be polarizing at times. Two options are fight and flight. We can discount the new information, claiming that it is completely wrong. Or we can simply ignore the information, believing that it doesn't apply to us. A third option requires more work. We can conduct research, analysis, and synthesis. "Then, and only then, are we logically capable of making a decision about the information."[20]

A THIRD WAY: THE NONLINEAR WORLD

Scholars have carefully studied the effects of the Information Revolution on the human brain. They have confirmed what any person with basic observation skills already knows. Our attention spans are becoming shorter, we are becoming more impatient, and less able to sit still for long periods of time. We question everyone and everything, based on information (whether good or bad) that we obtain on the internet. We make up our minds, and then surround ourselves with information and sources that support our worldview.

The Information Revolution is digitally and scientifically based. Computer programming, even in simple online learning management systems, is distinctly nonlinear. In science, nonlinear systems abound, where output does not equal input. In mathematics, linear equations of two variables can be graphed as a straight line. Nonlinear equations produce various curved lines. How we receive and process information follows the same nonlinear modes. We receive information via our computers, mobile phones, social media, television, radio, print materials, friends, family, and organizations, to name but a few. A lot of information, coming at us at lightning speed and not all verified, requires nonlinear skills of processing. Connecting dots does not all occur along a linear plane. Even our recreational outlets sometimes replicate this nonlinear world. Computer games require excellent perception and superb mind–body coordination skills. New synapses are bridged in the neurons of our brains, and these new circuits begin connecting to other cells.

THE TRINITY AND NONLINEAR THINKING

Three dimensions, virtual reality, and time as a fourth dimension—these are all fascinations of our time period. And all share the similarity of nonlinear thinking. Unity in diversity is yet another example of nonlinear thinking.

For years, the Roman Catholic Church has believed in unity in diversity, as expressed in the Trinity. How can there be three persons in one God? No matter what we prefer to call the Trinity—traditionally, the Father, Son, and Holy Spirit, or more contemporarily, the Creator, Redeemer, and Sustainer—the concept seems overwhelming. Yet, the very scientific discoveries of modern times, from Einstein's relativity of time to the mapping of the human genome, prove that time and space are merely relative, and that unity in diversity is present in the human condition itself.

UNITY IN DIVERSITY: THE TRINITY, THE SOUL, AND THE EUCHARIST

Likewise, the Roman Catholic Church teaches that, in the sacrament of the Eucharist, the bread and wine truly become the body and blood of Jesus Christ, called transubstantiation. Throughout history, this mystery has been the subject of many theological debates, including consubstantiation (the belief that the bread and wine become the body of blood of Jesus in essence only, not in external form) and memorialization (the belief that the Eucharist is merely a ceremony memorializing Jesus's death). The realities of the relativity of time and place, as well as of unity in diversity, may assist us in understanding the Eucharistic mystery. The Eucharist is God's union with all of us. In essence, it is the perfect—and most radical—expression of God's unquenchable love and grace for us.

Considering the literal communion of the sacrament of Eucharist, in bringing all of us closer to God, it is surprising how the Roman Catholic Church in the United States is continuing to impose barriers to the reception of this important sacrament. At weddings and funerals, for example, it has become more commonplace to hear priests disinvite those not Catholic from receiving the Eucharist. Further, unleavened bread used for the Eucharist must have some percentage of gluten, despite the fact that humankind's genetic mutations of wheat have undoubtedly led to greater gluten intolerance in many people. Gluten-sensitive people are told to partake of low-gluten hosts, or the wine instead, the latter an interesting quandary for those who may be alcoholic as well. Grape juice cannot be offered as an alternative for those who do not indulge in alcohol. Those in mortal sin are not supposed to receive the Eucharist. And while the advice for divorced and remarried Catholics without an official church annulment currently seems in flux, in the past the church's discouragement has made many feel unworthy and unwelcome including LGBTQ+ individuals in committed and monogamous relationships.[21] And the list goes on and on. To a conscientious person, the array of rules is stultifying. To the easy-going, run-of-the-mill Catholic, the rules seem artificial and antiquated, and are largely ignored. To thoughtful Catholics, all of these matters are part of a larger debate about salvation.[22]

UNITY IN DIVERSITY: THE SALVATION DEBATE

Martin Luther, encountering the abuse of the sale of indulgences in the early sixteenth century, reminded Christians that salvation and heaven could not be bought in the early sixteenth century. According to Lutherans, humans possess free will, but God's gifts of faith and grace are freely given to those who seek God. The Roman Catholic Church's position, in response to Luther, was that both faith and good works were essential to salvation. Lutherans, and many other Protestants, on the other hand, asserted that no human can *earn* salvation. Yet, they were left with the problem of how to control bad behavior and encourage good deeds if salvation were a gift from God. The Lutherans and others argue from the viewpoint of gratitude. Because we are saved by God's love, we should act gratefully, loving God in return, and loving our fellow humans. We love and obey because God loves us.

The Roman Catholic position on grace and free will, on the other hand, is more nuanced. It presupposes that an individual's informed conscience will enable them to balance out the intricacies of their life. I offer a simple scenario as an example. When I was young, I was a smart but nervous little boy. Sometimes, I had trouble sleeping. My mother would tell me, "Say your rosary, and you'll fall asleep." The first time she gave me that advice, I asked, "But what if I fall asleep before I finish my rosary?" "Your guardian angel will finish it for you," she replied lovingly.

In essence, that is what grace is. God completes our incomplete actions. God gives us the courage we lack, and provides us with friends, family, and colleagues to help us fill in life's voids. All of us should help one another in connecting the dots, solving problems, and facing challenges. Grace is that inexhaustible pool of God's unconditional love where you seek wisdom, patience, strength, and solace. Best of all, grace is free for the asking. There are no strings attached. Whether you're divorced and remarried, straight or LGBTQ+, female or male, black, white, brown or yellow, it does not matter to God. We are all God's children, made to love and be loved, and called by grace to do so.

Sadly, at times the Roman Catholic Church has misinterpreted grace as something earned, at least in terms of who is worthy or unworthy to receive the sacrament of Eucharist. However, the biblical definition of grace is not entrapped within a box. Grace is not an either/or proposition. If grace is earned, then it is not grace. Rather, it would be payment. Jesus made the difference quite clear, especially in his Parable of the Laborers in the Vineyard, which only appears in the Gospel of Matthew. In Matthew 20: 1–16, the wealthy owner of a vineyard hires laborers to work his vineyard at different times of the day, namely at dawn, nine o'clock in the morning, noon, three o'clock in the afternoon, and five o'clock in the early evening. Quitting time was at six o'clock in the evening, and at that time, the landowner paid the daily wages to the laborers. There is an ironic twist, however, which is clearly designed to shock us. Every laborer is paid the same daily wage, regardless of how many hours they worked. When one of the laborers who worked longer complained, the owner replied, "My friend, I am not cheating you, Did you not agree with me for the usual daily wage? Take what is yours and go. What if I wish to give this last one the same as you? [Or] am I not free to do as I wish with my own money? Are you envious because I am generous? Thus, the last will be first, and the first will be last."[23]

UNITY IN DIVERSITY: COGNITIVE DISSONANCE AND CHURCHES

This parable is a perfect example of cognitive dissonance. Inevitably, people and events enter our lives and demonstrate ideas and actions that do not connect to our vision of the world. Psychologists tell us that our brains dislike this kind of internal conflict. Cognitive dissonance can also appear when we least expect it, and from people and institutions that we may never have imagined as the source. In those cases, our basic faith may be shaken in that person or institution. For example, the clerical sexual abuse crisis in the Roman Catholic Church caused many lay people to question their leaders. Or perhaps a terrible accident or disease affects a loved one, and we begin to doubt whether a loving God exists. These are all normal human reactions to cognitive dissonance. Doubt is real, and, like many things, is inherently good.

Institutions also experience cognitive dissonance. We live in a world of vastly changing scientific and technological discoveries. Many of the innovations around us are double-edged swords. For instance, atomic bombs are capable of destroying the world. On the other hand, nuclear medicine saves lives. Computers and the internet allow humans to have access to more information in the palm of their hand than any of the world's largest libraries contain. Conversely, not all of this information is true or reliable, and some of it—for example, pornography—can dehumanize others.

Christian churches are likewise subject to cognitive dissonance. In fact, if they state that they are not, then either they are simply deceiving themselves, or choosing to ignore the world around them. Failing to share the Good News is not a viable option for churches, because that is their basic mission. Denying the need or even possibility of change is not helpful either. In fact, when I asked a priest-professor from a Catholic seminary recently about what the church might look like twenty years from now, he said that it would look exactly the way it looks today. If irrelevance and failing to share the Good News are the goals, then the professor was correct. If sharing God's love with everyone is a priority, then he is simply deceiving himself and others.

In the United States today, cognitive dissonance has invaded many of our Christian churches. The responses have been many and varied. Too often, however, on issues of deep importance to the lives of human beings, new approaches have been summarily rejected, without either serious reflection or consideration of the consequences of that rejection.

UNITY IN DIVERSITY: CHANGE AND RESISTANCE

Embracing change to solve problems is one of the principal ways that humans learn. Some people, of course, have difficulty understanding the importance and relevance of change in seeking the truth. Other people embrace change. "The differing reactions are not surprising, considering the fact that all change typically involves some sense of risk related to an unknown future." Sadly, "psychologists tell us that some people fear change so much that they will continue to engage in bad habits and addictions that make their lives unhappy rather than risk change."[24] It is precisely this fear that seems to paralyze the Catholic Church today, but institutional conscience may provide a path forward.

According to the *Catechism of the Catholic Church*, "Conscience is a judgment of reason whereby the human person recognizes the moral quality of a concrete act that he is going to perform, is in the process of performing, or has already completed." In addition, the *Catechism* states that "The education of the conscience is a lifelong task. From the earliest years, it awakens the child to the knowledge and practice of the interior law recognized by conscience. Prudent education teaches virtue; it prevents or cures fear, selfishness and pride, resentment arising from guilt, and feelings of complacency, born of human weakness and faults. The education of the conscience guarantees freedom and engenders peace of heart."[25]

While each of us has an individual conscience, we sometimes forget that institutions have a communal, that is, an institutional conscience. This institutional conscience helps groups—and churches—to make informed and rational decisions that seek the truth. Unfortunately, the institutional conscience of the Roman Catholic Church has been harmed by the clerical sexual abuse crisis. As a result, the legitimacy of the church's moral teachings has been impaired in the United States.

Nothing impairs a relationship as quickly as the lack of trust. When an institution or a person commits an action that breeds deceit and shatters trust, the consequences are far-reaching. The process of mourning the loss of trust is similar to that of a death. In 1969, American psychologist Dr. Elisabeth Kübler-Ross, "published a pioneering work entitled, *On Death and Dying*. In it, she postulated that terminally ill patients responded to their situations in a series of five stages, not necessarily in the same order."[26] The stages are usually referred to by the mnemonic of DABDA (Denial, Anger, Bargaining, Depression, and Acceptance).

The Clerical Sexual Abuse Crisis of the Roman Catholic Church in the late twentieth and the early twenty-first centuries was an important tipping point in church history, on a par with the Protestant Reformation of the 1500s. Although some church leaders, such as the former Pope Benedict XVI, have attempted to explain away the crisis by blaming it on the Sexual Revolution of the 1960s and the 1970s,[27] nothing could be further from the truth. The so-called Sexual Revolution in the United States was about sex between consenting adults, and also the associated use of birth control. It was not about pedophilia, a criminal offense involving sexual assault by an adult upon a child. Likewise, the pedophilia sexual abuse crisis in the Roman Catholic Church had little to do with homosexuality. Well-adjusted adult heterosexuals and homosexuals alike do not prey upon innocent children. Pedophilia is a serious criminal offense and, like rape, often involves psychological issues related to overpowering, harassing, and controlling others.

Studies have shown that the clerical sexual abuse scandal of the Roman Catholic Church has had a profound effect on people considering leaving the church. In March 2019, a new Gallup Poll of 581 U.S. Catholics included the following question, "As a result of the recent news about sexual abuse of young people by priests, have you, personally, questioned whether you would remain in the Catholic church, or not?" Of those polled, 37 percent answered, "Yes, have questioned," up significantly from 22 percent in 2002.[28]

Obvious reasons for those leaving the church because of the clerical sexual abuse scandal include mourning over family members and loved ones who were victims of abuse, as well as the loss of trust in the church and its hierarchy, as occasioned by the shroud of secrecy and lack of transparency that accompanied the pedophilia crisis. There is an understandable, and completely human, tendency for people to begin to question other aspects of the church and its teaching.

UNITY IN DIVERSITY: ESSENCE VERSUS ATTRIBUTES

Questioning, of course, is a rational process. It can lead the questioner to either greater doubt or deeper faith. In today's nonlinear world, however, our questioning needs to distinguish carefully between terminology. The essence of the Roman Catholic Church—the belief in a loving and merciful God who calls each individual to love God and one another—remains eternal, that is, unchangeable and timeless. On the other hand, decisions made by its clerics and rooted in time are changeable. Eternal truth does not have to be sacrificed in order for the church to adapt to new scientific theories. Clearly, the church was wrong about Galileo but correct about the very essence of Christianity. The church cannot—and indeed is incapable of—modifying the essence and nature of God. It is free, however, to change attributes or forms of church worship that it created in time, including policies regarding married priests, women priests, and open communion (i.e., extending the Eucharist to other Christians).

THE BARRIER TO CHANGE: STRUCTURAL SIN AND CLERICALISM

The history and extent of clericalism in the Roman Catholic Church has been studied by many scholars. The term "clericalism" derives from Latin and Greek sources referring to ministers or clergymen, quite literally "clerks." Today, clericalism has assumed the meaning of a religious hierarchy acting on behalf of—even sometimes opposed to—the laity, that is, those who are not priests, bishops, and the like.

The Roman Catholic Church has long attributed clerical authority to tradition and to a number of biblical passages, of which perhaps the most important and best expressed is Mathew 16:19: "I will give you the keys of the kingdom of heaven; and whatever you bind on earth shall have been bound in heaven, and whatever you loose on earth shall have been loosed in heaven." The God's Word translation offers another perspective: "I will give you the keys of the kingdom of heaven. Whatever you imprison, God will imprison. And whatever you set free, God will set free."[29]

As with all bible verses, we have to consider the context of Jesus's words, especially what transpired in the passages directly before them. In the beginning of chapter 16 of Matthew, the Pharisees asked Jesus for a sign, and he responded that they could forecast the weather. However, Jesus scorns the Pharisees for not being able to read the other signs all around them, particularly those that he is performing. Next, Jesus warns the disciples to beware of the leaven of the Pharisees and Sadducees, and in Mark 8:15, the warning is similar, to be cautious of the leaven of the Pharisees and of Herod. In Luke 12, Jesus actually refers to the Pharisees's leaven as hypocrisy.

Next, in Matthew 16, Jesus asked his disciples who they thought that he was. Simon responded that Jesus was the Messiah. At this point, Jesus stated that Simon would be known as Peter, the rock of the new church. Then, Jesus said, "I will give you the keys of the kingdom of heaven; and whatever you bind on earth shall have been bound in heaven, and whatever you loose on earth shall have been loosed in heaven."[30]

In the ancient world, locks were very expensive. Only the most important temples, government buildings, prisons, or storehouses would have featured sophisticated locks requiring complex keys. Door locks of that time period and in that area of the world were bolt mechanisms with "a number of holes into which fitted iron points in the door-post" and were "so arranged that they dropped into the corresponding holes as soon as the bolt was pushed into the opening made for it in the door-post."[31] Because of the expense of locks and keys, only the wealthiest, most powerful people could afford them. Possessing a key symbolized power and authority. Further, it was common knowledge in Jesus's time that Jewish rabbis officially "bound" and "loosed" obligations on people, particularly dealing with the 613 Jewish regulations in force. They also interpreted these regulations.

In addition to the context of Matthew chapter 16, we should also consider the overall views of Jesus. Throughout the gospel accounts, Jesus is unmistakably critical of many of the Jewish leaders, and how they had misinterpreted God's laws and misled others. He recognized how greed and hypocrisy had entered the inner sanctums of religion, even within the temple at Jerusalem. Further, Jesus disregarded many of the Jewish regulations regarding purification. He was not afraid of associating with sinners and those considered unclean. He refuted any and all theories blaming people for their own, or their children's, sicknesses or disabilities. He touched wounds and blood, in contravention of Jewish law. He even told a parable, the Good Samaritan (Luke 10:25–37), about how a Samaritan man (despised by Jews) helped a Jewish victim along the road, while a Jewish priest and a Levite passed by, because they feared touching the man and making themselves unclean.

Let's consider the New American Standard translation of the text again: "I will give you the keys of the kingdom of heaven; and whatever you bind on earth shall have been bound in heaven, and whatever you loose on earth shall have been loosed in heaven." "I will" is the future tense. "Shall have been" is what is called the future perfect tense, a rather complex way of stating that something will continue to happen for quite some time. In ancient Koine Greek of Jesus's time, the future perfect tense was used, but only in the passive voice. Let's review the passive and active voices. In English active voice, we can state: I threw the ball to you. The noun is "I," the verb is the past tense of "throw," the direct object is "the ball," and "you" is the indirect object. In passive tense, we can state: The ball was thrown to you by me. The meaning is basically the same, but the focus of the sentence is different in each.

For centuries, this scriptural passage has been incorrectly translated from the future perfect tense of the Ancient Greek into the future tense of Latin, "whatever you bind on earth will be bound in heaven, and what you loose on earth will be loosed in heaven." However, the future tense has a completely different meaning from that of the Koine Greek future perfect tense: "I will give you the keys of the kingdom of heaven; and whatever you bind on earth shall have been bound in heaven, and whatever you loose on earth shall have been loosed in heaven." "Shall have been bound in heaven" means that the binding and loosing have already happened in heaven, and are continuing to happen now, and will happen in the future. The future perfect tense in Koine Greek "always implies past action, even though the emphasis is on the continuance of the results."[32] As a passive tense, as well, the noun is not the disciples, but God. The disciples are the messengers of the Good News of forgiveness, not the decision-makers determining who can be forgiven and who cannot.

Considering the context of Matthew 16, Jesus's warnings to the disciples about the hypocrisy (bad leaven) of the Pharisees, Simon's faith in Jesus as Messiah, the understanding of locks, keys, binding and "loosing" to the Jews, and the accurate translation of the passage from the Greek future perfect tense, the meaning of Matthew 16:19 becomes clearer. It is doubtful, knowing Jesus's basic philosophy and realizing that he had just warned his disciples about the hypocrisy of the Pharisees, that he would have been suggesting that the disciples add a whole new level of complications to the 613 regulations of Judaism at that time. Rather, Jesus was more likely stating that salvation was in God's hands, and that the disciples needed to share that Good News with others. In addition, the disciples needed to love and respect others, forgiving others as God forgave them. Thus, twenty-first-century clericalism has no biblical mandate. Indeed, clericalism stands in the way of the church moving forward.

UNITY IN DIVERSITY

Adherents to clericalism also maintain ties to longstanding, traditional practices that exclude women, members of the LGBTQ+ community, and others from active priestly roles. When members of their own patriarchy question this exclusion, debate is officially terminated. What is merely a practice is regarded as the equivalence of doctrine. For example, some theological arguments offered in support of male-only ordination are questionable at best. For instance, Rev. Wojciech Giertych, a theologian on the staff of Pope Benedict XVI stated that "The son of God became flesh, but became flesh not as sexless humanity but as a male." According to the author of the article, Francis X. Rocca, Giertych believed that "Men are more likely to think of God in terms of philosophical definitions and logical syllogisms," and further that they demonstrate understanding "about structures, about the buildings of the church, about the roof of the church which is leaking, about the bishops' conference, about the concordat between the church and the state." On the other hand, the theologian argued that "The mission of the woman in the church is to convince the male that power is not most important in the church, not even sacramental power."[33]

This so-called special role of women was a theme popular in nineteenth-century America. The cult of domesticity ideology maintained that women's special role was as a compassionate nurturer to her spouse and family, in addition to bringing peace and civilization to an otherwise cutthroat male world. The home was her special abode, where she presided over providing a respite from the cares and concerns of the outside world. World War II and the need for women to work in factories outside the home helped to unravel the simplicity of this cult of domesticity. So too did the Civil Rights movement of the 1950s and the 1960s, which rejected the subjugation of blacks, Latinx, Native Americans, and women to roles predetermined by white males. Likewise, the LGBTQ+ community demanded their dignity as well.

Scientific scholarship is slowing unlocking the secrets of homosexuality. Brain scans of adult gay men closely resemble those for heterosexual women. Likewise, MRIs of lesbian women are more akin to the brains of heterosexual men. Further, it seems quite plausible that these brain changes are likely the consequences of fetal development. Other studies are offering clear evidence that a pregnant mother's timely, or untimely, release of certain hormones and antibodies directly affects fetal sexual development. The evidence is becoming increasingly indisputable scientifically—homosexual humans are created in the womb.[34]

To the disappointment of many, in June 2019 the Vatican released a new document entitled *Male and Female He Created Them*.[35] This document refers to transgendered individuals as a trend. Further, in the case of intersex newborns, it recommends that the medical doctor present—not the parents—make the least invasive decision to determine the newborn's sexuality.[36] Current church teaching in relation to gender and human sexuality is seriously outdated in terms of the scientific evidence. The church's overreliance on natural law, and on defining sexuality as only related to procreation, is largely responsible for these flaws. Indeed, such a natural law determination is not corroborated by scientific evidence. Homosexual activities do, in fact, exist in many species in nature. Sex pheromones and other hormones play key roles in sexual attraction. Not every sexual act needs to include the possibility of procreation. In fact, the hormone oxytocin is released by couples engaged in sex, playing an integral role in building trust, stability, and monogamy.

Likewise, arguments that same-sex marriage somehow contributes to the disintegration of the American family are unfounded. In 2015, the U.S. Supreme Court approved same-sex marriage in the United States, decades after a period of increasing divorce rates. Unless a heterosexual couple divorces because one spouse has been a closeted homosexual, same-sex marriage has no effect whatsoever on heterosexual couples.[37] On the other hand, I have personally witnessed how gay and lesbian friends have adopted the children of heterosexual relatives unable to provide a loving home, for various reasons. In such instances, the children benefit from a stable home, access to educational and other opportunities, and plenty of love.

THE GRADATIONS OF CHANGE: UNITY IN DIVERSITY

As a professor, I am gifted by witnessing change many times throughout the academic year, but especially at graduation ceremonies. The word graduation derives from a Latin word meaning degree or step. If we think about it, every important change in our lives is a literal step. Throughout our lives, we will continue to climb stairs, one step at a time. Some of these steps will be more difficult than others, but all will involve looking up rather than down. To some extent, each change involves the passing of one part of our lives and the birth of a new opportunity. However, we still remain the same person, merely transformed. We are living testimonials to the Trinity—multiple parts yet unified. Change is from God, and God made all of us for change—change for the better of the world.

In centuries past, when scientific and cultural changes occurred more slowly, the need to amend church practices was less imperative than today. However, modern science and technology is rapid and all-pervasive. We, as church, need not apologize for adapting to it. The willingness to embrace change is proof that we value the gifts of wisdom and learning with which God has endowed us. The Kingdom of God is now. We are charged to spread the Good News of eternal truth—to love, forgive, and heal. We cannot leave anyone behind. No one owns God or the path to God. Those seeking God will find God, whether we lock them out, or guard the doors to Jesus's heart in the Eucharist. Our deep love of God beseeches us to love radically, to include everyone, and to seek the unity in diversity which God has so clearly displayed in all of creation.

NOTES

1. For official Roman Catholic versions of the Apostles' and the Nicene Creeds, see *Catechism of the Catholic Church*, accessed October 2019, http://www.vatican.va/archive/ccc_css/archive/catechism/credo.htm.

2. "Attendance at Religious Services," Pew Research Center, *2014 U.S. Religious Landscape Study*, accessed October 2019, https://www.pewforum.org/religious-landscape-study/attendance-at-religious-services/.

3. "Mass Attendance in U.S. Down in Recent Years, Gallup Poll Finds," *Crux*, April 11, 2018, accessed October 2019, https://cruxnow.com/church-in-the-usa/2018/04/11/mass-attendance-in-us-down-in-recent-years-gallup-poll-finds/.

4. Crane Brinton, *The Anatomy of Revolution* (New York, NY: Vintage Books, revised and expanded ed., 1965): 36.

5. "Heraclitus," *Stanford Encyclopedia of Philosophy*, accessed October 2019, https://plato.stanford.edu/entries/heraclitus/#Flu.

6. For an excellent overview of the life and works of Aristotle, see: "Aristotle," *Stanford Encyclopedia of Philosophy*, accessed October 2019, https://plato.stanford.edu/entries/aristotle/.

7. For an excellent overview of the life and works of Aquinas, see: "Saint Thomas Aquinas," *Stanford Encyclopedia of Philosophy*, accessed October 2019, https://plato.stanford.edu/entries/aquinas/.

8. Paul A. Tenkotte, *The United States since 1865: Information Literacy and Critical Thinking*. Online textbook (Dubuque, IA: Great River Learning, 2019), Chapter 3.10.

9. Paul A. Wallace, ed. *The Travels of John Heckewelder in Frontier America* (Pittsburgh, PA: University of Pittsburgh Press, 1958), 1.

10. For the history of the Habsburgs, see: Robert A. Kann, *A History of the Habsburg Empire, 1526–1918* (Berkeley, CA: University of California Press, 1974); Andrew Wheatcroft, *Habsburgs: Embodying Empire* (London, United Kingdom: Penguin Books, 1996); Edward Crankshaw, *The Habsburgs: Portrait of a Dynasty* (New York, NY: Viking Press, 1971); William Maltby, *The Reign of Charles V* (Houndmills, United Kingdom: Palgrave, 2002); and Martyn Rady, *The Emperor Charles V* (London, United Kingdom: Longman, 1988).

11. Heinrich August Winkler, *Germany: The Long Road West*, vol. 1, trans. Alexander J. Sager (Oxford, United Kingdom: Oxford University Press, 2013), 17.

12. W. R. Ward, *The Protestant Evangelical Awakening* (Cambridge, United Kingdom: Cambridge University Press, 1992); Koppel S. Pinson, *Pietism as a Factor in the Rise of German Nationalism* (New York, NY: Columbia University Press, 1934).

13. Paul A. Wallace, ed., *The Travels of John Heckewelder in Frontier America* (Pittsburgh, PA: University of Pittsburgh Press, 1958); W. R. Ward, *The Protestant Evangelical Awakening* (Cambridge, United Kingdom: Cambridge University Press, 1992); Paul Wemmer, *Count Zinzendorf and the Spirit of the Moravians* (Camarillo, CA: Xulon Press, 2013); *Bethlehem of Pennsylvania*, 2 vols.

(Bethlehem, PA: Bethlehem Book Committee,1968); R. Douglas Hurt, *The Ohio Frontier: Crucible of the Old Northwest, 1720–1830* (Bloomington, IN: Indiana University Press, 1996).

14. Peter Guilday, *A History of the Councils of Baltimore, 1791–1884* (New York: The Macmillan Company, 1932; reprint ed., New York: Arno Press and the New York Times, 1969), 10, 253; Joseph E. Ciesluk, *National Parishes in the United States* (Washington, D.C.: The Catholic University of America Press, 1944), 39–42.

15. Richard Black, "Species Count Put at 8.7 Million," *BBC News*, August 23, 2011, accessed September 2019, https://www.bbc.com/news/science-environment-14616161.

16. "Current World Population," worldometers, accessed September 2019, https://www.worldometers.info/world-population/.

17. "Growth Rate," worldometers, accessed September 2019, https://www.worldometers.info/world-population/#growthrate.

18. Roger Highfield, "DNA Survey Finds all Humans Are 99.9 pc the Same," *The Telegraph*, December 20, 2002, accessed September 2019, https://www.telegraph.co.uk/news/worldnews/northamerica/usa/1416706/DNA-survey-finds-all-humans-are-99.9pc-the-same.html.

19. "Global Warming of 1.5° C," The Intergovernmental Panel on Climate Change, United Nations, accessed November 2019, https://www.ipcc.ch/sr15/.

20. Tenkotte, Chapter 8.2.

21. Joshua J. McElwee, "Vatican Cardinal: 'Amoris Laetitia' Allows Some Remarried to Take Communion," February 14, 2017, accessed November 2019, https://www.ncronline.org/news/vatican/vatican-cardinal-amoris-laetitia-allows-some-remarried-take-communion.

22. Jessica M. Murdoch, "The New Jansenism," *First Things*, February 21, 2017, accessed September 2019, https://www.firstthings.com/web-exclusives/2017/02/the-new-jansenism.

23. Matthew 20:13–16, New American Bible (Revised Edition), Bible Gateway, accessed October 2019, https://www.biblegateway.com/passage/?search=Matthew+20%3A1-16&version=NABRE (accessed August 2019).

24. Tenkotte, Chapter 2.3.

25. Article 6, Moral Conscience, *Catechism of the Catholic Church*, accessed September 2019, http://www.vatican.va/archive/ccc_css/archive/catechism/p3s1c1a6.htm.

26. Tenkotte, Chapter 2.3.

27. Joshua J. McElwee, "In New Letter, Benedict Blames Clergy Abuse in Sexual Revolution, Vatican II Theology," *National Catholic Reporter*, April 11, 2019, accessed November 2019, https://www.ncronline.org/news/accountability/new-letter-benedict-blames-clergy-abuse-sexual-revolution-vatican-ii-theology.

28. Jeffrey M. Jones, "Many U.S. Catholics Question Their Membership Amid Scandal," *Gallup*, March 13, 2019, accessed September 2019, https://news.gallup.com/poll/247571/catholics-question-membership-amid-scandal.aspx.

29. Matthew 16:19, Bible Hub, accessed August 2019. https://biblehub.com/matthew/16-19.htm.

30. Matthew 16: 19, New American Standard Bible, Bible Hub, accessed November 2019, https://biblehub.com/nasb/matthew/16.htm.

31. Emil G. Hirsch and M. Seligsohn. "Key," *Jewish Encyclopedia,* accessed August 2019, http://www.jewishencyclopedia.com/articles/9294-key.

32. Wilbur T. Dayton, "John 20:23; Matthew 16:19 and 18:18 In the Light of the Greek Perfect Tenses," *The Asbury Seminarian* 2, no. 2 (June 1947): 77, accessed August 2019, https://pdfs.semanticscholar.org/d04d/a007a64e6536bbae60c22e2eb9c40ed00e80.pdf; Jeff Rydberg-Cox, "Lesson XX: Aorist, Perfect, Pluperfect, and Future Perfect Indicative Middle," *A Digital Tutorial for Ancient Greek*, accessed August 2019, https://daedalus.umkc.edu/FirstGreekBook/JWW_FGB20.html.

33. Francis X. Rocca, "Why Not Women Priests? The Papal Theologian Explains," *National Catholic Reporter*, February 5, 2013, accessed August 2019, https://www.ncronline.org/news/theology/why-not-women-priests-papal-theologian-explains.

34. Simon LeVay, *Gay, Straight and the Reason Why: The Science of Sexual Orientation.* 2nd ed. (New York, NY: Oxford University Press, 2017); Joan Roughgarden, *Evolution's Rainbow: Diversity, Gender, and Sexuality in Nature and People* (Berkeley, CA: University of California Press, 2013).

35. Paul J. Schutz, "A Response to the Vatican Document 'Male and Female He Created Them,'" *National Catholic Reporter*, June 24, 2019, accessed November 2019, https://www.ncronline.org/news/opinion/response-vatican-document-male-and-female-he-created-them.

36. Vatican Congregation for Catholic Education, *Male and Female He Created Them: Towards a Path of Dialogue on the Question of Gender Theory in Education*, Section 24, accessed November 2019, https://zenit.org/articles/new-vatican-document-provides-schools-with-guidance-on-gender-issues/; "Recent Catholic Statement Endangers Intersex Children," *Intersex and Faith*, accessed November 2019, https://www.intersexandfaith.org/news/2019/6/17/catholic-statement-endangers-intersex-children.

37. "Marriage and Divorce," *CDC Centers for Disease Control and Prevention*, accessed November 2019, https://www.cdc.gov/nchs/fastats/marriage-divorce.htm; Donesha Aldridge, "Divorce Rates Lower in States that Allow Same-Sex Marriage," The Williams Institute, UCLA School of Law, accessed November 2019, https://williamsinstitute.law.ucla.edu/press/in-the-news/divorce-rates-lower-in-states-that-allow-same-sex-marriage/.

BIBLIOGRAPHY

Bokenkotter, Thomas. *A Concise History of the Catholic Church.* Revised and expanded ed. New York, NY: Image Books of Doubleday, 1990.

———. *Church and Revolution: Catholics in the Struggle for Democracy and Social Justice*. New York, NY: Image Books of Doubleday, 1998.

———. *Dynamic Catholicism: A Historical Catechism.* New York, NY: Image Books of Doubleday, 1992 ed.

Boswell, John. *Christianity, Social Tolerance, and Homosexuality*. Chicago, IL: University of Chicago Press, 1980.

Carr, Anne E. *Transforming Grace: Christian Tradition and Women's Experience*. New York, NY: Harper and Row, 1988.

Crosby, Michael H. *The Dysfunctional Church: Addiction and Codependency in the Family of Catholicism*. Notre Dame, IN: Ava Maria Press, 1991.

Cullen, Jim. *Restless in the Promised Land: Catholics and the American Dream*. Franklin, WI: Sheed and Ward, 2001.

D'Antonio, William V., James D. Davidson, Dean R. Hoge, and Mary L Gautier. *American Catholics Today: New Realities of Their Faith and Their Church*. Lanham, MA: Rowman & Littlefield, 2007.

Dolan, Jay P. *Catholic Revivalism and the American Experience, 1830–1900*. Notre Dame, IN: University of Notre Dame Press, 1978.

———. *In Search of an American Catholicism: A History of Religion and Culture in Tension*. New York, NY: Oxford University Press, 2002.

———. *The American Catholic Experience: A History from Colonial Times to the Present*. Notre Dame, IN: University of Notre Dame Press, 1992.

———. *The Immigrant Church: New York's Irish and German Catholics, 1815–1865*. Baltimore, MD: The Johns Hopkins University Press, 1975.

Dupré, John. *Human Nature and the Limits of Science*. Oxford, UK: Oxford University Press, 2001.

Ellinger, Herbert. *Hinduism*. Valley Forge, PA: Trinity Press, 1995.

Ellis, John Tracy. *American Catholicism*. Second ed., revised. Chicago, IL: The University of Chicago Press, 1969.

Emery, Gilles. *The Trinity: An Introduction to Catholic Doctrine and the Triune God*. Washington, DC: The Catholic University of America, 2011.

Fitzgerald, Frances. *The Evangelicals: The Struggle to Shape America*. New York, NY: Simon and Schuster, 2017.

Fogarty, Gerald P., ed. *Patterns of Episcopal Leadership*. New York, NY: Macmillan 1989.

———. *The Vatican and the American Hierarchy from 1870 to 1965*. Wilmington: DE: Michael Glazier, 1985.

Fox, Thomas C. *Sexuality and Catholicism*. New York, NY: George Braziller, 1995.

Gollar, C. Walker. *American and Catholic: Stories of the People Who Built the Church*. Cincinnati, OH: Franciscan Media, 2015.

Hatch, Nathan O. *The Democratization of American Christianity*. New Haven, Ct: Yale University Press, 1989.

Hegy, Pierre. *Wake Up, Lazarus! On Catholic Renewal*. Bloomington, IN: Universe, 2012.

Hendry, Joy. *Understanding Japanese Society*. Second ed. London, UK: Routledge, 1995.

Hennesey, James. *American Catholics: A History of the Roman Catholic Community in the United States*. New York, NY: Oxford University Press 1981.

Hill, Brennan R. *Exploring Catholic Theology: God, Jesus, Church, and Sacraments*. Mystic, CT: Twenty-Third Publications, 4th printing, 2001.

Holland, Joe. *Roman Catholic Clericalism*. Washington, DC: Pacem in Terris Pres,
Hoffman, Lawrence A. *We Have Sinned: Sin and Confession in Judaism*. Nashville, TN: Jewish Lights. 2012.
Jordan, Mark D. *The Invention of Sodomy in Christian Theology*. Chicago, IL: University of Chicago Press, 1997.
Keenan, Marie. *Child Sexual Abuse and the Catholic Church: Gender, Power, and Organizational Culture*. Oxford, UK: Oxford University Press, 2012.
Kübler-Ross, Elisabeth. *On Death and Dying*. New York, NY: Macmillan, 1969.
Laqueur, Thomas W. *Solitary Sex: A Cultural History of Masturbation*. New York, NY: Zone Books, 2004.
LeVay, Simon. *Gay, Straight and the Reason Why: The Science of Sexual Orientation*. Second ed. New York, NY: Oxford University Press, 2017.
LaVerdiere, Eugene. *The Eucharist in the New Testament and the Early Church*. Collegeville, MN: The Liturgical Press, 1996.
Levine, Amy-Jill and Marc Zvi Brettler, eds. *The Jewish Annotated New Testament*. Second ed. New York, NY: Oxford University Press, 2017.
Liptak, Dolores. *Immigrants and Their Church*. New York, NY: Macmillan, 1989.
Malik, Kenan. *The Quest for a Moral Compass: A Global History of Ethics*. New York, NY: Melville House, 2014.
Martel, Frédéric. *In the Closet of the Vatican: Power, Homosexuality, Hypocrisy*. London, UK: Bloomsbury, 2019.
Martin, James. *Building a Bridge: How the Catholic Church and the LGBT Community Can Enter into a Relationship of Respect, Compassion, and Sensitivity*. New York, NY: Harper, 2017.
Marty, Martin E. *A Short History of American Catholicism*. Allen, TX: Thomas More Publishing, 1995.
Massa, Mark S. *Catholics and American Culture*. New York, NY: Crossroad, 1999.
Mich, Marvin L. Krier. *Catholic Social Teaching and Movements*. Mystic, CT: Twenty-Third Publications, 1998.
Moody, Raymond A., Jr. *Life after Life*. New York, NY: Bantam Books, 1975.
Muller, James E., and Charles Kenney. *Keep the Faith, Change the Church*. Emmaus, PA: Rodale, 2004.
Noll, Mark A. *A History of Christianity in the United States and Canada*. Grand Rapids, MI: William B. Eerdmans, 1992.
Oberman, Heiko A. *Luther: Man between God and the Devil*. New York, NY: Image Books of Doubleday, 1992.
O'Brien, David. *Public Catholicism*. New York, NY: Macmillan, 1989.
O'Brien, John A. *The Faith of Millions*. Huntington, IN: Our Sunday Visitor, 1974.
Owen, Adrian. *Into the Gray Zone: A Neuroscientist Explores the Border between Life and Death*. New York, NY: Scribner, 2017.
Ozment, Steven. *A Mighty Fortress: A New History of the German People, 100 B.C. to the 21st Century*. London, UK: Granta Books, 2004.
Perito, John E. *Contemporary Catholic Sexuality*. New York, NY: Crossroad Publishing, 2003.

Ranke-Heinemann, Uta. *Eunuchs for the Kingdom of Heaven: Women, Sexuality, and the Catholic Church*. New York, NY: Doubleday1990.

Rosenberger, Nancy R., ed. *Japanese Sense of Self*. Cambridge, UK: Cambridge University Press, 1992.

Roughgarden, Joan. *Evolution's Rainbow: Diversity, Gender, and Sexuality in Nature and People* Berkeley, CA: University of California Press, 2013.

Schoenherr, Richard A. and Lawrence A. Young. *Full Pews and Empty Altars: Demographics of the Priest Shortage in United States Catholic Dioceses*. Madison, WI: University of Wisconsin Press, 1993.

Schreck, Alan. *Rebuild My Church: God's Plan for Authentic Catholic Renewal*. Cincinnati, OH: Servant Books, 2010.

Shaw, Stephen J. *The Catholic Parish as a Way-Station of Ethnicity and Americanization: Chicago's Germans and Italians, 1903–1939*. New York, NY: Carlson, 1991.

Snelling, John. *The Buddhist Handbook*. Rochester, VT: Inner Traditions, 1991.

Spitz, Lewis W. *The Protestant Reformation, 1517–1559*. New York, NY: Harper and Row, 1985.

Sproul, R. C. *Faith Alone: The Evangelical Doctrine of Justification*. Grand Rapids, MI: Baker Books, 1995.

Thompson, Laurence G. *Chinese Religion: An Introduction*. Fifth ed. Belmont, CA: Wadsworth, 1996.

Turpin, Joanne. *Women in Church History*. Cincinnati, OH: St. Anthony Messenger Press, 1990.

Wilson, George B. *Clericalism: The Death of Priesthood*. Collegeville, MN: Liturgical Press, 2008.

Winkler, Heinrich August *Germany: The Long Road West*, vol. 1, trans. Alexander J. Sager. Oxford, United Kingdom: Oxford University Press, 2013.

Witham, Larry. *The Measure of God: Our Century-Long Struggle to Reconcile Science and Religion*. San Francisco, CA: Harper Collins, 2005.

Yancey, Philip. *What's So Amazing about Grace?* Grand Rapids, MI: Zondervan, 1997.

Chapter 3

Crises and Opportunities since Vatican II

Conscience, Social Action, and Transparency

Pierre Hegy

Three major events happened as a consequence of Second Vatican Council (or Vatican II, 1962–1965) that still affect us today. The first was the encyclical *Humanae Vitae* which raised the issue of obedience versus conscience. The second event was the development of liberation theology which quickly became a major spiritual force for change in the West but was repressed. The third and least known was the rewriting of the code of canon law which downgraded the sanctions for clerical sex abuse. These three events created deep crisis but were also opportunities for the Catholic Church (henceforth, "the church"). Finally, Pope Francis addressed none of these issues directly and systematically, but he laid the groundwork for their possible resolution.

The 1917 code of canon law has been called the greatest revolution in canon law since the time of Gratian in the 1150s. A universal codification of church law had been called for by the Council of Trent (1545–1563) and the First Vatican I Council (1870). Finally, in 1904 Pius X created a commission that created the 1917 code. Reflecting its historical setting—the time of the last European monarchies before World War I—this code identified Catholics as subjects of the church the way they were subjects of kings or emperors in the civil society; in all cases their main duty was obedience. In the 1983 code, the status of Catholics changed from subjects to members in the church, while in their civil societies they were citizens. Citizens are protected by laws and the courts while Catholic membership is not. By canon law, one becomes a member in the church through baptism and "by the bonds of the profession of faith, the sacraments and of ecclesial governance."[1] Membership does not entitle Catholics with legal rights while obedience remains the main duty. The problem is that in the antiestablishment culture of the 1960s to today, membership without rights is increasingly seen as an oxymoron. It is membership based on obedience versus citizenship guaranteed by legal rights that is at the core of the three crises to be discussed here, the ban of artificial birth control, liberation theology, and the cover-up of clerical sex crimes. The Catholics' experience of citizenship in their respective countries is also an opportunity for the church to reform itself. I will develop this thesis in the three crises just mentioned.

AUTHORITY VERSUS CONSCIENCE AND LEGAL RIGHTS

In *Humanae Vitae* (1968) Pope Paul VI reasserted the traditional teachings about church authority and obedience. His argument can be summarized in two points, one about doctrine and the other about obedience. According to the pope, there is an "inseparable connection, established by God, between the unitive significance and the procreative significance which are both inherent to the marriage act."[2] In simple terms, every sexual act must be open to procreation. The justification of this position is found in neo-Scholastic ecclesiology: "The Church is competent in her magisterium to interpret the natural moral law . . . [because] Jesus Christ communicated His divine power to Peter and the other Apostles [and] constituted them as the authentic guardians and interpreters of the whole moral law."[3] The encyclical ends with a call to "inward as well as outward [obedience] which is due to the magisterium of the Church." Because "the pastors of the Church enjoy a special light of the Holy Spirit in teaching the truth . . . [they] are bound to obedience."[4]

This teaching ran into strong opposition, even before it was published. The lay birth commission created by Paul VI had voted fifteen against four in favor of doctrinal change, and the commission of cardinals and bishops voted nine against three and three abstentions in favor of such change, but the minority persuaded the pope that "the church cannot change."[5] The day after the promulgation of the encyclical, theologians of the Catholic University of America in Washington DC published a declaration asserting the right of dissent which received 650 signatures from theologians of all over the world within a month. In their response to the encyclical, the national conferences of Germany, Belgium, Canada, Scandinavia, and France emphasized the rights of conscience. One of the Vatican's greatest powers is patience. Cardinal O'Boyle of Washington sanctioned about sixty of his dissenting priests, and over time everything quieted down.

The disciplinary measures against the opponents of *Humanae Vitae*, in particular the dismissal of theologian Charles Curran from his position at the Catholic University, raised intellectual questions which could not be easily dismissed: Is the teaching on birth control infallible? Is there room in the church for loyal dissent?[6] More radically, is the papacy itself infallible?[7] The hierarchy ignored these questions and silenced prominent opponents. Pope John Paul II created a new uproar with his teaching that "accordance with God's eternal plan" Christ only chose men to be priests.[8] To put an end to the public controversy, he promulgated canonical measures against dissidents: "Anyone who rejects those propositions which are to be held definitely is opposed to the doctrine of the Catholic Church" and shall be subject to punishment according to canons 1371 and 1436.[9] There can be no appeal, because there is no body of legal rights and no courts to enforce them.

The crisis of authority created by *Humanae Vitae* is still with us, and so is the opportunity to deal with it creatively. Let us briefly review the major declarations of human rights in the civil society which stand as a challenge to Catholic reform. The basic rights of freedom of speech and religion upheld by the Enlightenment have been institutionalized in various bills or lists of rights, mainly in the United States, France, and the United Nations. Are the declarations of rights natural rights or just civil rights? Are they enforced and enforceable by independent courts? In the United States' Bill of Rights, only the first (freedom of religion, speech, and the press) are natural rights, the others are civil rights. The French Declaration of the Rights of Man and of the Citizen (1789) added private property to the list of natural rights; it also included constitutional need for three independent branches of government following Montesquieu (1748). The United Nations' Declaration of Human Rights (1948) consists of thirty articles with about as many human rights; they are widely accepted but nonbinding in national courts. Finally, the various forms of consumer rights (e.g., the Act of Parliament of the United Kingdom of 2015) define the rights and obligations of specific groups. In reference to all these rights, laws were enacted that created innumerable opportunities for social development.

The Catholic Church has not been indifferent to these legal achievements, and in Vatican II it clearly asserted the principle of religious freedom and the rights of conscience: "Every man [sic] has the duty, and therefore the right, to seek the truth in matters religious in order that he may with prudence form for himself right and true judgments of conscience."[10] More specifically, "Conscience is the most secret core and sanctuary of a man. There he is alone with God, Whose voice echoes in his depths. . . . For man has in his heart a law written by God; to obey it is the very dignity of man; according to it he will be judged."[11]

Catholicism needs a bill of rights and was about to create one when this endeavor was abruptly rejected by Pope John Paul II. A quiet revolution had taken place within the Commission for the Revision of Canon Law. In 1967 its President, Cardinal Felici created a central committee to develop a set of constitutional principles (the *lex fundamentalis*) that should inspire the whole new code. A proposal in ten principles was submitted to and approved by the 1967 Synod of Bishops. A new draft was sent to the Congregation for the Doctrine of the Faith in 1969 and to all the bishops of the world in 1971. By then the idea of a constitution for the church was widely accepted; it had been approved by Paul VI as early as 1965. By 1972, the document consisted of 95 canons of principles, rights, and duties. Canons 3 to 5 affirmed the principles of basic equality, universal vocation, and religious freedom. Canons 10 to 25 outlined basic rights, more specifically the rights of freedom of speech and inquiry, the right of association, and various procedural and remedial rights. In its discussion of the proposed constitution, the1967 Synod of bishops had asked for a greater protection against arbitrary administrative decisions. Such measures were later included in the proposed *lex fundamentalis*, namely the right of administrative recourse, the creation of administrative courts (at least one per nation), and the plaintiff's right to counsel. In 1981, the proposed new code was examined by a special commission created by John Paul II, but a few months later it became known that no constitution and no bill of rights would be included in the new code, which after a personal review by Pope John Paul II went into effect in 1983.[12]

Given the near success of creating a Catholic constitution and a bill of rights, the issue can be brought up again. This is not the direction taken by Pope Francis who favors instead a more flexible understanding of canonical and moral laws. In the past and even today, moral laws are to be interpreted in the light of Tradition, that is, the norms and practices as defined by the hierarchy. But moral theologians have expanded the criteria of moral interpretation, from two (scripture and Tradition) to four: scripture as understood in historical criticism, the variety of Catholic and non-Catholic traditions, the findings of the social sciences about the circumstances and consequences of moral behavior, and the pastoral experience in applying moral laws.[13] This is also the direction taken by Pope Francis as we will see here.

LIBERATION THEOLOGY AND THE AUTONOMY OF CATHOLIC ACTIVISM

Liberation theology has been a major force for change since Vatican II. It originated and spread around the world independently of the hierarchy, which for the institution raised the fear of loss of control. I will briefly review its origin in the conference of Medellín in 1968, its development in the work of Gustavo Gutierrez, and raise the question of autonomy of Catholic activism.

At their second continental meeting in Medellín, Columbia, the Latin American bishops discussed "The transformation of Latin America in the light of the [Vatican II] Council." The first two chapters of their document, on justice and peace, summarize their message. From the very first pages the situation of Latin America is described as one of "injustice which cries to the heavens," a situation characterized by "unjust structures."[14] This characterization is justified in the name of church doctrine: Jesus Christ came to "liberate all men from the slavery which sin has subjected them: hunger, misery, oppression and ignorance, in a word, that injustice and hatred which have their origin in human selfishness."[15] This statement is buttressed by references to Vatican II and Paul VI's encyclical *Populorum progressio.*[16]

The Medellín document offers a very broad agenda for change. Liberal capitalism "militates against the dignity of the human person" and must be revised.[17] Many workers live in a situation "which borders on slavery."[18] Industrialization must preserve "the legitimate autonomy of our nation[s]."[19] Political reform must be seen as a prerequisite for any reform. Violence is endemic in unequal societies where the dominant classes resort to force to repress any attempt of change.[20] Quoting *Populorum progressio*, Medellín condemned the "international imperialism of money" and the unjust international order through which Latin American nations "always remain poor, while the industrialized countries enrich themselves."[21] In short, Latin America finds itself in a situation of institutionalized violence which comes from its unjust structures rather than from a rebellion against them. In response to this situation, the bishops called for the "conscientization" of all the active elements of the church and society.

While Medellín dedicated only about thirty pages to injustice, Gustavo Gutierrez developed the topic in 300 pages in his *Theology of Liberation* originally published in 1971. Development versus dependency was a major topic of contention at the time. It was addressed by Vice-President Nelson Rockefeller during his presidential mission to Latin America in 1969.[22] The economic theory favored by the United States was development through the transfer of technology but in Latin America this was seen as international dependency. In his book Gutierrez clearly took sides. In his very first pages he stated that "the term *development* does not well express [our] profound aspiration." What he proposes instead was "liberation."[23] For him, development is "synonymous with reformism," being "ineffective in the long run and counterproductive to achieve a real transformation." What was needed was "a radical break from the status quo, that is, a profound transformation of the private property system, access to power of the exploited classes, and a social revolution that would [lead to] a socialist society."[24] More specifically, "there *can be authentic development* for Latin America only if there is liberation from the domination exercised by the great capitalist countries, and especially by the Unites States of America."[25]

Gutierrez was a secular priest from the archdiocese of Lima and his archbishop happened to be a conservative. His sociopolitical proposal was not well received in Rome. The official response was given in the "Instructions on Certain Aspects of the Theology of Liberation" by Cardinal Ratzinger (who later became Pope Benedict XVI), then Prefect of the Congregation of the Doctrine of the Faith.[26] Liberation theologies were to be seen as "serious ideological deviations." The two main accusations leveled against them were the use of Marxist class analysis and the "subversion of the meaning of truth and violence." As stated in an interview, "What is theologically unacceptable here and socially dangerous, is this mixture of Bible, Christology, politics, sociology, and economics." What is needed is a return to an orthodox understanding of sin: "It is precisely personal sin that is in reality at the root of unjust social structures. Those who really desire a more human society need to begin with the root, not with the trunk and the branches."[27] For Ratzinger, no dialogue was possible with "theologians who cling to the myth of the class struggle as an instrument in creating a classless society."[28]

Marxism was seen as dangerous not only in the church by all authoritarian regimes of Latin America. Hence the Holy See was on the side of the national security dictatorships. Over the following two decades liberation theologians and social activists were marginalized, if not persecuted, by the central governments of both the church and the civil societies. In Chile, Argentina, Brazil, and Guatemala, thousands of priests and social activists were imprisoned or killed as communists and subversives. Many if not most prominent Catholic theologians were under investigation and/or sanctioned: Gustavo Gutierrez of Peru, Leonardo Boff of Brazil, Ernesto Cardenal of Nicaragua, Hans Küng of Switzerland, Charles Curran in the United States, Edward Schillebeeckx of the Netherlands, and quite a few others.[29] As a general rule, all priests were ordered to withdraw from politics, for example the U.S. senator and Jesuit priest, Robert Drinan.

What is also at stake here is the role of lay participation in the life of the church. The limits of lay initiatives are clearly spelled out in canon law. No ministry (e.g., a soup kitchen) "shall assume the name Catholic unless the consent of the competent ecclesiastical authority is given" (canon 216). Similarly, no association (e.g., the Catholic Workers) "shall assume the name Catholic unless" (canon 300); similarly, no school (canon 803) and no university (canon 803#3) shall call itself Catholic without authorization. Those who do can be prosecuted legally or administratively, and those who are not recognized are simply ignored. Such legislation does not favor lay initiatives.

The fate of the Dutch Pastoral Council which met six times between 1966 and 1970 is an example of administrative harassment. When Rome objected to the name "council" as having no legal authority, the Dutch bishops changed it to "Pastoral Dialogue." Then Rome argued that such body had only consultative voice; yet, the bishops continued consulting the laity. Finally, Rome appointed bishops opposed to this national initiative and under John Paul II, the Dutch process of consultation stopped.[30] Yet, this Pastoral Council had been an exceptionally effective application of the Vatican II call for collegiality and church renewal.

The Detroit Call to Action Conference is another example of lay taming. For the 1976 centennial, the U.S. bishops decided to hold a national consultation consisting of three steps: first a two-year consultation of the laity, next a three-day national convention in Detroit, and later a five-year plan to implement the recommendations of the convention. About 800,000 parishioners were involved in the preparatory discussions, in the most extensive consultation of the laity ever undertaken by the U.S. hierarchy. The October 1975 Detroit convention was attended by 1,340 representatives from 152 dioceses; 93 percent of them had been selected by their bishops, and nearly 100 bishops, one-third of the American hierarchy, attended. For many observers, the conference was a successful example of collegiality. But for the more conservative bishops the conference was "not representative of the church of this country."[31] Indeed by canon law, only bishops are representatives of their dioceses. One month later at their semiannual meeting in Washington, the bishops made no mention of the conference. The consultation was dead. There would be no five-year implementation. Canonically and in practice, private groups like the lay Call to Action and the Voice of the Faithful[32] have no legal existence, hence can be ignored. Implicitly the Detroit Call to Action became a call for lay inaction unless clerically supervised.

The church has always supported social justice and social action as long as it could keep control. Social action for change has been part of papal teaching since *Rerum novarum* on the Rights and Duties of Capital and Labor of 1891. John Paul II in *Centesimus annus* (1991) further developed the rights of workers. He became actively involved in social change in Poland and with President Reagan can be seen as a world champion of anti-communism through his speeches and diplomatic action. But privately he did not support many individual initiatives, for example those of archbishop Helder Camara, the "red bishop" of Recife, Brazil, and those of Oscar Romero of El Salvador, the defender of the defenseless. He supported social action but only under his leadership and control. The American bishops wrote a pastoral letter about "Economic Justice for All" (1981) but a few years before they had rejected the conclusions of the Detroit Call to Action Conference in which more than 100 bishops and 1,340 delegates had participated.[33]

With the social activism generated by Medellín and liberation theology, Catholics joined the general movement of social activism of the 1960s which were times of great transformation. In the arts, the Beatles and rock and roll revolutionized popular music. In politics, the French students toppled the government of General de Gaulle. In Poland labor unions opposed the dictatorship of General Jaruzelski. Social movements led to the end of communism in Eastern Europe and the collapse of the Soviet Union. In the United States the civil rights movements fostered the cause of minorities, African Americans, women, as well as members of the LGBTQ community. The Catholic hierarchy has generally been open to change but only as long as it could keep control—which is understandable in a centralized organization.

In the liturgical arts, post-Vatican II parishes implemented significant changes, but always under strict Roman control. In politics, Pope John Paul II became a recognized voice on the international scene and a strategic guide to Solidarity in Poland. In all things the Vatican tried to keep abreast of change by keeping control, even in small details. Here are some details about the local handling of liberation theology.

Gustavo Gutierrez was a member of the faculty of the Pontifical Catholic University of Lima of Peru (PUCP) and both were under the jurisdiction of the Archbishop of Lima. As a cleric, Gutierrez seemed easy to handle, until he joined the order of the Dominicans and thus evaded the archbishop's control. The PUCP also seemed easy to handle. The archbishop was its chancellor. The university and the archbishop were in conflict over university governance and a property over which the archbishop wanted more control. The conflict resulted in a standoff. In 2012 the Vatican withdrew the titles "Catholic" and "Pontifical" from the university.[34] Yet, the Vatican seemed to be the loser: the university would continue calling itself Catholic and Pontifical, as this was its social and legal identity in Peru.

The mandated firing of gay teachers in Catholic schools occasioned other conflicts about hierarchical control. In 2019 archbishop Thompson of Indianapolis issued a decree stating that the Brebeuf Jesuit Preparatory School would no longer be recognized as a Catholic school by the archdiocese because it had refused to fire a same-sex married teacher. This is a unique case, not only because the school refused to fire a homosexual, but more importantly because the school ignored the ecclesiastical sanction. Half of the student body of Brebeuf is non-Catholic, the school has no financial ties to the archdiocese, and as a Jesuit school it enjoys the moral support of the Jesuit organization.[35] Clearly the old sanctions of public condemnations do not work anymore. Excommunication was the dread of all good Catholics of the past, but today it is quite ineffective. Condemnations of schools as "non-Catholic" are reminiscent of the anti-American condemnations of McCarthyism and they are less and less effective.

Something needed to change. One year after the condemnation of PUCP, Benedict XVI resigned and Francis was elected pope. Only months after his election, Pope Francis sent a letter to PUCP's authorities in order to find a compromise.[36] A solution was found that was agreeable to both sides. Francis also invited Gutierrez to visit him at the Vatican, and the bad memories of the past were forgotten. This is the small steps strategy of Pope Francis. As to the Brebeuf school, the Vatican suspended the effect of the bishop's condemnation.[37]

What is at stake is the autonomy of social action in the church. Because there is no central control in Protestant denominations, religious entrepreneurship can thrive. It has been most successful in creating attractive megachurches and successful televangelism. In the Catholic Church few priests would take initiatives if they feel their bishop would not approve, and laypeople as members without legal rights receive little support for independent initiatives. The lack of clerical support for lay social action has cost the church dearly. One striking example is that of Catholic charismatics, who in Latin America were originally seen as dangerous Protestants. Having been publicly condemned and refused communion by their parish pastors, a few of them went to their bishop in Quetzaltenango, Guatemala, to plead their case. The bishop advised them to meet in private homes, never on church property. Since then and to this day, the Catholic charismatics of Guatemala tend to own or rent their meeting places and have their own agenda, independent of their parishes. They are still widely excluded from parish life because they pray in tongues and sing Pentecostal-type hymns using electric guitars, while parish priests pray from prayer books and prefer organ music. Pentecostalism is a wildfire in the Global South while traditional Catholicism is not. The 160 million Catholic charismatics worldwide could be the vanguard of the church but too often they are mainly marginalized groups. What is needed is lay empowerment for autonomous initiatives in all areas of Christian life, in devotions, charity work, social justice, politics, and much more. There is a long way to go from membership without legal rights to citizenship in the church entrusted with autonomous entrepreneurship—which is actually the legal status of religious orders within the church.

THE ECCLESIASTICAL COMPLICITY AND THE NEED FOR TRANSPARENCY

One key piece of information about today's sexual crisis is the change in canon law: in the 1917 code clerical sex with minors was to be punished with severe sanctions but in the 1983 code these sanctions have been lightened. Let us look at the texts.[38]

According to the 1917 code (canon 2359, #2), sex offenders involving minors under the age of sixteen "must be suspended, declared infamous, deprived of any office, benefice, dignity, and responsibility they may have, and in more serious cases they must be deposed." This canon applies to various kinds of serious sex offenses besides delicts against minors, namely "bestiality, sodomy, sex trade, incest with a blood relative or a relative in the first degree." To be "deposed" (*deponantur*) is one of the highest sanctions of the 1917 code; it refers to expulsion from the clerical state.

These sanctions were replaced in the 1983 code by the following: "if the delict was committed by force or threats or publicly or with a minor below the age of sixteen years, [the cleric] is to be punished with just penalties, not excluding dismissal from the clerical state *if the case so warrants*" (canon 1395#2; italics added). Clerical rape (sex "committed with force") and sex with minors are to be punished "with just penalties." Like what? The Commentary of the code suggests the following: "Great care should be exercised by church authorities in this delicate matter. Frequently the most beneficial approach is a therapeutic rather than a legal one."[39] It is the therapeutic approach that most bishops have embraced.

This indulgent attitude is also applied to clerics living in a marital relationship. In the 1917 code the rules were stiff: such clerics "are to be coerced into giving up their illicit relationship, repair the scandal" and be suspended *a divinis* (prohibited from administering the sacraments). In the 1983 code, the condemnation is conditional: "A cleric who lives in concubinage . . . which produces scandal is to be punished with suspension." From this text it appears that concubinage which does not produce scandal to the institution can be ignored. In summary, the 1983 code tends to promote a lax attitude toward sexual delicts, which reflects the lax sexuality of the 1960s.

The new code also implies a callous neglect of the victims. There is to be therapy for the criminal, but no help or compensation for the victims. This is what happened in most cases of clerical sex abuse that were reported since the report in the *Boston Globe*. Worse, this attitude recalls the story of the Good Samaritan in reverse. A Samaritan is beaten up by a thief and left half dead. Pass a Levite and a priest. However, if the Levite and the priest today were to notice that the thief was a cleric, they would promptly offer therapy by taking him to a nearby hospital. Clerics helping clerics can be seen as clericalism, but in the case of sex abuse it is worse. When bishops shelter criminals through transfers which in several instances allows them to continue their criminal activities, it is complicit. Moreover, abandoning the victims when they are most in need of help is a grave social injustice comparable to the abandonment of children by their parents.

The 1983 legal change in the handling of clerical sex crimes was not an isolated oversight, but part of generational trend of tolerance that affected the revision of the code throughout its process. The Commission for the Revision of Canon Law started working in 1966, divided into ten study groups to review the various aspects of the code. These groups prepared drafts that were circulated and evaluated by national conferences of bishops, which usually led to revisions. All preliminary proposals were combined in 1980 and submitted for review by a select committee of prelates. A final draft was submitted to John Paul II in 1981 who took one year to study it, make changes, and promulgated it in 1983.[40] Thus, the changes in canon law did not happen overnight but took fifteen years of intense debate, reflecting the changes in the church and society toward greater moral laxity. Moreover, the abandonment of victims of sexual abuse betrays a weakening or lack of moral judgment on the part of the hierarchy.

Can the legal changes toward clerical sexuality explain the spread of clerical sex abuse? Let us first look at statistics. The Center for Applied Research in the Apostolate (CARA) has summarized in a chart the distribution of 8,694 allegations of sexual abuse in the United States by date of occurrence from 1950 to 2017. This chart makes it plain that the vast majority of cases happened between 1960 and 1999, namely 6,458 cases. From 2000 to 2017 there were only 648 cases, that is, about ten times fewer allegations per year. Most incidents happened during the pontificate of Paul VI (1968–1978) and during the first years of John Paul II (1979–2005) when the number of sex scandals was about fifty to sixty times higher than today. During most of this time, the strict legislation of the 1917 code was still in effect but apparently was not applied. Moreover, Paul VI did nothing about the abuse, and John Paul II, ignorant like his predecessor of the facts, did nothing to stop it. We must conclude that the clerical sex abuse is a by-product of the moral laxity of the 1960s. But we must also conclude that the downgrading of sanctions in the 1983 code was a by-product of the 1960s laxity as well.

In 2002 the *Boston Globe* published shocking findings about sex abuse in the archdiocese of Boston. Many more such findings were published, but nearly all these cases, including the 2018 Pennsylvania report, present abuses that mostly happened between 1950 and 1999 with only few cases after the year 2000. The continued publication of archival data about abuse created the impression that the sexual epidemic was ongoing—which was false—hence the general clamor: "Protect our children!" The Catholic hierarchy had taken serious steps in 2002 in the Dallas charter, and more measures were taken in the following years. Yet, these measures—which should have been taken forty years before—did not address the ineffective handling of the problem by the hierarchy, namely complicity and abandonment of victims.

The Maciel sex scandal is an example of Roman practices. Marcial Maciel was a Mexican priest who had founded the Legion of Christ in 1941. At the time of John Paul II, he was much admired in Rome for being a tremendous fundraiser. But it had progressively been revealed that he sexually abused boys and young men and maintained relationships with at least two women. In 1956 (under Pius XII) he had been investigated for morphine addiction, but he was exonerated for lack of witnesses, because he made the legionnaires promise by vow to say nothing negative about him. In 1976 (under Paul VI) a letter of accusations involving twenty-two victims was sent to Rome but received no reply; the victims were ignored, and the abuse continued. Maciel was well honored in the church and John Paul II embraced him publicly in St. Peter's Square, heralding him an "efficacious guide to youth."[41] Formal charges were filled by nine men in 1998, but the following year the Vatican chose not to prosecute Maciel. Just three years later, the *Boston Globe* revealed the scope of sexual misconduct in Boston; Cardinal Law accused of cover-up had to resign. Following the policies of John Paul II, his cover-up was not investigated; Cardinal Law was not reprimanded but honored with a prestigious position in Rome. Again, Rome did nothing for the victims. One of the first major decisions of Pope Benedict XVI was to reopen the Maciel case. The abuser was forced into retirement, officially called "a life of prayer and penance," but there would be no public investigation to avoid scandal to the institution, and no mention of the victims.

In the United States, according to the Pennsylvania Report, "Many accused priests were sent for treatment in a clinical approach to the abuse rather than what should have occurred—criminal reporting. Once these treatments were considered complete, abusers were often returned to ministry in new assignments. The allegations were rarely, if ever, disclosed publicly." Did the bishops know? No doubt about it: "The bishops weren't just aware of what was going on; they were immersed in it. And they went to great lengths to keep it secret."[42]

The bishops' handling of sex scandals is often labeled cover-up, but legally it is more accurately called complicity. This is the opinion of French courts which sent three prelates to prison so far. The most prominent case is that of Cardinal Barbarin, the archbishop of Lyons and the primate of the Gauls, hence the highest-ranking French prelate. In 2019 he was given a suspended sentence of six months in prison for "non-denunciation" of sex abuse of minors. He had informed the Vatican about it but not the district attorney. He was also accused of complicity with the perpetrator and abandonment of the victims.

A priest from Lyons, Bernard Preynat, had abused boy scouts in the 1970s and 1980s (like most sex crimes reported earlier). One of his victims came to Barbarin in 2014 to uncover the abuse. Preynat assured Barbarin that he had not committed any sex crimes since 1991, so the cardinal did nothing. Case closed for the church, but not for the victims. Preynat has abused about seventy boy scouts who now requested justice and their stories galvanized public opinion. In the view of the court Barbarin was guilty of "inaction" (*inertie*) because "his functions allowed him to have access to all kinds of information" about the crimes and their consequences but he did nothing.[43] This is what accomplices do: nothing while the criminals continue their work.

A prison term for the "non-reporting" of sex crimes of thirty years ago is harsh, but it is a partial answer to the victim's call for justice which they did not find in the church.

No criminal charges have been filed against U.S. bishops in contrast to the victims' numerous civil lawsuits seeking compensations. A total of about $3 billion has been awarded them, which emphasizes the culpability of the hierarchy in its abandonment of the victims.[44]

In nearly all cases of clerical sex abuse, the lack of transparency is obvious and was often mentioned in the press. Bishops have access to all kinds of information, but they are seldom told what they do not want to hear. There is no independent diocesan press due to episcopal control and the lack of autonomy of social action discussed earlier. The social movement Voice of the Faithful was founded in Boston after the revelations of the *Boston Globe* in order to help the church. Most of the founding members were from the Vatican II generation, practicing Catholics educated in Catholic schools, and active members in their parishes. Their banner was "Keep the Faith, Change the Church."[45] The movement spread all over the country with chapters in most dioceses. Their stated goals are to support the victims and seek greater participation of the laity in the life of the church. Their effort has generally not been well received by the hierarchy who generally prefer to hire lawyers rather than listen to lay advocates for change. Their impact has been minimal in comparison to the impact of court decisions, which implies that Catholics seeking justice should go to civil courts rather than church authorities. Transparency in the Catholic Church is an oxymoron because secrecy is one of its main tools of power. It is a legacy of eighteenth-century absolutism which is still the model of Catholic governance.

From the preceding discussion we can conclude the following. (1) The strict sanctions of the 1917 code were no deterrents to abusers and were not enforced under Paul VI and John Paul II. (2) In the United States and the Vatican, the appeal to the police is seen as a major and necessary step, which is an implicit recognition that canon law and the hierarchy are unable to handle church delinquents, having no appropriate courts, no bill of rights, and little credibility. (3) The hierarchy generally failed in moral judgment by allowing sexual abuse to continue for years and doing nothing for the victims until taken to court. On these issues Pope Francis has little to contribute except by nominating bishops with a greater concern for social justice.

POPE FRANCIS'S SILENT TRANSFORMATIONS

Francis is an exceptional example of pastoral leadership, but he is not the institutional reformer most liberals hoped for. He has, however, stretched the boundaries of traditional Catholicism through his emphasis on *synodality* (or collaborative leadership) in church government, compromise in cases of conflict, dialogue with non-Christians especially Muslims, concern for the environment, and openness to the Global South which holds the future of Christianity. I want to describe briefly two examples of minor steps which may lead to important changes in the future: his compromised solution for communion to divorced and remarried Catholics, and his reorganization of the Curia.

The discussions at two world synods of bishops of 2014 and 2015 progressively led to a consensus about communion to the divorced and remarried through the "internal forum," as opposed to the external forum of the divorce courts. In the internal forum a responsible penitent discusses the situation with a responsible pastor in an effort to search for God's will. Francis presented this solution toward the end of his post-synodal exhortation *Amoris laetitia* (#300), in the form of a quotation from the Synod's conclusions rather than in his own terms.

While this exhortation was generally well received, although with little enthusiasm, it generated vocal dissent in defense of traditional orthodoxy among conservative laypeople and bishops. Four cardinals publicly disagreed with the new policy. In 2019 *The Catholic World Report* launched a scholarly rebuttal of "five serious problems" or errors in the papal exhortation, most importantly its "inconsistency with the teaching of Trent on grace."[46] Shortly after the Pennsylvania grand jury report, Archbishop Carlo Maria Vigano accused publicly Pope Francis of sexual cover-up and requested his resignation. This overt dissent of conservatives at the highest levels revealed the strength of the opposition.[47] This is a paradoxical situation: it is the conservatives who always clamored for obedience to church authority who now take positions of opposition and defiance. For ages it seemed inconceivable that cardinals openly criticize the pope. What has changed?

The recourse to the internal forum opens a door that can lead to wider changes. Gay marriage came rapidly to be accepted by public opinion and the legislators. Can the internal forum be applied to gay couples? The Synod on the family reflected on Catholic families as if they consisted of two parent homes which is not the norm anymore in the West. In the United States the marital situation is very diverse: there are cohabiting couples raising children, divorced parents entering cohabiting relationships, multiethnic and multi-confessional families, single parents, gay couples raising children, etc. Can the internal forum be applied to all of them? Today the prospect of a "responsible penitent" discussing the situation with a "responsible pastor" seems unrealistic, mainly because most people today make up their minds by themselves, after consultation with friends and relatives, but seldom with priests who in most parishes are too busy to be available.

In his presentation of the internal forum, Francis set forth a general principle: "If we consider the immense variety of concrete situations, it is understandable that neither the Synod nor this Exhortation could be expected to provide a new set of general rules, canonical in nature and applicable to all cases (#300)." In short, there can be no universal laws applicable to all situations. But this principle contradicts the traditional Roman practice of interpreting laws only in the light of scripture and Tradition. Today moral theology is more inclusive. All traditions, within and outside the church, should be considered, as well as the findings of the social sciences and the lessons of experience. Pope Francis's moral teachings espouse this broader perspective. This broader understanding of moral and ecclesiastical law is likely to be applied more generally, especially if the Francis's reform of the Curia will succeed.

Francis Jorge Bergoglio was elected pope with the mission of reforming the Curia. Shortly after his election he set up an advisory group for this purpose. Six years later, the first draft of a new apostolic constitution, *Praedicate Evangelium*, has been circulated for comments before its publication. The main structure of the document is clearly spelled out. I will point to three aspects: emphasis on evangelization, downgrading the Congregation of the Doctrine of the Faith, and decentralization.

As indicated by the title of the constitution, a missionary spirit is to animate the Curia and the whole church in the spirit of *The Joy of the Gospel* of 2013. The new constitution will not promote proselytism, that is, the effort to convert people to their own beliefs. Moreover, in Catholic parlance, "gospel" usually refers to the four gospels and the ideals of the Sermon of the Mount—a model of conduct—while for Protestants it more often refers to the doctrine of salvation as in Paul's letters—a model of belief. This missionary emphasis should turn the church to the outside world, away from internal narcissistic concerns. It should also turn the tide of the moral and religious laxity inherited from the 1960s.

A new super-dicastery (a clerical word for "department") for evangelization is to be created by merging the Congregation for the Evangelization of Peoples and the Pontifical Council for the New Evangelization. All other departments (or dicasteries, as they will be called) are equal in importance but subordinate in spirit to evangelization. Hence the Congregation for the Doctrine of faith is demoted.[48] This is a very important move. The Supreme Sacred Congregation of the Roman and Universal Inquisition was created in 1542 as part of the Catholic Counter-Reformation against the spread of Protestantism. It was renamed the Holy Office in 1908 and received its current name in 1965. The emphasis on strict orthodoxy and the eradication of heresy have been guiding principles of Catholic life since the Council of Trent. Moreover, all Roman Congregations worked under the guidance of the Doctrine of the Faith and thus could control the whole church within strict orthodoxy. The end of Counter-Reformation orthodoxy is seen with concern by conservatives and without the guidance of the Congregation of the Doctrine of Faith, the various dicasteries might fall into chaos. A major but implicit message of *Praedicate Evangelium* is that the Counter-Reformation and its emphasis on doctrine are over. The future will be one of evangelism and decentralization.

Freed from the oversight of the Doctrine of the Faith, national conferences will be responsible for making some doctrinal decisions. It is indeed the primary responsibility of bishops and bishops' conferences for the particular churches to use their genuine doctrinal authority. This is not well received by conservatives. That the German church will be different from the Italian or Spanish churches seems unacceptable in the Tridentine perspective which has always envisioned unity as uniformity.

So far, the reform of the Curia is stalled. Moreover, conservative opposition has grown recently about the possibility of priestly ordination of a few select "mature men" in the wilderness of the South American Amazon. Clerical celibacy is a matter of discipline, not doctrine; it could be abrogated by a simple papal decree, but this would be anathema for the Catholic rear guard. What is new is not opposition within the church but the acerbic, acrimonious, and even violent tone of some of its protagonists—similar to the hate language found among some populist Trump supporters and politicians. Would it be that Catholic conservatives have espoused the ideology and rhetoric of American political conservatives?

Ideology could explain much of what was discussed in this chapter. Vatican II espoused many of the liberal ideals of the 1960s. Authority versus conscience and legal rights is a liberal agenda. Liberation theology and the Latin American crusade against injustice were noble liberal goals at a time when papal policies favored traditional and conservative positions. As shown in the CARA compilation of clerical sex violations, the vast majority of cases happened between 1960 and 1999, that is, at the time of general sexual laxism in the West, and then stopped by itself. The bishops' overindulgence as well as the indulgent provisions in the 1983 code of canon law may also have been affected by this cultural laxism. With the recent explosion of populism in the West, the ideological tide has changed again; now it is the conservatives who are most vocal; Catholic conservatives seem to have adopted their language and tactics. The presence of ideology in religion is also a theological and administrative problem that is seldom raised. How should Rome handle opposition? Fr. James Martin is a well-known writer who took an open-minded position in his 2017 book *Building a Bridge: How the Catholic Church and the LGBT Community Can Enter into a Relationship of Respect, Compassion, and Sensitivity*. He was widely and even bitterly attacked for it. What can Rome do? Pope Francis invited him for a brief audience in the private library of the Vatican palace where he meets heads of states, international organizations, cardinals, and bishops' conferences.[49] This is a new, non-disciplinary, and more evangelical way of dealing with opposition, but it is only a beginning.

The proposed new apostolic constitution, *Praedicate Evangelium*, could also be a new beginning for the issues raised in this chapter. The two emphases on mission instead of orthodoxy and decentralization in favor of local churches are likely to affect the three issues discussed here: conscience, autonomy in action, and transparency. It will be remembered that after the publication of *Humane Vitae* most national conferences took positions in favor of the primacy of conscience, only to be rebuked by the Curia. Had the church been decentralized then, the conflict of conscience versus obedience would have been avoided. Had the Congregation of the Doctrine of the Faith not publicly condemned liberation theology as dangerously Marxist, it would have flourished, bloomed, and faded away like all intellectual trends in a pluralistic church. Hence the small steps of Pope Francis in the reorganization of the Curia are likely to have lasting effects. Only time will tell. What does it mean to be a Catholic today? Citizenship in the church? No. Membership without legal rights? Yes, most likely. But preferably according to Francis: missionary discipleship of Jesus Christ. This is the unexpected turn brought forth by Pope Francis. It is not what liberals expected, but it offers a major opportunity for the future of the church.

NOTES

1. James A. Coriden, Thomas J. Green, and Donald E. Heintschel, *The Code of Canon Law: A Text and Commentary* (New York: Paulist Press, 1985) canons 96 and 205.
2. Paul VI. *Humanae Vitae*. Encyclical Letter of July 25, 1968, http://w2.vatican.va/content/paul-vi/en/encyclicals/documents/hf_p-vi_enc_25071968_humanae-vitae.html, 12.
3. Paul VI *Humanae Vitae*, 4.
4. Ibid., 28.
5. Robert Hoyt, *The Birth Control Debate* (Kansas City, MO: Herder and Herder, 1968).
6. Charles E. Curran, ed., *Contraception. Authority and Dissent* (New York: Herder & Herder, 1969) and Charles E. Curran, *Faithful Dissent* (New York: Sheed & Ward, 1986).
7. Hans Kung, *Infallible? Une interpellation* (Paris: Desclé de Brouwer, 1971).
8. John Paul II, *Apostolic Letter Ordinatio sacerdotalis. On Reserving Priestly Ordination to Men Alone*, 1994, http://w2.vatican.va/content/john-paul-ii/en/apost_letters/1994/documents/hf_jp-ii_apl_19940522_ordinatio-sacerdotalis.html/.

9. John Paul II, *Apostolic Letter Motu Proprio Ad Tuendam Fidem by Which Certain Norms Are Inserted into the Code of Canon Law*, 1998, http://w2.vatican.va/content/john-paul-ii/en/motu_proprio/documents/hf_jp-ii_motu-proprio_30061998_ad-tuendam-fidem.html/, 4.

10. Walter M. Abbott, General Editor. *The Documents of Vatican II* (New York: Guild Press, 1966). Decree on Religious Freedom, 3, http://www.vatican.va/archive/hist_councils/ii_vatican_council/documents/vat-ii_decl_19651207_dignitatis-humanae_en.html/.

11. Abbott. *The Documents of Vatican I*. Pastoral Constitution on the Church in the Modern World, 16, http://www.vatican.va/archive/hist_councils/ii_vatican_council/documents/vat-ii_const_19651207_gaudium-et-spes_en.html/

12. Thomas Green, "The Revision of Canon Law: Theological Implications." *Theological Studies*, December 1, 1979, http://journals.sagepub.com/doi/abs/10.1177/004056397904000401/

13. Todd A. Salzman and Michael G. Lawler, *Introduction to Catholic Theological Ethics: Foundations and Applications* (New York: Orbis Books, 2019).

14. Second General Conference of Latin American Bishops, *The Church in the Present-Day Transformation of Latin America in the Light of the Council* (Washington, DC: USCCB, 1973) 40.

15. Second General Conference of Latin American Bishops. *The Church in the Present-Day Transformation of Latin America in the Light of the Council*, 41.

16. Paul VI. *Populorum progressio. On the Development of People*, 1967, http://w2.vatican.va/content/paul-vi/en/encyclicals/documents/hf_p-vi_enc_26031967_populorum.html/

17. Second General Conference of Latin American Bishops. *The Church in the Present-Day Transformation of Latin America in the Light of the Council*, # 10.

18. Ibid., 45.

19. Ibid., 47.

20. Ibid., 55.

21. Ibid., 56.

22. Nelson A. Rockefeller, *The Rockefeller Report of the Americas: The Official Report of a United States Presidential Mission for the Western Hemisphere* (Chicago: Quadrangle Books, 1969).

23. Gustavo Gutierrez, *A Theology of Liberation: History, Politics and Salvation* (New York: Orbis books, 1973), x.

24. Gutierrez, *A Theology of Liberation*, 26.

25. Ibid., 88. Italics in the text.

26. Joseph Ratzinger, "Instructions on Certain Aspects of the 'Liberation Theology.'" 1984, http://www.vatican.va/roman_curia/congregations/cfaith/documents/rc_con_cfaith_doc_19840806_theology-liberation_en.html/

27. Vittorio Messori, *The Ratzinger Report. An Exclusive Interview on the State of the Church. Joseph Cardinal Ratzinger with Vittorio Messori* (San Francisco: Ignatius Press, 1985), 190.

28. Messori, *The Ratzinger Report*, 189.

29. *National Catholic Reporter*, "The List." February 25, 2005, http://natcath.org/NCR_Online/archives2/2005a/022505/022505h.php/

30. Eric O. Hanson, *The Catholic Church in World Politics* (Princeton University Press, 1987) 87.

31. Call to Action. History of the Movement, http://cta-usa.org/history/#

32. William D'Antonio and Anthony Pogorelc, *Voices of the Faithful: Loyal Catholics Striving for Change* (New York: Herder & Herder, 2007).

33. Call to Action. History of the Movement, http://cta-usa.org/history/#

34. *National Catholic Reporter*, July 23, 2012. "Vatican Withdraws Recognition of Peru University as 'Catholic,'" https://www.ncronline.org/news/parish/vatican-withdraws-recognition-peru-university-catholic/

35. *New York Times*, June 21, 2019. "Jesuit School, Defying Archdiocese, Refuses to Remove Teacher in Same-Sex Marriage," https://www.nytimes.com/2019/06/21/us/fire-gay-teacher-jesuit-school.html/

36. *The Catholic World Report*, July 19, 2019. "The Holy See and the Catholic University of Peru Reach an Agreement," https://www.catholicworldreport.com/2016/10/24/the-holy-see-and-the-catholic-university-of-peru-reach-an-agreement/

37. "The Vatican For Now Won't Penalize a Jesuit School for Refusing to Fire a Married Gay Teacher," *CVV*, September 24, 2019, https://www.cnn.com/2019/09/24/us/brebeuf-jesuit-preparatory-school-catholic-church-trnd/index.html

38. 1917 Code of Canon Law in English, https://www.wipo.int/edocs/lexdocs/laws/en/va/va001en.pdf /

39. Coriden, Green, and Heintschel, *The Code of Canon Law*, 929.

40. Ibid., 4–8.

41. *Medium,* August 28, 2017. "The Demon at the Center of the Roman Catholic Sex Abuse Scandal," https://medium.com/@theacropolitan/father-marcial-maciel-the-demon-at-the-center-of-the-roman-catholic-sex-abuse-scandal-f9d3f46e7e27/

42. Pennsylvania Grand Jury Report, 2018, https://www.attorneygeneral.gov/report/

43. *La Croix*, March 3, 2019. "La justice condamne le cardinal Barbarin," https://www.la-croix.com/Religion/justice-condamne-cardinal-Barbarin-2019-03-07-1201007220/

44. *National Public Radio*, August 18, 2018. "The Clergy Abuse Crisis Has Cost the Catholic Church $3 Billion," https://www.npr.org/2018/08/18/639698062/the-clergy-abuse-crisis-has-cost-the-catholic-church-3-billion/

45. D'Antonio and Pogorelc. *Voices of the Faithful.*

46. *The Catholic World Report*, July 20, 2019. "Five Serious Problems with Chapter 8 of *Amoris Laetitia*," https://www.catholicworldreport.com/2016/04/22/five-serious-problems-with-chapter-8-of-amoris-laetitia/

47. Associated Press, "Sanctions, Sex Abuse and Silence: A Primer on the Pope Saga." September 9, 2018, https://www.yahoo.com/news/sanctions-sex-abuse-silence-primer-081340314.html/

48. *Catholic News Service*, April 23, 2019. "Curia Reforms Put Priority on Evangelization, Synodality, Cardinals Say," https://www.catholicnews.com/services/englishnews/2019/curia-reforms-put-priority-on-evangelization-synodality-cardinals-say.cfm/; *Catholic News Agency*, July 2, 2019. "Analysis: New Vatican Constitution to Centralize Power in State Secretariat," https://www.catholicnewsagency

.com/news/analysis-new-vatican-constitution-to-centralize-power-in-state-secretariat-15873/

49. "Pope Francis Meets with Father James Martin in Private Audience." *America Magazine*, September 30, 2019, https://www.americamagazine.org/faith/2019/09/30/pope-francis-meets-father-james-martin-private-audience/

BIBLIOGRAPHY

Abbott, Walter M., General Ed. *The Documents of Vatican II*. New York: Guilt Press, 1966.

America Magazine. "Pope Francis Meets with Father James Martin in Private Audience," September 30, 2019, https://www.americamagazine.org/faith/2019/09/30/pope-francis-meets-father-james-martin-private-audience/.

Associated Press. "Sanctions, Sex Abuse and Silence: A Primer on the Pope Saga," September 9, 2018, https://www.yahoo.com/news/sanctions-sex-abuse-silence-primer-081340314.html/.

Call to Action. History of the Movement, http://cta-usa.org/history/#/.

Catholic News Service. "Analysis: New Vatican Constitution to Centralize Power in State Secretariat," July 2, 2019, https://www.catholicnewsagency.com/news/analysis-new-vatican-constitution-to-centralize-power-in-state-secretariat-15873/.

———. "Curia Reforms put Priority on Evangelization, Synodality, Cardinals Say," April 23, 2019, https://www.catholicnews.com/services/englishnews/2019/curia-reforms-put-priority-on-evangelization-synodality-cardinals-say.cfm/.

The Catholic World Report. "Annulment Nation," April 28, 2011, https://www.catholicworldreport.com/2011/04/28/annulment-nation/.

———. "Five Serious Problems with Chapter 8 of *Amoris Laetitia*," July 20, 2019, https://www.catholicworldreport.com/2016/04/22/five-serious-problems-with-chapter-8-of-amoris-laetitia/.

———. "The Holy See and the Catholic University of Peru Reach an Agreement," July 19, 2019, https://www.catholicworldreport.com/2016/10/24/the-holy-see-and-the-catholic-university-of-peru-reach-an-agreement/.

CNN. "The Vatican for Now Won't Penalize a Jesuit School for Refusing to Fire a Married Gay Teacher," September 24, 2019, https://www.cnn.com/2019/09/24/us/brebeuf-jesuit-preparatory-school-catholic-church-trnd/index.html/.

Coriden, James A., Thomas J. Green, Donald E. Heintschel, eds. *The Code of Canon Law: A Text and Commentary*. New York: Paulist Press, 1985.

Curran, Charles E. ed. *Contraception. Authority and Dissent.* New York: Herder & Herder, 1969.

———. *Faithful Dissent*. New York: Sheed & Ward, 1986.

D'Antonio, William and Anthony Pogorelc. *Voices of the Faithful. Loyal Catholics Striving for Change.* New York: Herder & Herder, 2007.

Green, Thomas. "The Revision of Canon Law: Theological Implications." *Theological Studies*, December 1, 1979, http://journals.sagepub.com/doi/abs/10.1177/004056397904000401/

Gutierrez, Gustav. *A Theology of Liberation. History, Politics and Salvation.* New York: Orbis Books, 1973.

Hanson, Eric O. *The Catholic Church in World Politics.* Princeton University Press, 1987.

Hoyt, Robert. *The Birth Control Debate.* Kansas City, MO. Herder and Herder, 1968.

John Paul II. *Apostolic Letter Motu Proprio Ad Tuendam Fidem by which Certain Norms Are Inserted into the Code of Canon Law*, 1998, http://w2.vatican.va/content/john-paul-ii/en/motu_proprio/documents/hf_jp-ii_motu-proprio_30061998_ad-tuendam-fidem.html/.

———. *Apostolic Letter Ordinatio sacerdotalis on Reserving Priestly Ordination to Men Alone*, 1994, http://w2.vatican.va/content/john-paul-ii/en/apost_letters/1994/documents/hf_jp-ii_apl_19940522_ordinatio-sacerdotalis.html/.

Kung, Hans. *Infallible? Une interpellation.* Paris: Desclé de Brouwer, 1971.

La Croix. "La justice condamne le cardinal Barbarin." March 3, 2019, https://www.la-croix.com/Religion/justice-condamne-cardinal-Barbarin-2019-03-07-1201007220/.

Medium. "The Demon at the Center of the Roman Catholic Sex Abuse Scandal." August 28, 2017, https://medium.com/@theacropolitan/father-marcial-maciel-the-demon-at-the-center-of-the-roman-catholic-sex-abuse-scandal-f9d3f46e7e27/.

Messori, Vittorio. *The Ratzinger Report. An exclusive Interview on the State of the Church. Joseph Cardinal Ratzinger with Vittorio Messori.* San Francisco: Ignatius Press, 1985.

National Catholic Reporter. "Full Text and Explanatory Notes of Cardinals' Questions on 'Amoris Laetitia,'" November 14, 2016, http://www.ncregister.com/blog/edward-pentin/full-text-and-explanatory-notes-of-cardinals-questions-on-amoris-laetitia/.

———. "The List." February 25, 2005, http://natcath.org/NCR_Online/archives2/2005a/022505/022505h.php/.

———. "Vatican Withdraws Recognition of Peru University as 'Catholic,'" July 23, 2012. https://www.ncronline.org/news/parish/vatican-withdraws-recognition-peru-university-catholic/.

National Public Radio. "The Clergy Abuse Crisis has Cost the Catholic Church $3 Billion." August 18, 2018, https://www.npr.org/2018/08/18/639698062/the-clergy-abuse-crisis-has-cost-the-catholic-church-3-billion/.

New York Times. "Jesuit School, Defying Archdiocese, Refuses to Remove Teacher in Same-Sex Marriage," June 21, 2019, https://www.nytimes.com/2019/06/21/us/fire-gay-teacher-jesuit-school.html/.

Paul VI. *Encyclical Letter Humanae vitae*, 1968, http://w2.vatican.va/content/paul-vi/en/encyclicals/documents/hf_p-i_enc_25071968_humanae-vitae.html/.

———. *Populorum progressio. On the Development of People*, 1967, http://w2.vatican.va/content/paul-vi/en/encyclicals/documents/hf_p-vi_enc_26031967_populorum.html/.

Pennsylvania Grand Jury Report. 2018, https://www.attorneygeneral.gov/report/.

Ratzinger, Joseph. "Instructions on Certain Aspects of the 'Liberation Theology,'" 1984, http://www.vatican.va/roman_curia/congregations/cfaith/documents/rc_con_cfaith_doc_19840806_theology-liberation_en.html/.

Rockefeller, Nelson A. *The Rockefeller Report of the Americas. The Official Report of a United States Presidential Mission for the Western Hemisphere*. Chicago: Quadrangle Books, 1969.

Salzman, Todd A. and Michael G. Lawler. *Introduction to Catholic Theological Ethics: Foundations and Applications*. New York: Orbis Books, 2019.

Second General Conference of Latin American Bishops. *The Church in the Present-Day Transformation of Latin America in the Light of the Council.* Washington, DC: USCCB, 1973.

World Intellectual Property Organization. 1917 Code of Canon Law in English, https://www.wipo.int/edocs/lexdocs/laws/en/va/va001en.pdf/.

Chapter 4

Grave Injustice and Great Deception

The Ban on Women Priests Never Rested on Theology

Miriam Duignan

The Roman Catholic Church's ban on women's ordination is not about priesthood, it's about prejudice. The exclusion of women was based on a creeping cultural misogyny that infected Christianity and which led to the slow and steady decline the Roman Catholic Church is crippled with today. There can be no hope for reform until women resume their rightful place.

In this chapter, I will not attempt to present a systematic account of all the evidence for women's ordination, for this can be found in many studies elsewhere.[1] I will instead highlight the inconsistency of the arguments used to justify the ban on women priests which directly contradict the most visible historical tradition of the Early Church as well as its ethical teaching. I will also reflect on how the banishing of women is based on an unjust law and that, as long as we uphold this law, we tacitly condone the ancient misogyny that underpins it and we sustain the institutional prejudice and global harm that results from it.

Where did Catholic patriarchy come from? Let us first examine the official ban on women priests and how, in barring women from the altar, we know they must have been there in the first place: The Christian Church did not start off as a patriarchal institution. But, as ancient cultural prejudices against women were allowed to creep into Christianity, patriarchy and its prejudices against women then became a defining characteristic of every aspect of the official Catholic Church's administration, teaching and policies. This was a direct consequence of the adoption of Christianity in the fourth century by the militaristic and patriarchal Roman Empire. As it struggled to fit the teachings of Jesus Christ into the new official state religion, the egalitarianism of Christ's message was intentionally erased, and the liberating words of the Gospel were reinterpreted to help maintain power and social order. That social order included needing to keep women in what was considered to be their rightful place—as subordinate to men. In the subsequent centuries, as women became more and more regarded as inferior, unclean, and sinful, church leaders sought to stamp out the practice of women in ministry in line with the model of all-male leadership in society and politics of the time. They finally enshrined the expulsion of women in written law in the year 1150 stating: "Only a baptized male can be validly ordained."[2]

But as lay Catholics become more and more educated, there is growing awareness that women did serve in ministerial leadership for centuries in the early Christian communities which were famously egalitarian.[3] Women are documented as having been named as apostles, prophets, and deacons and many performed what is now recognized as a priestly role. Women were the leaders of early church communities and had a thriving ministry for the first 300 to 400 years, to the extent that the Romans considered Christians to be radically counter cultural in their inclusion of women in leadership roles. What is clear now is that the steady decline of women's participation only set in as the virulent sexism of the surrounding culture was adopted by the newly established religion of the Roman Empire and that this sexism did not originate in our faith tradition.

The debate about women's ordination tends to focus on whether women were or were not sacramentally ordained into the same roles as men in the early church. The fact is that the Christian Church, in the first three centuries, did not have the ecclesiastical structure which now exists in Catholicism and there was no hierarchy that ranked "ordained" priests above "lay" people; baptism had created a priesthood of all believers and no officially "ordained" bishops, priests, or deacons can be found in the New Testament.[4] There were, however, three layers of leadership from the first century on: *episcopoi* (bishops), *presbyteroi* (elders), and *diakonoi* (deacons). They were designated to their tasks by the imposition of hands, but the concept of "sacred" priesthood did not exist in the early community. This came into the church from Roman religion whereby the priest was subsequently elevated to level of *sacerdos*—a so-called sacred person.[5] It is this belief in the sacred, special nature of priesthood that gave rise to the concept of clericalism, considered by many to be the root cause of the issues in the church due to an all-male and elitist caste of priests whose loyalty to the hierarchy and each other is all important.[6] But the elevated status of the priest today is not in keeping with the early egalitarian communities and those seeking to reform the church believe the time has come to reprise the original, Early Church, understandings of ministry, honoring their biblical origins and scope—with men and women, single and married exercising their full baptismal authority.[7] And that by transforming current ecclesiology via restoring women to an equal leadership that reflects justice, the church can be free of the damaging products of centuries of clericalism.

Despite women being officially banned from the altar via Canon Law in 1150, there is evidence of women in ministry up until the 1400s. Those later examples were mostly Abbesses of enclosed orders who still enjoyed a lot of authority, including hearing confessions—something only an ordained male priest can do now. The local bishop had no say over such religious territories, and many wrote letters of complaint about women flouting the ban on ministry. Defenders of the Vatican policy on women claim this doesn't constitute "priestly authority" because they were nuns acting in isolation. But what matters is that women were administering sacraments that are today strictly restricted to men, thus disproving claims that women never acted in this capacity and so, never should.[8]

What is clear is that the ban on women priests is not a 2,000-year-old mandate from Jesus, but rather a medieval misogynist coup to oust the female half of the congregation from spiritual leadership and full participation in their own church. The continued opposition to women's priesthood mostly comes from those who consider themselves "Traditionalists" and who claim a loyalty to an unaltered history dating directly to Christ. However, all the evidence points to the fact that the immediate followers of Jesus recognized women as liturgical leaders in what was, at the time, considered an example of radical equality inspired by his teachings. This makes any claims to tradition mistaken and those campaigning for a return to equality must provide constant and persuasive reminders of this truth.

Is there light at the end of the tunnel? There are occasional hopes of a breakthrough for women and one of these came in 2016 when, in response to a question posed during a meeting with superiors of women's religious congregations in Rome, Pope Francis agreed to create a commission to study the historical presence of women deacons in the church. After the twelve members concluded three years of discussing the evidence, Pope Francis announced, in May 2019, that the commission was not able to unanimously agree and called for yet more evidence, saying: "If the Lord didn't want a sacramental ministry for women, it can't go forward. I cannot make a sacramental decree without a theological, historical foundation."[9]

This conclusion creates an unfortunate technical bind because, in the current structure, there can be no change without consensus. In a commission containing many strong believers in all-male ministry and whose members will likely never all agree, the next commission could be delayed for years debating the finer points of sacramental ordination rites and essentially tied up in theological knots. The decision seems to betray Pope Francis's own fears about how to persuade the Catholic hierarchy that the church is ready to open up roles for women and suggests he, too, is mistakenly attached to the belief that only men were welcomed into the sacrament of ordained ministry in the church's history.

What is striking is that all evidence points to the historical fact that women deacons received the exact same Sacrament of Holy Orders in the Early Church as their male counterparts.[10] And, if wondering whether women deacons were part of biblical revelation, Pope Francis need look no further than St Paul who, in his Epistle to the Romans (verses 16:1–2) names Phoebe as a Deacon and entrusts her as his emissary to deliver a letter to the church in Rome and praises her as a church leader.

Can pictures speak louder than words? Shortly after Pope Francis called for more proof that women held equivalent roles to men in the Early Church, new evidence was published showing that early Christian artists portrayed women leaders inside the sanctuary spaces of some of the most important basilicas in the Christian world and look to have been capturing images that they saw in everyday liturgical life.

The new research, unveiled at the International Society for Biblical Literature in July 2019, proved that, not only do the three oldest surviving images of Christians worshipping at church altars all show women in official liturgical leadership roles, but they also happen to be located in the three most important churches in early Christendom. It is worthy of note that there is no surviving Christian art from this time that shows a man alone at the altar without a woman alongside him enacting parallel, equal roles and therefore we can conclude that the solitary male priest is a relatively new invention.

In the illustrated book *Mary and Early Christian Women: Hidden Leadership* (Palgrave Macmillan, 2019), the author, Ally Kateusz, shows how the two very oldest iconographic artifacts—both dating from around 430—are carved liturgical scenes on sculptures found in Old Saint Peter's Basilica in Rome and in the Hagia Sophia Church in Constantinople (Istanbul). One is an ivory reliquary box which depicts the sanctuary of Old St. Peter's in Rome—that is the first church built above the tomb of St. Peter. This image of a scene from the altar depicts a man and a woman standing on either side, facing each other and each raising what appears to be a chalice in a gesture recognized as a liturgical act performed by priests. The other is a stone sarcophagus front from the Hagia Sophia in Constantinople and shows a male and a female figure standing on either side of the altar, holding their arms up in the *orans* pose—a gesture recognized as priestly presiding over the Eucharist at the altar and which again shows male and female bodies with gestures mirroring one another in a parallelism indicative of their equality in liturgical roles.

The third oldest artifact provides yet more proof to combat the false modern imagination that men, and only men, were priests in the early Christian era. It is an ivory box dating from the 500s, called *Pyx with women at Christ's tomb* and portrays the Church of the Holy Sepulcher in Jerusalem. The sculptor carved women, and only women, in a liturgical procession to the altar and it is the very oldest artifact to depict only one sex at the altar—with only women. The oldest surviving art to depict men alone at the altar of a real church is centuries later, on a ninth-century ivory tablet. The two oldest artifacts apparently only survived because they were buried and then excavated in the twentieth century and we can surmise that there must have been others depicting the gender parallel liturgy but were likely censored later as women were officially banished from serving in a "priestly" capacity.

These images are windows into the early Christian liturgy because virtually no manuscripts survived from the first seven centuries of Christianity in relation to ordination and who led the liturgy in those early centuries. As the author Ally Kateusz says: "If the sculptors had portrayed only men at these church altars, everyone would assume that they had important liturgical roles . . . the artworks illustrate that early Christian women routinely performed as clergy in orthodox churches."[11]

If any doubt remains about how these findings directly contradict the Vatican's claim that there is no evidence of a tradition of women in liturgical leadership roles, you only need to look at their reaction when asked to explain the discovery of what appeared to be a woman in a priestly pose in the heart of Catholic Rome. In 1941, in a vain attempt to prove that the ivory sculpture that depicted a woman at a church altar was not at the altar of Old Saint Peter's Basilica, the Vatican excavated beneath the modern Saint Peter's high altar. Beneath it, excavators discovered the second-century shrine and stone table that had been dedicated to Peter on the site of his martyrdom. The ivory sculptor had carved the woman at this very table. The Vatican admitted that the ivory represented the shrine and its table—but instead of admitting that a woman had been at the altar in Old Saint Peter's, the Vatican argued that Old Saint Peter's had to have had a portable altar, trying to dismiss the significance and suggest it must have been in some hidden away side chapel.[12]

The hierarchy seeks to define away women in iconography via scholars associated with the Vatican who assert that, when it comes to a woman portrayed in a priestly way, it simply isn't possible. One famous example comes from the Catacombs of Priscilla in Rome, dating from the second to fifth centuries, where recent renovations drew attention to the fact that underground chapel frescoes included female figures portrayed as liturgical leaders. One image shows a woman wearing a liturgical garment and a stole in a priestly pose and another shows women with their arms outstretched around a table celebrating Mass. Professor Fabrizio Bisconti, the superintendent of the Vatican's religious heritage archeological sites, said that such interpretations of the images were "sensationalist . . . a fairy tale . . . and a legend." He asserted that the fresco of a woman in a gesture of priest-like prayer was actually "a depiction of a deceased person now in paradise" and that the women at the table were "taking part in a funeral banquet" and not a Eucharistic gathering.[13]

In making such efforts to deny their existence, the Vatican reveals the fragility of their theory that, from Jesus onward, women were excluded from leadership and therefore they have no authority to include women now. In the face of this evidence, the Vatican must be encouraged to recognize and admit that there were women in equal ministry to men and we must resist getting bogged down in distracting debates about what title those women held then in comparison with the current roles that only men were allowed to grow into. The fact is that, whatever men did in the first several hundred years of the church, women did too—as equals and not subordinate assistants. And because traditional-minded Catholics believe that "if it has been done, it can be done," there is overwhelming proof available to show that the equality of men and women is the true tradition of the Catholic Church and should have remained a constant practice had medieval misogyny not muddied the baptismal waters.

So, what "proof" does the Vatican cling to? Despite a huge body of evidence showing women as leaders among the immediate followers of Jesus, the official church clings to its entrenched position that a male-only priesthood is a sacred tradition that cannot be changed. I examine two of their justifications here as they are the most frequently cited and also perfectly illustrate the contradiction inherent in the ways the Bible has been intentionally distorted to suit a sexist, entrenched position.

We are told that Jesus chose only twelve men as his apostles and therefore must have intentionally excluded women forevermore from exercising ministry in his name.[14] This, despite the fact that Paul calls a woman, Junia, "outstanding among the apostles" in the Early Church (Rom., 16:7). Some say Jesus "ordained" the men as the first priests at the Last Supper meal, whereas historians will point out that there was no formal ordination or formal priesthood until approximately 400 years later and that the Last Supper meal was a typical Passover gathering with families and could not have been just twelve men shut together in that Upper Room.[15] When Jesus said "Do this in memory of me," he was saying this to all his followers with women sitting right there with him. And, most important in dispelling the narrative of men only chosen as apostles, it was Mary Magdalene who, in all four Gospels, was documented as the first witness to the most important event in Christianity—the resurrection of Jesus Christ. And the definition of the title, apostle, is simply: "a messenger who is sent forth." On account of this, Mary Magdalene is acknowledged as an apostle even by the official church who elevated her memorial to a feast day in 2016 with a decree that was titled "Apostle of the Apostles." The Early Church devotion to Mary Magdalene as a leader among Jesus's followers is evidenced by the sixth-century writing of

Gregory of Antioch who portrays Jesus's message to women as: "Be the first teacher to the teachers. So that Peter who has denied me, learns that I can also choose women as apostles."[16]

Mary Magdalene was the devoted apostle to whom Jesus chose to deliver his "Good News" of renewed life and a new mission to his followers, male and female. If we are to accept that Jesus chose only twelve men as the first priests then, by the same analogy, in choosing a woman to teach them Mary Magdalene was appointed by Jesus as the first bishop. And yet, defenders of the all-male priesthood reject this analysis by claiming it was one isolated example and we cannot infer that Jesus wanted to include women among his chosen messengers for all time.

Compare and contrast the aforesaid conclusion with the letter in which St. Paul seems to be telling women to be quiet in church. We are told that this was not just an isolated incidence in history but that he did mean all women, for all time. In response to the directive in 1 Timothy 2:12, "I permit no woman to teach or to have authority over men. She is to keep silent," the opponents of women priests will argue that this verse contains teaching that must be held as definitive, including Pope Paul VI, who wrote: "Through this, he established a permanent norm—which excludes women from the priestly ministry" (*Inter Insigniores* § 9–12).[17]

But many qualified studies question the authorship of this famous letter and are certain that Paul, the leader of the first generation of Early Christians, did not even write these words himself.[18] Many scholars believe that the author is imposing a prohibition on a group of women in the Ephesian church because of a conflict over disputed teaching they wanted included. It was most certainly a local and temporal request and cannot be considered a universal Christian norm used to permanently silence women.[19]

We also know for sure that Paul himself actively encouraged women to speak prophetically in church (1 Corinthians 11,5) and warmly praised a woman, Phoebe, as a "deacon," which, at the time, would have been the leader of a church community, tasked with teaching, preaching, and leading the Eucharistic meals, therefore equivalent to what a priest would do today.[20]

For as long as the male-only hierarchy of the church cling to their rejection of women, we are crippled as a faith that cannot properly interpret the Bible to see the true message of equality and fellowship that is intended. Although Jesus was born into a patriarchal faith tradition, he challenged the cultural norms of his time to welcome women into his community of friends and followers, treating them with respect and equality. One of the tragedies of the misogyny that took root in the structures of the church centuries ago is that the equality Jesus promoted is still not being preached from the pulpit or seen at any level of leadership. And in Paul's writings, we see evidence of men and women working together in church communities that mirrored the ideas and wisdom that Jesus put forward during his life. But instead of continuing with these models of shared spiritual leadership, it was this one edict concerning a woman's subservient place in the church that was misrepresented to justify the strict limitations placed on women in the next phase of the Christian religion.

And what about those medieval men? When studying the medieval theologians whose writings have been used to justify the ban on women priests, what is striking is that only seven out of twenty-nine are on record as attributing Christ as responsible for women's exclusion. The rest are unanimous in believing women to be unfit for priesthood because of what most referred to as their "defective, inferior nature."[21] It is the writings of Aquinas and Augustine which had the most influence on church teaching and whose theories of women's inferiority and connection to sin live on in the theories of gender roles and women's place in church teaching today. Thomas Aquinas in his *Summa Theologiae*, a body of work still studied by trainee priests today, asserts that woman is defective in her humanity and that her creation made sin possible but that she is still necessary in the hierarchy of nature to help man in the work of procreation. Aquinas declared in writings that have justified church prejudice through the ages, that it was women's inherent inability to hold any authority that made ordination impossible: "since it is not possible in the female sex to signify eminence of degree, for a woman is in the state of subjection, it follows that she cannot receive of the Order."[22]

And so, when the church claims it is guided by a universal and constant tradition, it is correct. But it is not a *sacred* tradition, but rather the unfortunate human tradition of prejudice against women, inherited from centuries of ignorance and social prejudice that it still cannot break free from.

The assertion that "Jesus was a man and only chose men" is still the story we are being told despite the fact it does not stand up to scrutiny. The Vatican's doubling down on the ban on women priests intensified in the 1970s when momentum began to build within some churches of the Anglican Communion to ordain women to the priesthood. The Vatican was reluctant to reckon with its own past and fearful of also being forced to make changes.

In November 1975, Pope Paul VI sent a letter to the Archbishop of Canterbury, Donald Coggan, expressing concern about the direction the Anglican Communion was taking with regard to its openness to ordaining women. The pope stated that the permanent position of the Catholic Church is that it is not admissible to ordain women to the priesthood, citing: "The example recorded in the Sacred Scriptures of Christ choosing his Apostles only from among men; the constant practice of the Church, which has imitated Christ in choosing only men; and her living teaching authority which has consistently held that the exclusion of women from the priesthood is in accordance with God's plan for his Church."[23]

And yet a few months later, in April 1976, the Vatican's own Pontifical Biblical Commission concluded unanimously that using the New Testament by itself did not permit a permanent settlement of the question of ordaining women. The members of the commission voted 12–5 in favor of the view that the Bible alone *does not exclude* the ordination of women, and 12–5 in favor of the view that the church could ordain women to the priesthood without going against Christ's original intentions.[24] This extraordinary admission that has been contradicted and obscured since then must stand forever as testament to how, when examining the evidence, the ban on women priests is only upheld by the Vatican via a lingering legacy of inherited sexism, intentionally distorted teachings and hidden history.

In a continuing pattern of doubling down on this position of denial, Pope John Paul II issued the apostolic letter *Mulieris Dignitatem* in 1988, stating: "In calling only men as his Apostles, Christ acted in a completely free and sovereign manner. . . . This is clear and unambiguous when the sacramental ministry of the Eucharist, in which the priest acts 'in persona Christi,' is performed by a man."[25] In focusing on how maleness plays the primary role in ordination, it leads to some frightening imagery about genitals that debase the role of the priest and is offensive to those who see their vocation as a spiritual path and not that their primary qualification is having a male body.

Attempts to shut down debate that would expose these inconsistencies and increase pressure to change escalated in 1994 when Pope John Paul II issued his letter, *Ordinatio Sacerdotalis* that stated: "We declare that the Church has no authority whatsoever to confer priestly ordination on women and that this judgment is to be definitively held by all the Church's faithful."[26] And thus the Vatican began a phase where any discussion of women's ordination to the priesthood was officially and forcefully banned. Priests who mentioned the subject were defrocked and financially cut off. Theologians who wrote about women priests were fired from teaching positions in Catholic institutions. The document claimed that the teaching was "founded on the written Word of God"—that is, the Bible, which is a blatant contradiction of the 1976 findings of the Pontifical Biblical Commission that tried but failed to find anything in the New Testament to justify banning women from full participation.[27]

This stubborn refusal to change an incorrect position can partly be blamed on misguided loyalty and a clerical duty to uphold the positions held by predecessors. Pope Francis has made several statements where he rejected calls to discuss the ordination to women and his most forceful justifications are based, not on theology, but on adherence to the teachings of previous popes. Francis has said that his predecessor, Pope John Paul II: "was clear and closed the door" to women becoming priests, explaining "you can't do anything because dogmatically it doesn't go. I won't turn. It was a serious thing, not capricious."[28] It is serious to him because his predecessor said so and he will not discuss a glaring injustice against women out of reverence to papal authority and precedent. Is it fear that his own changes and teachings might one day be challenged after his papacy? Whatever the motivations, a grave injustice cannot be allowed to stand for all time to protect and preserve papal prejudice and ignorance. The ban on women priests is in direct contradiction to the teaching and practice of Jesus and is therefore disloyal to his legacy. It is instead a continuous act of loyalty to the teachings of early misogynist church theologians and subsequent popes who couldn't face questioning this legacy. Women have been sacrificed at the altar of a stubborn refusal to confront the sin of sexism.

What about Catholic ethics? The sustained barrier to women pursuing a vocation to the priesthood is based on the preposterous suggestion that Jesus, a famed feminist, would not want women to celebrate Mass in memory of him. And that Jesus, who chose women to communicate his teaching multiple times, would refuse a woman the chance to proclaim the Gospel. Despite the Vatican still clinging to the claims that Jesus is to blame for excluding women, what is clear is that the early Christian communities followed Paul's teaching in Galatians 3:28 as their golden rule for leadership in spiritual and sacramental matters. This famous declaration that: "There is neither Jew nor Greek, neither slave nor free, neither male nor female: for you are all one in Christ Jesus" asserts a fundamental teaching of the Catholic faith which is that baptism makes us all equal and that gender differences are irrelevant. In the risen Christ, Christians believed that there was no essential distinction between women and men any more than there was between Jew and Greek or slave and free. This runs contrary to the now official church assertion that a priest must resemble the physical maleness of Christ as if this was his most defining and divine characteristic and as if his message was somehow tied to his maleness.

Every trainee priest and student of Catholic theology must complete a course on Christian ethics as well as Catholic social justice teaching based on the Gospel message of equality, dignity, and liberation. Yet, this teaching stands in such stark contrast to the current treatment of women and the deeply unethical, unchristian ban on women's expression of spiritual leadership that it is a source of shame for the church and all it claims to stand for.

The exclusion of women from equal participation means upholding a ban based on the medieval belief in divinely ordered subjugation and the natural inferiority of women. It strips women of equal dignity and suggests that the Roman Catholic Church still believes that it would be scandalous for a woman to administer sacraments because they were born in the "wrong body." The influence of these prejudices serves to rationalize reserving priestly ordination to men, a practice that is not faithful with what Christ intended. And as this practice rests on the prevailing belief in women's natural inferiority, it does not adhere to the church's constant tradition because it has since strongly repudiated this discrimination.

In 1965, the Second Vatican Council called for all discrimination to be eliminated: "every type of discrimination . . . based on sex . . . is to be overcome and eradicated as contrary to God's intent."[29] But despite the church trying to reckon with its history of prejudice against women, it still fails to follow this through to its just conclusion and remove its most visible legacy of discrimination against women via the ban on ordination.

In 1995, Pope John Paul II wrote a letter in which he apologized to women for the church's part in their suppression throughout history:

> When it comes to setting women free from every kind of exploitation and domination, the Gospel contains an ever relevant message which goes back to the attitude of Jesus Christ himself. Transcending the established norms of his own culture, Jesus treated women with openness, respect, acceptance and tenderness. In this way he honored the dignity which women have always possessed according to God's plan and in his love. As we look to Christ at the end of this Second Millennium, it is natural to ask ourselves: how much of his message has been heard and acted upon?[30]

This letter should stand for all time as the guiding ethical position the church must adopt when it comes to women. If the Vatican has repudiated the evil of misogyny, it must also be obliged to eliminate the structural sin formed by it. The Vatican still avoids referring to women as equal to men but says instead that we have "equal dignity." But let's look at the word dignity from an ethical perspective. The fact is that declaring women unfit for priesthood is inconsistent with women having equal dignity to men and the current situation is intrinsically undignified. The Catholic Church is demonstrating the ultimate subordination of women in its own leadership and ministry structure and contributes to the further "othering" of women by rendering them unworthy to speak as equals to men in the church.

What is clear from examining Catholic theology is that the exclusion of women is a church practice that can be changed without threatening the creed of our faith. It is not an unchangeable, fundamental doctrine of the church. We can look back now and see how other false beliefs were enshrined in church practice that have since been cast aside because they were based on prejudicial, medieval misinterpretation of the Bible and "natural law." This includes the church's support and justification of slavery and their failure to end the practice in its own properties until long after slavery was banned.[31]

Catholic teaching tells us that we can infer Jesus's decision from the proven practice of the Early Church. But based on overwhelming evidence, the Vatican cannot prove a constant practice of a male-only priesthood. The exclusion we have today is based on reasons the Roman Catholic Church has categorically rejected and those are reasons of sexism alone. It is the pagan imposter of ancient misogyny masquerading as a divine commandment.

What are the consequences of this all-male leadership? The Catholic Church is more than a faith tradition. It is also the largest nongovernmental health care provider in the world and runs one quarter of the world's schools. Through the Vatican State's embassies and observer status at the United Nations, the hierarchy of the church is a visible and active presence on the world stage. But while church leaders are also involved in aid efforts, peace keeping missions and providing care for the poor all over the world, it is their influence and interference in issues related to gender and women's reproductive health that come under the most scrutiny and criticism and detract from the good works the church seeks to do.

It is the all-male leadership's entrenched misunderstanding about women's subordinate role and a natural law view of the purpose of sex for procreation that have led to a seemingly obsessive focus on marriage and motherhood on the global stage. Pope Francis himself declared a commitment to getting more women in leadership but also admitted a predicament in being able to reconcile obvious imbalance while still being tied to an ancient theology of motherhood as women's divine purpose: "How is it possible to grow the effective presence of women in public life . . . where the most important decisions are made and at the same time maintain a presence and a preferential attention for the family?"[32]

As the church hierarchy cling to teaching from the medieval era, they refuse to update their policy on the banning of contraception and their insistence that women's destiny is to mothering roles. In their global infrastructure and via influence on the world stage, the Catholic Church exerts huge influence in how women are seen, spoken about, and treated. But while ordained priesthood is a prerequisite to decision-making power in the church, not one woman has the opportunity to challenge and change these doctrines, policies and moral arguments that directly impact the lives and bodies of women around the world. The Roman Catholic Church is burdened with a legacy of an all-male clerical caste who have never been allowed to get to know women as multidimensional and fully human equals. Many never studied alongside women or had a female teacher and none of them benefit from the input of women in any of the important decisions being made that impact the global church. It is this absence of female influence and perspective that has contributed to theology being stuck in the middle ages and has created a closed loop of men talking to each other, making decisions about women.

And so, despite the power and potential of the Catholic Church, it has lost its moral authority in refusing to back down and change its more damaging positions and policies on human sexuality and the role of women. Its potential influence in talking compellingly about the dangers of climate change, eradicating poverty as well as its impressive peacekeeping efforts are constantly distracted from. In the secular environment of the United Nations, the Holy See (the Vatican's embassy with a permanent observer status at the UN) does not talk about the details and origins of its theology on women and sexuality but refers instead to the more modern concept of "complementary" to justify its positions and its preoccupations. Gender complementarity is how the Vatican refers to their belief that God intended women to have different roles to men that are "complementary" to each other and create a "natural order" in the family, society, and the church. Women are told they are only capable of those roles directly derived from their biological capacity as mothers, that is strictly caring and nurturing roles. Whereas men's roles are not limited to those connected to biological fatherhood or defined by fathering qualities alone, but rather on the ancient patriarchal belief that men are destined to lead, make decisions, and exercise authority in all realms. This includes insisting that men and women belong in heterosexual marriages, that same sex unions are destructive to society, that contraception is a sin, and that motherhood is women's destiny. This divine order also dictates that clerical hierarchies mean male priests can be leaders with the power to administer sacraments and participate in decision-making in church policy and teaching, whereas religious sisters and lay women must occupy a nurturing and supportive role, and will never be considered the peer of a priest and never hold a position of authority. This means that, despite the strong presence of so many women religious at the UN, not one of them can speak on behalf of the church or influence their brother priests at the Holy See office to change their focus and end the policies and interventions that cause so much harm to Catholics around the world.

But insistence on change is coming from Catholics themselves. In March 2019, a group comprised of Catholic organizations and networks, called "Catholics for Human Rights," organized an event during the Commission on the Status of Women at the UN where they presented an appeal calling for the revocation of nonmember state permanent observer status from the Roman Catholic Church due to the incompatibility of an all-male religious institution having a seat at the table when nondiscrimination on the basis of sex has been a mandate of the United Nations since its inception. The Commission on the Status of Women was founded to promote women's rights in political, economic, social, and educational fields and yet the church's hierarchy systematically excludes women from positions of leadership and influence: "The Holy See is a completely male dominated institution. Every facet of Church governance and Holy See diplomacy is led entirely and only by ostensibly celibate men. In both the Vatican's teaching authority and the Holy See's system of governance, women have never had a voice in developing doctrine or any decision-making authority."[33]

The group pointed out the great irony that it is in the areas of women's rights and health that the exclusively male leadership of the Holy See has the most visible and vocal involvement in. And it is this hypocrisy and obvious imbalance that must be urgently addressed to bring about a change in direction.

What is the reality of Catholic life for women? The Roman Catholic Church is a global faith where gender difference clearly confers power to some over others. This is the norm that is still being modeled in churches, schools, and hospitals in every country on earth. Women learn this injustice via absorbing the constant message that Jesus rejected women and so does the institutional church. Without questioning the theology, women and men see the example of how being male must have some kind of natural, enhanced entitlement, that women are not equal and must expect to be subordinated as their divinely mandated role. The 1.2 billion Catholics and the surrounding culture learn these lessons from Catholicism and it counts as a spiritual stamp of approval and conditioning for disordered male–female relations that contribute to negative, sexist socialization.

There is a growing sense of urgency and realization of the consequences of upholding an artificial barrier to the vocations and contributions of women, based on sexist beliefs. In tolerating the ongoing ban on women priests, the world's largest and most globally influential religion is allowed to claim that Jesus rejected women. And in failing to challenge the unjust law, Catholics tacitly condone the oppression of women via the Vatican's real-world interference in hospitals, schools, and legislative bodies based on theology and teaching that has remained unchanged for centuries and has never had the input of a single woman.

Despite all the damage done, the Catholic Church is here to stay and will remain a global powerhouse of wealth, influence, and institutional control for many years to come. Although there is an exodus of women who can no longer tolerate their obviously inferior status, many do stay and see the church as their spiritual home and as a force for good that is stronger than its legacy of cruelty and corruption.

There will continue to be discussions about whether there is more evidence of women deacons than women acting in the equivalent role of today's priests and bishops and it is highly likely that the first step to inclusion will come via a limited role for women that is a watered down version of a diaconate ministry. This ring-fenced role will not be a sacramentally ordained and empowered member of the full spectrum of church leadership structures but rather a subordinate role to assist the priest. Of course, there is no such thing as partial equality and the half measure of a deaconess ministry should not be acceptable to anyone. But this inevitable "Deaconess" role will begin the necessary process of incremental change and will be welcomed as the first brick to fall from the wall that has kept women sidelined and silenced for centuries. The fact is that once people, including priests, get used to seeing women on the altar even in a limited ministry, there will be no turning back from an even stronger push for and acceptance of full sacramental authority for women.

It is current church workers who are likely to step into any future deaconess ministry role and it is these women who are currently carrying out the church's mission via ministering in parishes, hospitals, and schools in every corner of the Catholic world. These are women who will sit for days praying with a dying patient but will have to call in a priest to administer the sacrament of the last rites. These are the nuns in remote areas who cannot lead their communities in celebrating Sunday Mass without having had a male priest first bless the Eucharist for them. These are the parish catechists who work for months to prepare parents and children for baptism and first holy communion but are not allowed to administer those sacraments with the families they are closest to, they must sit to one side and allow the male priest to step in.

These ludicrous scenarios should render every Catholic incandescent with rage at such degrading displays of discrimination. Clericalism has meant that people now associate priesthood with power and status, but the average priest's job is hard and often heartbreaking work. And it is women who are also doing this real work and are supplementing the current shortage of priests in parishes throughout the world. But yet, they are not allowed to complete their work and administer sacraments that are key to the Catholic faith because their female body is still deemed unworthy of representing the legacy of Jesus that they are personally living every day. A man must always step into every sacramental situation and take over from these women who cannot be allowed to act alone and unsupervised.

And how about listening to the testimony of women themselves? There are thousands of women around the world who know that their true vocation in life is to be a priest and their spiritual calling and talent for priesthood is real. Catholics pray for vocations for men and warmly receive new ordinands to the church believing that their vocation is real but when expressed in a woman, the establishment response is that they are "clerical and power hungry" as if women are seeking only privilege and access to power rather than an authentic call to serve a parish in a role that is not easy and not particularly high status.

The Vatican is so threatened by challenges to their authority and teaching that it demonizes those who seek to highlight the early Christian teaching of radical equality. Brave nuns, priests, theologians, and campaigners who have spoken out have been censured and punished—removed from ministry, cut off financially, and lost their positions in Catholic institutions. Women who have sought ordination through the Roman Catholic Women Priests movement are immediately excommunicated. This sounds like an archaic punishment, but it still holds real-world consequences for devout Catholics—for example, they cannot get married in a Catholic Church and cannot be buried in a Catholic ceremony alongside their family members.

And yet, it is my observation that the majority of priests are uncomfortable with the church's treatment of women and know that the ban on women priests is based on bogus theology and distorted teachings. They do not want to be seen as complicit in an institution labeled as a bastion of misogyny but are paralyzed by the official leadership's inability to reverse their entrenched teaching and cannot challenge the authority of papal pronouncements. The choice for these men is to take a stand against injustice and lose their ministry or stay and trust that they can do more good inside the institution than outside.

So how will change come about? The tipping point will be reached when there is a critical mass of people willing to speak out and take a stand against the grave injustice of institutionalized sexism and all the damage it has done and continues to do. Priests and all clerics must be inspired to follow the church's own teaching and demand dignity for women; parishioners must recognize when they are witnessing the degrading treatment of women who are effectively ministering without a license to act alone. If Catholics prioritized the teaching of Jesus and the practice of the early church as the model of the faith they want to follow, the push to reinstate women as priests would become an unstoppable force.

The Roman Catholic Church can only recover and reform when it confronts the sins of sexism and includes women at every level of ministry and administration. The Vatican leadership must be persuaded that the push for women's ordination is not a conspiracy against them but rather the arc of justice bending strongly toward truth and reconciliation via the rehabilitation of the outcast, othered women the church has missed the talents and contribution of for centuries.

The decline of the Catholic Church started with sexism and it can only be saved by ridding itself of sexism. We must engage with the church's own teaching on justice and apply it to women. We must expose the church's own history to model what real equality looks like and we must confront the church hierarchy to ask why they are ignoring the will of their own constituents who have seen through the great deception and will no longer tolerate this grave injustice. A new era could be on its way for Catholics who have an authentic desire to follow the radical equality taught by Jesus and the practices of his inspired early followers.

NOTES

1. See, for instance, Arlene Swidler and Leonard Swidler, eds., *Women Priests, a Catholic Commentary on the Vatican Declaration* (Paulist Press, 1977); Kelley Raab, *When Women Become Priests* (Columbia University Press, 2000); and John Wijngaards, *The Ordination of Women in the Catholic Church* (Darton, Longman & Todd, 2001).

2. Canon Law 1024—from the Roman Catholic Church's code of written laws: http://www.vatican.va/archive/cod-iuris-canonici/cic_index_en.html.

3. One of the best collection of essays on the topic is the two-volume work Carroll D. Osburn, ed., *Essays on Women in Earliest Christianity*, 2 vols (Joplin, MO: College Press, 1995).

4. Herbert Haag, *Clergy & Laity: Did Jesus Want a Two-Tier Church?* (Tunbridge Wells: Burns & Oates, 1998).

5. Frank Viola and George Barna, *Pagan Christianity? Exploring the Roots of Our Church Practices* (Carol Stream, IL: Barna, 2008).

6. On a recent attempt by the Vatican Congregation for Divine Worship to reintroduce "sacrality" on all levels, see John Wijngaards, *Don't Cage the Sacred*, in *The Tablet*, September 23, 2000, pp. 1256–1257.

7. Lynn Cohick, *Women in the World of the Earliest Christians: Illuminating Ancient Ways of Life* (Baker Academic, 2009).

8. Joan Morris, *The Lady Was a Bishop: The Hidden History of Women with Clerical Ordination and the Jurisdiction of Bishops* (New York: Macmillan, 1973), available on www.womenpriests.org; Gary Macy, *The Hidden History of Women's Ordination: Female Clergy in the Medieval West* (Oxford University Press, 2007).

9. Joshua McElwee, *National Catholic Reporter*, May 10, 2019.

10. Full evidence provided by John Wijngaards, *The Ordained Women Deacons of the Church's First Millennium* (Canterbury Press, 2011). The ancient ordination rites have also been published online on www.womendeacons.org.

11. Sarah MacDonald, Interview in the *National Catholic Reporter*, July 13, 2019.

12. Ally Kateusz, *Mary and Early Christian Women: Hidden Leadership* (Palgrave Macmillan, 2019), 169–174.

13. Philip Pulella, *Reuters*, November 20, 2013.

14. One of the most comprehensive rebuttals of such a contention is still Elisabeth Schüssler Fiorenza, "The Twelve and the Discipleship of Equals," in *Discipleship of Equals: A Critical Feminist Ekklesia-Logy of Religion* (London: SCM Press, 1993), 104–16.

15. On women being present at the last supper, see Suzanne Tunc, "Meals of the Community," in *Des Femmes Aussi Suivant Jésus* (Paris: Desclée de Brouwer, 1998), ch. 4.

16. Ann Graham Brock, *Mary Magdalene, the First Apostle: The Struggle for Authority* (Cambridge: Harvard University Press, 2003), xviii and 235.

17. Many Vatican documents are available online. See, for instance, http://www.vatican.va/roman_curia/congregations/cfaith/documents/rc_con_cfaith_doc_19761015_inter-insigniores_en.html.

18. Anthony T. Hanson, *Studies in the Pastoral Epistles* (SPCK, 1968); M. Dibelius and H. Conzelmann, *The Pastoral Epistles* (Fortress Press, 1972).

19. B. Thurston, "1 Timothy 5.3–16 and Leadership of Women in the Early Church," in *A Feminist Companion to the Deutero-Pauline Epistles*, ed. Amy-Jill Levine and Marianne Blickenstaff (London: T&T Clark International, 2003).

20. While it is anachronistic to understand the term "deacon" in Rom., 16:2 as referring to the contemporary office of deacons, still it is likely it referred to fulfilling important tasks: elsewhere in the New Testament deacons such as Philip and Stephen show, as preaching, teaching, baptizing, and performing miracles and exorcisms (Acts 8:4–8). Indeed, the first seven deacons (Acts 6) appear to have been tasked not with distributing food or serving at tables during common meals, as it has long been mistranslated, but rather with preaching to foreign widows in their homes and in their own language. See John N. Collins, *Diakonia Studies: Critical Issues in Ministry* (Oxford University Press, 2014).

21. Texts available online: http://www.womencanbepriests.org/theology/overv_th.asp.

22. Aquinas, *Summa Theologica,* Suppl, Q39, A1.

23. Text at http://www.womencanbepriests.org/church/cant1.asp.

24. Swidler and Swidler, eds., *Women Priests,* 25–34.

25. The document can be found at http://w2.vatican.va/content/john-paul-ii/en/apost_letters/1988/documents/hf_jp-ii_apl_19880815_mulieris-dignitatem.html.

26. The document can be found at http://w2.vatican.va/content/john-paul-ii/en/apost_letters/1994/documents/hf_jp-ii_apl_19940522_ordinatio-sacerdotalis.html.

27. Robert J. Egan, "Why Not? Scripture, History & Women's Ordination," *Commonweal*, April 3, 2008.

28. Philip Pulella, *Reuters,* November 1, 2016.

29. Vatican II, *Gaudium et Spes,* § 29.

30. The document can be found at https://w2.vatican.va/content/john-paul-ii/en/letters/1995/documents/hf_jp-ii_let_29061995_women.html.

31. John Wijngaards, *Did Christ Rule out Women Priests?* (McCrimmons, 1986) 18–20.

32. John Allen, *National Catholic Reporter,* January 24, 2014.

33. Catholics for Human Rights, *Report on the Holy See at the United Nations,* March 2019.

BIBLIOGRAPHY

Brock, Ann Graham. *Mary Magdalene, the First Apostle: The Struggle for Authority*. Cambridge: Harvard University Press, 2003.

Cohick, Lynn. *Women in the World of the Earliest Christians: Illuminating Ancient Ways of Life*. Baker Academic, 2009.

Collins, John N. *Diakonia Studies: Critical Issues in Ministry*. Oxford University Press, 2014.

Dibelius, M. and Conzelmann, H. *The Pastoral Epistles*. Fortress Press, 1972.

Egan, Robert J. "Why Not? Scripture, History & Women's Ordination." *Commonweal*, April 3, 2008.

Fiorenza, Elisabeth Schüssler. *Discipleship of Equals: A Critical Feminist Ekklesia-Logy of Religion*. London: SCM Press, 1993.

Haag, Herbert. *Clergy & Laity: Did Jesus Want a Two-Tier Church?* Tunbridge Wells: Burns & Oates, 1998.

Hanson, Anthony. *Studies in the Pastoral Epistles*. SPCK, 1968.

Kateusz, Ally. *Mary and Early Christian Women: Hidden Leadership*. Palgrave Macmillan, 2019.

Macy, Gary. *The Hidden History of Women's Ordination: Female Clergy in the Medieval West*. Oxford: Oxford University Press, 2007.

Morris, Joan. *The Lady Was a Bishop: The Hidden History of Women with Clerical Ordination and the Jurisdiction of Bishops*. New York: Macmillan, 1973.

Osburn, Carroll D., ed. *Essays on Women in Earliest Christianity*, 2 vols. Joplin, MO: College Press, 1995.

Raab, Kelley. *When Women Become Priests*. New York: Columbia University Press, 2000.

Swidler, Leonard and Swidler, Arlene, eds. *Women Priests, a Catholic Commentary on the Vatican Declaration*. Paulist Press, 1977.

Thurston, B. "1 Timothy 5.3–16 and Leadership of Women in the Early Church." *A Feminist Companion to the Deutero-Pauline Epistles*, edited by Amy-Jill Levine and Marianne Blickenstaff. London: T&T Clark International, 2003.

Tunc, Suzanne. *Des Femmes Aussi Suivant Jésus*. Paris: Desclée de Brouwer, 1998.

Viola, Frank and Barna, George. *Pagan Christianity? Exploring the Roots of Our Church Practices*. Carol Stream, IL: Barna, 2008.

Wijngaards, John. *Did Christ Rule out Women Priests?* McCrimmons, 1986.

———. *The Ordained Women Deacons of the Church's First Millennium*. Canterbury Press, 2011.

———. *The Ordination of Women in the Catholic Church*. London: Darton, Longman & Todd, 2001.

Chapter 5

The Deconstruction of Clerical Hegemony

Ending the Moral Dissonance and Abuse of Power

Sylvia Hübel

Besides my lived experiences as a feminist theologian, there have been some specific events unfolding during the last couple of years reminding me that the censorship and silencing of women's voices have been to date very powerful in the Catholic Church. I took note of these cases from the media, first in the spring of 2018 when *Voices of Faith (VOF)*, an international Catholic women's group was hindered in the organization of an event advocating a more significant role for women in the church. This meeting has been held at the Vatican yearly since 2014 around International Women's Day. However, in 2018, the head of the *Dicastery for Laity, Family, and Life*[1] refused to approve some of the speakers. The personal profile and activities of the targeted speakers were showing in the direction of the issues that the church treats as taboos, non-topics, or where usually some form of silencing is imposed: feminist scholarship and activism; pro-choice stance; lesbian and gay advocacy. Finally, the organizers countered this act of censorship by relocating the event to the Jesuit Curia, a few blocks away.[2]

Around the same time, the beginning of March 2018, a women's monthly supplement of *L'Osservatore Romano*, titled *Women Church World*—published testimonies of women religious denouncing their widespread exploitation as housekeepers for the clergy. They reported that religious sisters were treated like servants, ordered to do domestic work and the highly educated ones were given chores with no relationship to their intellectual formation and vocation. This magazine continued delivering groundbreaking work during the following year. They also played a crucial role in breaking the taboo around the sexual abuse of religious sisters and nuns.[3] Nevertheless, after a series of publications revealing the culture of power abuse ruling in the church, the staff of the magazine has been put under so much pressure that they decided to resign with the whole editorial group. In her open letter addressed to Pope Francis, founder and editor Lucetta Scaraffia quoted among the main reasons a campaign of progressive discrediting and delegitimization directed toward them: "We throw in the towel because we feel surrounded by a climate of mistrust and progressive delegitimization, by a gaze in which we do not feel the esteem and credit necessary to continue our collaboration. . . . Now it seems to us that a vital initiative is reduced to silence and that we return to the antiquated and arid custom of choosing from above, under direct male control, women deemed reliable. In this way, a positive work and a beginning of frank and sincere relationship, an occasion of parresia, is discarded in order to return to clerical self referentiality."[4]

Last but not least, in the current climate, I could not overlook another silenced group, namely the victims of sexual and power abuse of clergy and those who tried to speak up for them, who were often women.

EPISTEMIC INJUSTICE

These cases brought me to reflect on the hostility proved by the officials of the church toward women's agency and voice. It gave me the impulse to analyze how this stubborn bastion of patriarchy with its system of gender apartheid still censors and silences the testimonies of women who take the courage to utter the inconvenient truths. Nothing new under the very low glass ceiling of the Vatican—one could say. Teaching and being listened to, decision-taking positions are still privileges not readily available to most women. Even if they represent the vast majority of practicing Catholics attending mass daily or volunteering in myriad church activities, women are barred from most forms of authority.

This sort of harm and injustice has been coined by the British philosopher Miranda Fricker as *epistemic injustice*. She defines this situation as a distinctive type of injustice when someone is wronged specifically in her capacity of knower, informant, or participant in the community's sharing of knowledge.[5] The three scenarios quoted earlier are in fact textbook examples of how epistemic injustice operates. Hence, I believe the concept of epistemic injustice can have an invaluable contribution to our discussions of the intersections of clerical power, knowledge/or claim to knowledge, and gender.

In her theory, Fricker brings together in an innovative way the issues of power, knowledge, and participation to knowledge production and sharing. Her attention goes primarily to the ethical and political dimensions of processes of knowledge exchange. This is one of the most influential theories to have emerged in philosophy in recent years. The impact of her work has been enormous, and her conceptual frame has been used in many contexts: from human rights issues in general or specific forms of discrimination (based on gender, racial, or other elements), in the healthcare context or for the analysis of concerns regarding climate change.

In this chapter, I will connect Fricker's theory with the sources and manifestations of this injustice, as well as the mechanisms that kept it going for so long in the institutions of the church. I will demonstrate why this conceptual framework lends itself so well to women's situation in the Catholic Church. Further, I would like to refer to the examples of feminist scholarship and lay activism which have been resisting and countering these injustices.

HERMENEUTICAL INJUSTICE

Fricker distinguishes two forms of epistemic injustice: hermeneutical and testimonial. The first one, hermeneutical injustice belongs to the domains of understanding and interpretation, and it refers to situations when due to unequal power relations, some people are denied the access to epistemic goods (such as education, knowledge, or interpretive discourses). They are unable thus to formulate their experiences and interpret their world due to lacunae in their conceptual resources. Fricker defines this as: "the injustice of having some significant area of one's social experience obscured from collective understanding owing to structural identity prejudice in the collective hermeneutic resource."[6] This hermeneutic marginalization has further as a direct consequence the lack of active participation in the pool of social meanings.

In our case, although women represent the majority group in the active life of the Catholic community, the ones without whom the pews would be empty, and most activities would be stagnating, they also represent the category with the most limited access to knowledge shaping and sharing tasks. Due to longstanding patriarchal ideas, practices, and implicit biases, women members of the church in general and women theologians, in particular, have been positioned as less than competent knowers. They have been hermeneutically marginalized and their testimonies systemically dismissed. As a consequence of the fact that the whole doctrine of the church has been formulated by male clergy, it failed to capture the experiences of lay people in general and women in particular. Hence, women also lacked the conceptual means and opportunities to articulate their lived experience. Moreover, religious discourse has been used for centuries to justify women's invisibilization and silencing. This sort of disadvantage constitutes in Fricker's understanding hermeneutical injustice.

Throughout history, women were judged as not corresponding to gender norms if only they expressed a wish for knowledge, reading and studying, sharing ideas, or speaking up in a public context. Up to the twentieth century, such gender norms have been regulating the production and dissemination of knowledge. Anyone deviating from these norms was considered dangerous, hence, persecuted, sanctioned, or robbed of their lives. The church in the role of social influencer and shaper of morals has played for long centuries a significant role in initiating, orchestrating, and conducting the persecution of women who expressed a desire or claim to knowledge. Women were prevented from participation in creating and shaping hermeneutical understanding in the church, simply because they were excluded from theologizing or interpreting the Bible. The clergy's hegemonic claim to truth and knowledge has thus caused enduring epistemic violence against women.

TESTIMONIAL INJUSTICE

Testimonial injustice occurs when due to structural inequalities, a hearer fails to treat the speaker as a source of knowledge, systemically questioning, censoring, or finally discarding her testimonies. Fricker argues that this form of injustice is primarily a matter of credibility deficit, due to the lower social status of the epistemic agent or the prevailing negative stereotypes around her person. Those who do not possess a certain social standing are ignored or dismissed, so they cannot participate in the production or exchange of knowledge.

Testimony occupies a central place in the tradition of the Catholic Church, consequently credibility is a central issue. Women's testimonies and voices have been dismissed since the dawn of resurrection. The resurrection narrative itself, which represents the cornerstone of Christian faith, is women's story, their lived experience which has been officially told, transmitted, and interpreted only by men.

Testimonial injustice can occur in a one-on-one transactional exchange when, for instance, a member of the clergy does not personally give credit to the knowledge of a woman due to the prejudices deeply embedded in his education or culture.[7] However, instead, we would rather zoom out to the systemic manifestations of testimonial injustice on a structural level. We use the context of testimony in a broad sense, as being able to speak and to be heard, to narrate and interpret, to participate, to dissent, and to be believed. Even though these are crucial prerogatives of membership in any community, the lay faithful are to date prevented from participating in fair epistemological exchanges in the institution of the church. We will focus not only on the silencing of women's voices in theology but also on all acts of restricting their access to knowledge, interpretation of their own experiences, and the sharing of knowledge across the centuries.

Feminist philosopher Kristie Dotson identified a subcategory of testimonial injustice, called *testimonial smothering* when the speaker self-silences for fear that her testimony will be misinterpreted or rejected, when one "perceives one's immediate audience as unwilling or unable to gain the appropriate uptake of proffered testimony."[8] For instance, although the first extensive reports on the abuse of nuns in the church go back to the 1990s, the scale at which the reports come up today confirms the fact that most of the victims kept silent for fear of the consequences. Personal narratives reveal that raped nuns did not dare to complain to their superiors, because they knew they would not be given credit or even worse, they would be blamed for seducing a member of the clergy. Cases from India, Africa, and Europe confirmed that those who finally spoke up revealing the abuse they suffered, have been intimidated, ostracized, dismissed from their communities even when pregnant.

THE SOURCES OF EPISTEMIC INJUSTICE IN THE CHURCH

The Negative Stereotypes and Prejudices about Women

With all the aforementioned forms of epistemic injustice in mind, we will further explore the sources of epistemic injustice, using examples from historical and contemporary cases. Some very significant sources of epistemic injustice are the negative stereotypes or the prejudices against women. Theological tradition has, implicitly or explicitly, provided a negative characterization of "women" and the "feminine" centuries long. Religious discourse has been used to justify the exclusion of women from knowledge production and sharing.

Already, during the first centuries of Christianity, the church fathers created and sustained very negative stereotypes about women, their weak, sinful nature, questioning even their humanity. The patriarchal exegesis of the creation story reinforced the idea that the woman was the cause of the original sin. As a consequence, our theological tradition was built on the dichotomy of female sinfulness versus male salvific action. One of the most used and abused texts in this regard was a pronouncement from the First Letter of Paul to Timothy (1:2,11–14) stating that women were not allowed to teach nor communicate their faith in public, due to their inherent sinfulness and moral corruption: "A woman must receive instruction silently and under complete control. I do not permit a woman to teach or to have authority over a man.

She must be quiet. For Adam was formed first, then Eve. Further, Adam was not deceived, but the woman was deceived and transgressed."[9]

The patristic influence on later thinking was so profound that the idea of women's inferiority and their vilification were reiterated and reinforced by the teachings of Saint Augustine and Saint Thomas Aquinas as well. Thus, women suffered a significant credibility deficit, labeled as not trustworthy testimonies and their experiences have been discounted, invalidated, or silenced. What was the harm perpetrated, in these cases? First of all, their lived experiences of religious life, their understanding of God and faith have been dismissed by the dominant group. Second, not being taken seriously as a knowing subject/knower meant not being respected in a fundamental human capacity. The harm and damage incurred were at once moral and epistemological. In this regard, Fricker emphasizes that while at instances testimonial injustice might have minor consequences, the harm is growing in gravity when it is persistent and systematic.

Hermeneutic Marginalization and Invisibilization

Women have been unable to contribute to the processes through which knowledge and meanings were produced and exchanged in the Catholic Church for almost 2000 years. Being deprived of access to education or theological knowledge implied as well that they absented from the development of hermeneutical and epistemic tools (language, concepts, symbols of theology, liturgy, and Christian life). They could not participate in the areas which created the official discourse of the church and its hermeneutical understanding, simply because they were excluded from theologizing.

In most places, they have been admitted to theological training only in the second part of the twentieth century. For instance, the Gregorian University opened its doors to women's training in 1965, the first Ph.D. defended by a woman was in 1973. The timing was approximately the same in other Western European countries, such as Germany and Belgium. In the United States the admission happened a bit earlier, as specific training opened to women already in the fifties and by the eighties, some women theologians enjoyed a particular position and voice in the academia.

Another, more hidden strategy of epistemic silencing and invisibilization was prescribing passivity, sacrifice, and selflessness as typically feminine virtues. All through the centuries of our history, the vast majority of female saints canonized by the church and set as role models for women, kept silent in the face of abuse or suppression, being examples of endurance, humility, and obedience. To date, even the official teaching of the church on women and their role in the world and family has been dictating a passive, servile role as well.

Scrutiny, Canonical Warnings, and Censorship

A more aggressive way of epistemic silencing is the exercise of doctrinal authority. Critically inquisitive or dissenting voices have never really been appreciated in the Catholic Church, nor tolerated as expressions of a sincere quest for meaning. The church has a long and disheartening history of silencing, ostracizing, and removing those who raised issues, which could shake the structural foundation of power concentrated in the clergy. Throughout this history, bishops exercised control over all theological conversations, claiming that their office succeeds to the authority of the apostles as guardians of the faith. Various levels and forums were set up to monitor and admonish theological work, from local or regional doctrinal committees to centralized ones such as the Congregation for the Doctrine of the Faith. These were charged with prescribing disciplinary actions whenever they deemed to discover doctrinal irregularities.

To date, many of women's theoretical and practical preoccupations, such as the concerns for inclusivity and social justice have been scrutinized, censored, and silenced by doctrinal forums at both national and Vatican levels. To mention just a few cases: the investigation of the Leadership Conference of Women Religious in the United States started in 2012 under the authorization of Pope Benedict. This scrutiny concluded that the sisters had challenged the church teaching on homosexuality, the ordination of women, and healthcare reform. Similar action was often taken against the theological work of individuals. The Congregation for the Doctrine of the Faith, after the scrutiny of Professor Margaret Farley's work *Just Love: A Framework for Christian Sexual Ethics* (2006), contended that her theological method was not consistent with authentic Catholic theology, as was her interpretation of the role of the Magisterium. Many more women theologians who addressed what the church perceives as thorny issues in the fields of sexual or medical ethics received warnings, sanctions, or they have even been excommunicated.

Clerical Status: The Basis for Epistemic Privilege and Credibility Excess

Even though all the elements mentioned before contributed to epistemic injustice in the church, the primary source from which all of them originate is the two-tiered lay-clergy structure itself. This asymmetry created two epistemic classes, one of knowers and the other of sub-knowers, which have been sustained to date. According to the official doctrine of the church, the community is made up of a teaching part (*docens*) and a taught part (*discens*): "In the dominant episteme, the laity made up the *ecclesia discens*, or that element of the church taught by the hierarchy, and the hierarchy existed as *ecclesia docens*, or the teaching church."[10] While the clergy received all the authority of knowledge production and sharing, lay people have been placed in a passive, receptive position, and this prescribed a leader/follower dynamic.

In order to contextualize this power dynamics operating to date inside the Catholic community, we need to look into the development of clerical status itself. Christianity started as an equality-based community. However, it has been gradually transformed into a hierarchical structure and the tasks initially shared among the members have been later concentrated on the person of the priest. A mere glimpse into the history of the church reveals that during its first millennium, priesthood comprised a more restricted territorial and ministerial jurisdiction. According to theologian Yves Congar, up to the twelfth and thirteenth century, ordination meant being entrusted with leadership and liturgical role for a specific community; it encompassed at the same time election as its starting point and consecration as its term. The term *ordinatio* signified the fact of being designated and consecrated to take up a certain place, or better a certain function, ordo, in the community and at its service.[11] Besides, it initially covered all the other roles of service (lectors, acolytes, superiors of religious communities, and kings were all ordained for their specific role). This definition has gradually shifted and by the twelfth century ordination came to signify the investment with an irrevocable power to be exercised in any community in the universal church. Along the centuries, as a result of the epistemic privilege and credibility excess enjoyed by the members of the clergy, a whole set of attitudes and practices had been constructed around priesthood. Therefore, we need to have a look at the essential points of the theology of priesthood as well.

A very powerful source of epistemic privilege is the triple office priests are granted in ordination, namely the office of *sanctifying (munus sanctificandi)*, *teaching (munus docendi)*, and *governing (munus regendi)*. Through their ordination and the so-called concomitant ontological change they undergo, priests are formed to act as alter Christus—other Christs. They "are configured to Christ in such a way that they are able to act in the person of Christ the head" (*Lumen gentium*, n. 28 and *Presbyterorum ordinis*, n. 2 and 13).[12]

The teaching *munus* implies that they possess a transcendental warrant to claim knowledge over what is truthful and right in issues of faith and morals. When they speak in the name of Christ and the church, when they preach and teach, they do this with an authority that no member of the laity can ever enjoy (*Presbyterorum ordinis*, n. 5). Further, the priest, as a sharer in Christ's kingship, can also exercise a governing function (*Presbyterorum Ordinis*, n. 6–7). The conferred pastoral power covers the legislative, judicial, and punitive aspects in the life of the community. Also, through the sacerdotal power invested on them in ordination, they become mediators of God's grace or forgiveness in the sacraments.

These transcendental dimensions of priestly vocation and status have been deeply embedded in the Catholic public imagination through the discourses which could reach the faithful. As such, if Catholic priests are seen as mediators between God and humans, linking the human and divine realms, their role is indispensable. The theologically uneducated laypeople are exposed to the essential points of the theology of priesthood every time they participate in a liturgical service. The overemphasis on the divine selection, indelible mark, and ontological difference acquired in the order become thus the bedrock of clerical identity and their status in the communities.

Further, even the metaphorical language used in the official discourse and liturgy of the church serves to obscure the asymmetrical power relations. French sociologist Pierre Bourdieu argues that euphemisms and a very abstract vocabulary play a crucial strategy in the Catholic Church's reproduction of inequality between the hierarchy and the laity. The language of piety and obedience is used to mystify, deny, and to distract from this reality. Church officials use this language "to inoculate themselves from acknowledgment of the real truth of church practices and to convince the laity (and others) that there is nothing arbitrary about hierarchical power and the clerical privilege it embeds."[13] Epistemic authority is further reinforced by rituals and practices, which increase the sense of authority of the leaders. These rituals and the elevated language used to describe almost all actions and relationships in the church service obscure power relations.

Until the second half of the twentieth century, the laity hardly enjoyed any access to formal theological education. This knowledge differential facilitated clerical abuse of power. By ordination and the powers invested in them, the members of the clergy played the role of institutional gatekeepers of knowledge production and sharing, claiming unique access to truth and its interpretation. This fact produced undue credibility inflation. It allowed priests to rule over communities unfairly, and their practices could go unpunished for centuries. Moreover, historically, the exercise of clerical powers extended much beyond the institution of the church, reaching equally the cultural, social, and political spheres. The church leaders and the clergy were by their office in a position to define morality and regulate or influence practically all essential aspects of lay life—from family and community relations, the attitudes toward material goods and property, work ethics, and even the most intimate aspects of marital life such as sexuality or reproduction.

Last but not least, the idea of the priest as someone set apart due to his divine calling has also been closely associated with him as a person endowed with particular virtues. However, this moral authority and credibility were not necessarily based on personal virtues, but on the power invested in ordination and the constructs emerging from this. As the sacrament of order endowed the member of the clergy with a sanctifying grace enabling them to lead a holy life, the role of personal morals would be minimized or lost out of sight. Also, the sacramental powers operated "mechanistically," meaning that the personal merit of the priest would not affect the perceived quality of the sacraments conferred by him.

Not only power imbalance but also the image of the members of the clergy as trustworthy, moral figures facilitated sexual and other forms of abuse of power. For instance, through the sacrament of reconciliation and the practice of spiritual guidance, they came in the possession of intimate knowledge, revealing parishioners' vulnerability, innocence, lack of sexual experience, and understanding. All public revelations of cases of sexual abuse of minors or even adults start as a competition between the word of a clergy member to be trusted by virtue of his divine selection and his assumed moral superiority and the word of a child or lay adult.

Clericalism and the Abuse of Power

The economy of credibility is a rather complicated issue and a site of numerous intersecting aspects. For instance, today, the members of clergy enjoy quite varying degrees of authority and credibility in different regions of the world. In the Western world, their societal influence and authority have significantly declined already in the second part of the twentieth century. However, in more traditional societies from Eastern Europe to Latin America or African countries, the clergy has been enjoying until recently a quite authoritative role. This positioning has partly contributed to the delayed outburst of the abuse crisis in these areas. If we only look at the example of the recent outburst of the abuse crisis in Poland, we will understand that the more traditionally Catholic is a country, the harder it is to break through the layers of taboo and cover-up. Even though the cases coming to the light today are at least as old as the ones revealed in other parts of the world much earlier, in traditional settings, they surface with greater difficulty. On many sites around the world, this drama has not even managed to unfold.

Further, understanding clericalism is crucial for grasping the various manifestations of abuse of power, as well as the epistemic harms suffered by all those who advocated for the discriminated or silenced groups in the church. In a report on the causes and context of the Sexual Abuse Crisis, the Voice of the Faithful (VOTF)—a lay movement started in Boston in 2002, defined clericalism as: "an overriding set of beliefs and behaviors in which the clergy view themselves as different, separate, and exempt from the norms, rules, and consequences that apply to everyone else in society."[14] So, it is the manifestation of an attitude of entitlement and privilege of a member of the clergy placing himself above the status of the other baptized members of the community.

The divide between the class of clerics possessing all the governing power and the laity restricted to a followers' obedient role resulted as we know in a plethora of abusive practices and unethical behavior patterns. These abominable conditions could be sustained for such a long time due to a well-established culture of obedience on which the pastoral relations were built. If the priest was the man of God who continued Christ's ministry on earth, he was also perceived as the one who could cut people off from the kingdom of God.

Part of the problem is priestly training in itself. For many generations, young seminarians have been taught that they are aspiring to a higher status not available to the laity, a position from which they will have the authority to teach, sanctify, and govern those below. This approach was perceived and meant as a sort of insulation from worldly influences. However, the overemphasis on ontological difference contributed to a somehow aloof attitude, the sense of superiority and entitlement prevailing among some ordained men. Besides, the demographic reality of priest shortage has given rise to lowered selection criteria and minimalist expectations concerning the moral, spiritual, and intellectual character of the candidates for the priesthood. The authenticity of their priestly calling has been preserved as the primary criterion, to be tested and judged by the superiors. Also, this in itself has been often based on a submissive attitude, while the candidates with a critical stance have been discouraged or dismissed in the process.

As a consequence, the clergy has become a counter-image to its true vocation and the spirit of the Gospel. The clerical mentality has been trumping the needs of the church community. For instance, as a solution to clergy shortage, church administrators chose to close down parishes, rather than share ministerial functions with the lay people willing to serve their communities.

Pope Francis himself has repeatedly denounced clericalism, calling it an ugly perversion of the church. In *Evangelii Gaudium*, he referred to Jesus's example, who did not distinguish himself by assuming a dignitary role in the synagogue and he expressed his concern that in priesthood the sacramental power has been often confused with power in general. Instead, he described the priest as a servant and pastor of the community, not a bureaucratic official.[15] He warned about the fact that clericalism could be fostered by laity as well if they show excessive deference assuming the moral superiority of the clergy: "Clericalism, whether fostered by priests themselves or by laypersons, leads to an excision in the ecclesial body that supports and helps to perpetuate many of the evils that we are condemning today. To say 'no' to abuse is to say an emphatic 'no' to all forms of clericalism."[16]

Epistemic Silencing: Cover-Ups, Lack of Accountability

When analyzing the meaning and practice of ecclesial authority, the work of Michel Foucault can represent an excellent starting point for our ecclesiological critique. Foucault's theorization of regimes of power/knowledge intersects with Fricker's central concerns and can serve as a resource for our discussion of epistemic injustice.[17] For Foucault, power is always linked to knowledge: "There is no power relation without the correlative constitution of a field of knowledge."[18] In his account of disciplinary power he refers to the operations that produce disciplined subjects and knowledge: selection, normalization, hierarchization, and centralization.[19] Drawing on Foucault's approach on power, Steven Ogden argues that, at least since Constantine, the church has been enmeshed with monarchical forms of power and church leaders play the role of guardians of knowledge. Ecclesial discourses highlight this epistemological centrality of church leaders, determining who can speak, and decide what counts as true. Due to the drive toward maintaining a unitary discourse, dissenters are marginalized or silenced.[20]

Cover-up has been a part of the Catholic institutional culture and the commonly used policy in cases of clerical misconduct. The responses to the abuse crisis revealed that the institution of the church protected the clergy at all costs, hiding their crimes as long as it was feasible. The mere acknowledgment of the problems would have meant exposing the system to critique and weakening their absolute power. Under the guise of protecting the good name of the church, they were, in fact, defending the authority and sovereign power of clergy; they deemed these as more important than the protection of the most vulnerable or the commitment to the values of the Gospel.

The strategies of covering up scandals have proved to be strikingly similar around the globe: relocating the accused to another parish, region or even country; shuffling them around even several times when needed; offering them higher positions in church hierarchy or administration; sending them to poorer, remote parishes as places of banishment; temporary "treatment" in church-owned healthcare institutions; or if the perpetrator was too visible and highly placed, a hideaway in a luxurious monastery under the guise of a life of penance. Conversely, everything has been done to silence the victims and their families: dissuading them at all costs from filing official complaints, imposing legal clauses in settlements.

The culture of secrecy, internal protocols, the closed circuits of communication such as those revealed in *Crimen Sollicitationis* (1962) enabled these strategies.[21] One such example would be that in situations of scandal, members of the clergy have often misused the sacrament of confession to silence not only the victims, but also fellow priests and superiors. From the moment they had to listen to the confession of a perpetrator, colleagues and superiors were bound to secrecy and restricted in any communication about the case. Besides, evidence surfaced about the common practice of quieting the victims through the imposition of a secrecy associated misleadingly with the seal of confession.

The reactions of disbelief and the unwillingness of church officials to acknowledge or handle the cases of abuse were nothing else than expressions of profound testimonial injustice. Epistemic smothering is the reason why in most cases no complaints or no criminal charges have been filed. Survivors have been searching for listeners among those whose role would have been by virtue of their ministry to support the vulnerable. Instead, they have been blamed even with outright accusations of seduction. Moreover, when a member of the clergy or the entire group invested with such moral authority denied the lived experience of survivors, they were re-experiencing epistemic injustice. Personal stories of survivors confirmed that the repeated experience of testimonial injustice—being questioned, dismissed, blamed often resulted in new traumas. This was especially damaging to their spiritual lives, causing a crisis of faith and alienation from their communities.

Unfortunately, quite often even the lay members of their parishes reproduced these injustices, being blinded by clericalism. While the victims and their families had been often ostracized in their communities, the abusers preserved their respected position. Lay parishioners reproduced these injustices largely because of submissive behaviors inculcated in their education at home, school, and church. But these behaviors also protected the church from the blemish of scandal. More importantly, they gave more credibility to a member of the clergy than to any layperson.

Personal responsibility and accountability have been minimized in all cases when sexual abuse has been proved. Church leaders have resisted both individual and institutional responsibility. If we have a closer look at the discourse used by both the superiors and the perpetrators, we sometimes discover the medical terminology of uncontrollable conditions or illness, as euphemisms to cover the nature of their acts or to deculpabilize them.

The history of the church contains a long row of evidence regarding the fact that priests have not been held to professional standards, either to their vows, and their misconduct has rarely been punished in a commensurate way. The structures of clerical accountability are missing to date from the system of governance of the church. They still do not have a binding professional code of ethics with concrete sanctions in proportion with the gravity of their misconduct.

RESISTING AND COUNTERING EPISTEMIC INJUSTICE

The Role of Feminist Scholarship

Women's voice and testimony have been questioned, censored, discarded ever since the dawn of resurrection. Until the end of the twentieth century, women could not participate in the areas that created hermeneutical understanding in the church, thus, feminist scholarship came first of all, as an expression of resistance to the patriarchal regime of truth.

During the initial stage of formal feminist endeavors, starting with the 1970s, feminist scholars tackled primarily what we defined in the previous as hermeneutic injustice. They set out to identify and address the various forms of exclusion and infringement on the epistemic agency of women which reduced their ability to participate in the epistemic community of the church. They set out to identify, examine, and denounce the patriarchal knowledge practices and the political strategies of silencing women's voices. In order to achieve this, they revisited the mainstream concepts and methods of theologizing. They approached the biblical and historical sources with *hermeneutics of suspicion* and created tools to uncover and reconstruct *herstory* (women's version of history) from under 2000 years of ideological debris.

The *hermeneutics of suspicion*—a term coined in the 1970s by Paul Ricoeur—has become synonymous with a deconstructive practice of inquiry and interpretation. According to this theoretical approach, there can be no objective or absolute knowledge of the meaning of texts (including literary, philosophical, or even biblical texts).[22] It rejects the objectivist illusion or academic myth that all scientifically based interpretation, including that of the Scriptures, is objective and value-free. This reading strategy is critically subversive of all forms of power and domination hence its aim is to reveal not only the structures of domination inscribed in texts but as well in their interpretations. Needless to say, the *hermeneutics of suspicion* has been widely used by feminist Bible interpretations. For instance, a pioneer in this field, biblical scholar Elisabeth Schüssler-Fiorenza, emphasized that a feminist reading of the biblical texts should be as well rooted in suspicion and it should ask whose interests and point of view do these interpretations support in the earthly realm.

The primary aim of feminist theology was to deconstruct the hegemony of the male-made discourse of theology. Further, feminist theologians intended to create a more inclusive hermeneutical climate, deconstructing the sources of women's unequal position in the community. Deconstruction was not at all a synonym of destruction, but a critical look questioning what has been long taken for granted even in the Scriptures and their interpretation. They challenged centuries-old misinterpretations of religious texts that have justified gender inequality in religious communities. Awareness-raising of the mechanisms of epistemic marginalization was an important step in order to change malestream epistemological frameworks. They revealed their ideological role in legitimating and inculcating oppressive structures and women's exclusion from knowledge creation and sharing.

Moreover, the language, the doctrine of the church as well as its imagery and liturgy, created an overwhelming sense of God as male. For this reason, feminist theology set out to create its own epistemological approaches, an inclusive language, taking a firm methodological commitment to women's experience. They designated women's experience as a central methodological concept and the starting point for theological reflection: "the lens through which one does theology," and "a filter through which theological sources must pass in order to be included in the doctrine."[23]

Feminist theologians are not so much prevented from the process of knowledge production today, but they continue to be impacted by the authoritative forms of sharing it. Feminist contributions have been to date disregarded, devalued, and systematically dismissed as not real scholarship. As Foucault's theorizing of the power/knowledge nexus puts it, their contributions "have been disqualified as nonconceptual knowledges, as insufficiently elaborated knowledges: naïve . . . hierarchically inferior knowledges . . . that are below the required level of erudition and scientificity."[24] Accordingly, the feminist efforts have been more recently redirected toward unveiling the persistent testimonial injustice.

Also, feminist scholars extended their focus and concerns from the patriarchal power relations to other forms of domination—racism, colonialism, religious exclusion, poverty, heterosexism.[25] Feminist theology is a liberation theology, sensitive to the intersections of power with gender, race, social, and economic vulnerabilities, educational level: "In order to get hold of the complex nature of oppression, feminist ideology critique cannot limit itself to the category of sex/gender but must always include an analysis of race, class, and colonialism because women as wo/men are determined by these power structures and ideologies. Consequently, Gal 3:28 is best understood as espousing a counter ideology to that of kyriarchy. It does not just announce the invalidity of kyriarchal gender ideology but also of ethnic, religious, and status differences."[26]

Kyriarchy is a term coined by Elisabeth Schüssler-Fiorenza in her groundbreaking work *But She Said: Feminist Practices of Biblical Interpretation* (1992). It is a neologism derived from the Greek κύριος (kurios—lord, master) and ἄρχειν (archein—to rule, to dominate) by which she described all interconnected and intersecting systems of domination based on the rule of a lord/master. By this definition she extended the focus from sexist relations of discrimination in a patriarchal system to all other forms of oppression.

Feminist theologies demonstrated sensitivity to the multiplicity of perspectives, and they advocated for the inclusion of all lay perspectives in the doctrinal process and ministry practices of the church. Feminist scholars have been committed not only to the elimination of women's subordination but also to inclusivity toward all other oppressed or vulnerable groups—all *wo/men*. Elizabeth Schüssler-Fiorenza introduced this spelling to express that feminist concern was directed to all marginalized, women and men equally, independently of race, class, or religion. "Hence the spelling wo/men seeks to communicate that whenever I speak of wo/men I mean not only to include all women, but also to speak of oppressed and marginalized men. Wo/men must be therefore understood as an inclusive expression, rather than as an exclusive universalized gender term."[27]

Feminist critiques noted that Catholicism was based on a typically patriarchal discourse in its insistence on the singularity of meaning. The main preoccupation of malestream theology was the preservation and adherence to the fundamental doctrine of the church, which implied dismissing, discrediting liberation theologies—among which are feminist ones.[28] Bioethical questions, especially around beginning and end-of-life, ministry to the LGBTQ community or the care for HIV patients, advocacy for social justice or supporting the survivors of sexual abuse have been treated as the minefields of theoretical and practical preoccupations. So, in many real-life challenges the church abandoned its people, not answering the needs of our contemporary world. Nevertheless, feminist theologians, wo/men, religious sisters have been pioneering in these areas. They tackled the thorny issues, trying to answer the needs and challenges facing real people's lives today. Feminist scholars lent their voice to the voiceless, marginalized and ostracized of our societies. They have attended to contemporary human experience and the empirical reality of social inquiry, raising difficult questions regarding official teachings that seemed at variance with believers' deepest intuitions and experiences. As a reaction to this they were confronted with investigations and various severe sanctions from the suspension of their activities and tasks to excommunication.[29] Feminist scholars argue that theology should be an open conversation grounded in the experiences of our existence. Hence, they urge the church community to open conversations engaging in authentic dialogue, practicing the virtue of epistemic justice to restore the credibility of the church.

Feminist scholarship accomplished very much in these few decennia of struggle against epistemic injustice; they did plenty in order to prevent and mitigate epistemic harm. The delivered work encompasses all sectors of contemporary life: from biblical studies to systematic theology, social ethics, human rights issues, bioethics to environmental issues. They managed to lessen the effects of epistemic injustice and create a more inclusive hermeneutical climate. However, they have not reached yet the impact they should have on mainstream theological discourses and church practices. They still lack epistemic authority, they remain marginal in the discourses of the church and they are still not in the position to share knowledge authoritatively or participate in decision-making. However, I firmly believe that partly, thanks to their monumental scholarly and advocacy work, we are testimonies of an encouraging momentum.

THE EMERGENCE OF LAY REFORM MOVEMENTS: FROM KYRIARCHY TO A DISCIPLESHIP OF EQUALS

In our days, women and men, youth and elderly equally, from Germany to the United States are leaving the church in impressive numbers because they feel they are not being heard. Besides, in the rows of the remainers we are testimonies of an unprecedented crisis, as the dissenting voices are getting louder, and a highly visible reform movement is being born. A great number of lay initiatives have emerged during the recent years, all trying to address the moral dissonance they experience between the teachings of the Gospel and clerical abuse of power. They are urging to combat the various manifestations of clericalism, misogyny and the unfair treatment of various groups in the Catholic Church. Many compare this moment to the eve of the Reformation.

This crisis of morals has revived in theological circles the discussions around the role of the magisterium. There is also a renewed interest in the meaning, purpose, and manifestations of *sensus fidei* (sense of the faith). Surveys done all around the world have repeatedly confirmed the vast disconnect between the stance of the magisterium and the lived experience of laypeople. For instance, decisions related to healthcare and biomedical ethics are affecting the lives of families and the average Catholic is not trained to face such difficult moral issues. Despite the contributions of Vatican II in this regard, the sense of the faithful has been overlooked, dismissed ever since, and this qualifies as yet another manifestation of testimonial injustice. As the church authorities disconnect with real life grows, the laity feels left in the cold and chooses following their consciences in moral matters.

The International Theological Commission of the church issued in 2014 a study urging for an appropriate answer to the situations, when the reception of magisterial teaching meets with difficulty and resistance in the rows of the faithful: "Alerted by their sensus fidei, individual believers may deny assent even to the teaching of legitimate pastors if they do not recognize in that teaching the voice of Christ, the Good Shepherd."[30] They advanced the idea that laity is not supposed to obey the church authorities blindly and they defined the *sensus fidei* as: "a sort of spiritual instinct that enables the believer to judge spontaneously whether a particular teaching or practice is or is not in conformity with the Gospel and with the apostolic faith." They referred to the authority of St. Thomas Aquinas on this point, who taught that even if a believer lacks theological competence, it is licit and proper for him to resist in virtue of his sensus fidei his bishop, or pope if they are preaching heterodox things. Further, they based this argument on the Code of Canon Law (canon 208–223), which ascribes to the laity the responsibility of intervening in the problems of the church:

> According to the knowledge, competence, and prestige which they possess, they have the right and even at times the duty to manifest to the sacred pastors their opinion on matters which pertain to the good of the Church and to make their opinion known to the rest of the Christian faithful, without prejudice to the integrity of faith and morals, with reverence toward their pastors, and attentive to common advantage and the dignity of persons.[31]

Pope Francis himself has stressed the importance of listening to the *sensus fidei*: "the *sensus fidelium* must be listened to because it is a locus theologicus, a place where the revealing God can be heard speaking to the church today. Why listen to the *sensus fidelium*?—To find out what the Lord asks of his Church today."[32] Besides, in both *Evangelii Gaudium* and *Amoris Laetitia*, he brought to the moral forefront the Catholic doctrine on the authority and inviolability of personal conscience.

The newly emerged lay initiatives proposed various fresh ecclesiological models as most of them agree that the old model of governance is unsustainable. The critical voices are all directed toward the current bureaucratic structure the church inherited from the Roman Empire and the feudalism from the Middle Ages. Some groups argue for dismantling completely the hierarchical system, replacing it with egalitarian, function-based, structures that conform to the Gospel and answer the needs of the twenty-first-century community. They share the vision of a more democratic church governance and collaborative leadership aiming to transform the Catholic Church from a *kyriarchy* into *a discipleship of equals*, using the terminology introduced by Elisabeth Schüssler-Fiorenza.[33]

Other central concepts around which the idea of renewal is being built is the *synodality* of the church and *decentralization.* During his pontificate Pope Francis has strengthened the power of the Synod of Bishops and initiated many meetings in this regard: two synods on the family (2014 and 2015), the synod on "Young People, the Faith and Vocational Discernment" in 2018, and the recent so-called Amazon Synod in October 2019. These events are meant as steps in a process of implementing transformations, such as renewed collaborative ways of functioning, giving more leadership to the lay and more autonomy to the local churches in dealing with regional challenges. Pope Francis expressed repeatedly the intention to sustain the implementation of the Second Vatican Council in order to answer adequately to the needs of the church in the third millennium.

Synodality has become synonymous with a journey made together, referring back to its Greek etymological roots: the prefix, *syn-* ("together") and the word *hodos* ("road") to mean a "common journey." In *Evangelii Gaudium* Pope Francis shared a vision for a more collegial and "listening" church. He referred to a more decentralized institutional organization, in which local bodies have a high degree of decision-making power in church governance. At the same time a group of Catholic scholars made a public statement with several concrete proposals in this regard such as: giving laity an active role in church governance at all levels and electing bishops more locally and democratically as in the beginnings of the church; give them more autonomy; admitting independent, professional advisers to the Congregation for the Doctrine of the Faith.[34]

Further, while some reform groups call for abolishing the clerical status in its current form, others are voicing the wish to keep clerical ministry with a renewed theology of clerical ministry. However, combatting clericalism, changing clerical attitude will only be possible if we address the formation, tackling the elements where the emphasis on ministry and service have been replaced by privileges and sacerdotal powers. A scholarly group at Boston College has issued a statement on priesthood and ministry in the contemporary Catholic Church. In order to uproot the deeply embedded clerical culture and eradicate the clerical culture, they proposed a thorough reexamination of the formation process, reimagining the ministerial priesthood with an emphasis on collaborative leadership.[35]

Even though the proposed models and solutions differ in some points regarding their practical implementation, they all have the goal of a profound ecclesial transformation. They all admit that a redistribution of ministries will be crucial in order to be able to answer the needs of the community in the twenty-first century. The church in its role of meaning-making community has created and sustained unfair differentials in epistemic authority and this injustice is insurmountable in the form in which church governance, doctrine and regulation of morals happen today. Genuine epistemic transformation and the correction of injustices will only be made possible through concrete actions and renewed practices.

José Medina and other theorists of epistemic resistance refer to the imperative of epistemic interaction manifested in various forms of activism and political resistance. They all underscore the importance of genuine dialogue between groups requiring an attitude of respect, recognition, enabling "mutual resistance and beneficial friction."[36] Epistemic justice and equality will not be accomplished, until the counterparts do not lend a listening ear and take a genuinely receptive attitude to the imperative of equality inside religious communities. In order to transform the Catholic Church from a *kyriarchy* into a *discipleship of equals* we need epistemically virtuous men like the Jesuits who opened their Curia in Rome to welcome the censored speakers of the VOF event; or like the priests who assumed their suspension from ministry just because they advocated equality for women. We need to engage and persist in epistemic disobedience, challenging the privileged group to unlearn their ignorance and become aware of their oppressive norms and practices. The momentum asks for more epistemic friction.

NOTES

1. A dicastery (from Greek δικαστήριον, law court) is a department of the Holy See. Together with other units (such as the Secretariats, the Congregations, the Pontifical Councils), they form the Roman Curia, or the central body assisting the Pope in governing the Catholic Church. Pope Francis created this specific department in 2016 to unite the work of two older units focusing on the life and apostolate of the lay faithful and the pastoral care for families. Ironically, through a statute modification, this dicastery received the unique mission of promoting "ecclesial reflection on the identity and mission of women in the church and society, promoting their participation" in April 2018, just one month after the censoring of the VOF event. For this modified statute, see: *Statutes of the Dicastery for Laity, Family and Life*, http://press.vatican.va/content/salastampa/en/bollettino/pubblico/2018/05/08/180508a.html (accessed November 14, 2019).

2. This is the administrative center of the Society of Jesus (SJ) or the Jesuit Order.

3. In daily language use, the terms "nun" and "religious sister" are used interchangeably to imply women who have professed the vows of poverty, chastity, and obedience. However, the term "nun" strictly speaking refers to women living a contemplative life in a cloistered (enclosed) or semi-cloistered monastery. The other category of "religious sisters" refers to women engaging in "active" forms of ministry within the world. The precise term implying both categories would be "women religious." Considering that the journalistic accounts of these cases of abuse are not considering this difference, we might also use them interchangeably.

4. Lucetta Scaraffia, *Open Letter to Pope Francis*, https://www.futurechurchnews.org/article/scarrafias-open-letter-to-pope-francis (accessed November 13, 2019).

5. Miranda Fricker, *Epistemic Injustice: Power and the Ethics of Knowing* (Oxford University Press, 2007).

6. Fricker, *Epistemic Injustice*, 155.

7. Fricker distinguished between transactional and structural varieties of testimonial injustice, and she focused mainly on the one-on-one individual exchanges.

8. Kristie Dotson, "Tracking Epistemic Violence, Tracking Practices of Silencing," *Hypatia* 26, no. 2 (2011): 244.

9. *The New American Bible*, Revised Edition (Saint Benedict Press, 2010).

10. Mark Kowalewski, *All Things to All People. The Catholic Church Confronts the AIDS Crisis* (SUNY Press, 1994), 132.

11. See Yves Congar, "My Path-findings in the Theology of Laity and Ministries," *The Jurist* 32 (1971): 180.

12. See: Dogmatic Constitution on the Church, *Lumen Gentium* (1964), http://www.vatican.va/archive/hist_councils/ii_vatican_council/documents/vat-ii_const_19641121_lumen-gentium_en.html (accessed November 11, 2019); *Decree on the Ministry and Life of Priests* (1965), http://www.vatican.va/archive/hist_councils/ii_vatican_council/documents/vat-ii_decree_19651207_presbyterorum-ordinis_en.html (accessed November 11, 2019).

13. Michele Dillon, "The Catholic Church's Euphemization of Power," *National Catholic Reporter*, February 15, 2019, https://www.ncronline.org/news/accountability/catholic-churchs-euphemization-power (accessed August 15, 2019); See also: Pierre Bourdieu, *Practical Reason: On the Theory of Action* (Stanford University Press, 1998).

14. VOTF is one of the leading reform-minded lay organizations active at the moment. They are involved in collaborative projects directed towards bridging the gap between clergy and laity in order to address the crisis in our Church. This year they have published a report jointly with the Association of United States Catholic Priests (AUSCP), titled "Confronting the Systemic Dysfunction of Clericalism," https://www.futurechurch.org/sites/default/files/Model%204%20A%20-AUSCP%20White%20Paper-Systemic%20Dysfunction%20Clericalism.pdf (accessed August 5, 2019).

15. He is echoing at this point Eugen Drewermann's critique on priests as bureaucratic functionaries.

16. *Letter of His Holiness Pope Francis to the People of God*, August 20, 2018, Vatican City, http://w2.vatican.va/content/francesco/en/letters/2018/documents/papa-francesco_20180820_lettera-popolo-didio.html (accessed July 28, 2019).

17. Amy Allen, "Foucault and Epistemic Injustice," in Ian James Kid et al. (eds.), *The Routledge Handbook of Epistemic Injustice* (Routledge, Taylor and Francis Group, 2017), 187–194.

18. Foucault, *Discipline and Punish: The Birth of the Prison*, trans. Alan Sheridan (New York, NY: Vintage Books, 1978), 27.

19. Allen, "Foucault and Epistemic Injustice," 191.

20. Steven G. Ogden, *The Church, Authority, and Foucault: Imagining the Church as an Open Space of Freedom* (London: Routledge, 2017).

21. The Supreme Sacred Congregation of the Holy Office, *Instruction on the Manner of Proceeding in Causes involving the Crime of Solicitation* (Vatican Polyglot Press, 1962), http://www.vatican.va/resources/resources_crimen-sollicitationis-1962_en.html (accessed September 6, 2019).

22. For an introduction and definition of the term, see: Hans-Georg Gadamer, "The Hermeneutics of Suspicion," in Gary Shapiro and Alan Sica (eds.), *Hermeneutics:*

Questions and Prospects (University of Massachusetts Press, 1984), 63; G. D. Robinson, "Paul Ricoeur and the Hermeneutics of Suspicion: A Brief Overview and Critique," *Premise* 8 (1995): 12, http://individual.utoronto.ca/bmclean/hermeneutics/ricoeur_suppl/Ricoeur_Herm_of_Suspicion.htm (accessed November 12, 2019); David Stewart, "The Hermeneutics of Suspicion," *Journal of Literature and Theology* 3 (1989): 296–307.

23. Elizabeth A. Johnson, *She Who Is: The Mystery of God in Feminist Theological Discourse* (New York: Crossroad, 1992), 15.

24. Michel Foucault, *Society Must Be Defended: Lectures at the Collège de France, 1975–1976*, trans. David Macey (New York: Picador Press, 2003), 7.

25. Elisabeth Schüssler-Fiorenza, *Discipleship of Equals: A Critical Feminist Ekklēsia-logy of Liberation* (New York, NY: Crossroad, 1993), 341–342.

26. Elisabeth Schüssler-Fiorenza, *Rhetoric, and Ethics. The Politics of Biblical Studies* (Minneapolis: Fortress, 1999), 153.

27. Elisabeth Schüssler-Fiorenza, *Jesus: Myriam's Child, Sophia's Prophet: Critical Issues in Feminist Christology* (London: The Continuum International Publishing Group, 1994), 191.

28. Schüssler-Fiorenza, *Jesus: Myriam's Child, Sophia's Prophet*, 177–178.

29. For instance, Sister Margaret McBride, a hospital executive and member of St. Joseph's Hospital Ethics Committee in Phoenix, Arizona was relieved of her position and excommunicated for approving the termination of the life-threatening, eleven-week pregnancy of a twenty-seven-year-old mother of four. Or, Sister Jeannine Gramick spent three decades building a pioneering ministry to the gays and lesbian community, despite relentless and unsuccessful efforts made by then Cardinal Ratzinger to silence her and ban her work.

30. This International Theological Commission studied the nature of *sensus fidei* and its place in the life of the Church between 2011 and 2014. For the final document, see: *Sensus Fidei in the Life of the Church* (2014), http://www.vatican.va/roman_curia/congregations/cfaith/cti_documents/rc_cti_20140610_sensus-fidei_en.html (accessed November 17, 2019).

31. Code of Canon Law, Canon 212, http://www.vatican.va/archive/ENG1104/_PU.HTM (accessed November 17, 2019).

32. *Address of His Holiness Pope Francis during the Meeting on the Family* (Vatican City, October 4, 2014), http://w2.vatican.va/content/francesco/en/speeches/2014/october/documents/papa-francesco_20141004_incontro-per-la-famiglia.html (accessed November 17, 2019).

33. See: Schüssler-Fiorenza, *Discipleship of Equals*.

34. Catholic Scholars' Declaration on Authority in the Church opened for endorsement on October 11, 2012 on the occasion of the 50th anniversary of the opening of the Second Vatican Council, see: http://www.churchauthority.org/jubilee-declaration.asp.

35. Boston College Seminar on Priesthood and Ministry for the Contemporary Church, "To Serve the People of God: Renewing the Conversation on Priesthood and Ministry," https://www.bc.edu/content/dam/bc1/schools/stm/faculty-research/BC%20Priesthood%20document%20-%20Origins%20-%2027%20Dec%202018.pdf (accessed November 14, 2019).

36. José Medina, *The Epistemology of Resistance: Gender and Racial Oppression* (Oxford University Press, 2012).

BIBLIOGRAPHY

Address of His Holiness Pope Francis during the Meeting on the Family (Vatican City, October4, 2014), http://w2.vatican.va/content/francesco/en/speeches/2014/october/documents/papa-francesco_20141004_incontro-per-la-famiglia.html (accessed November 17, 2019).

Allen, Amy. "Foucault and Epistemic Injustice." In *The Routledge Handbook of Epistemic Injustice*. Edited by Ian James Kid et al., 187–194. Routledge, Taylor and Francis Group, 2017.

Boston College Seminar on Priesthood and Ministry for the Contemporary Church. *To Serve the People of God: Renewing the Conversation on Priesthood and Ministry*, https://www.bc.edu/content/dam/bc1/schools/stm/faculty-research/BC%20Priesthood%20document%20-%20Origins%20-%2027%20Dec%202018.pdf (accessed November 14, 2019).

Bourdieu, Pierre. *Practical Reason: On the Theory of Action*. Stanford University Press, 1998.

Catholic Scholars' Declaration on Authority in the Church, 2012, http://www.churchauthority.org/jubilee-declaration.asp (November 17, 2019).

Code of Canon Law, Canon 212, http://www.vatican.va/archive/ENG1104/_PU.HTM (accessed November 17, 2019).

Congar, Yves. "My Path-findings in the Theology of Laity and Ministries." *The Jurist* 32 (1971): 169–188.

Decree on the Ministry and Life of Priests (1965), http://www.vatican.va/archive/hist_councils/ii_vatican_council/documents/vat-ii_decree_19651207_presbyterorum-ordinis_en.html (accessed November 11, 2019).

Dillon, Michele. "The Catholic Church's Euphemization of Power." *National Catholic Reporter*, February 15, 2019, https://www.ncronline.org/news/accountability/catholic-churchs-euphemization-power (accessed August 15, 2019).

Dogmatic Constitution on the Church. Lumen Gentium (1964), http://www.vatican.va/archive/hist_councils/ii_vatican_council/documents/vat-ii_const_19641121_lumen-gentium_en.html (accessed November 11, 2019).

Dotson, Kristie. "Tracking Epistemic Violence, Tracking Practices of Silencing." *Hypatia* 26, no. 2 (2011): 236–257.

Foucault, Michel. *Discipline and Punish: The Birth of the Prison*, trans. Alan Sheridan. New York: Vintage Books, 1978.

———. *Society Must Be Defended: Lectures at the Collège de France, 1975–1976*. trans. David Macey. New York: Picador Press, 2003.

Fricker, Miranda. *Epistemic Injustice: Power and the Ethics of Knowing*. Oxford University Press, 2007.

Gadamer, Hans-Georg. "The Hermeneutics of Suspicion." In *Hermeneutics: Questions and Prospects*. Edited by Gary Shapiro and Alan Sica. University of Massachusetts Press, 1984.

International Theological Commission. *Sensus Fidei in the Life of the Church* (2014), http://www.vatican.va/roman_curia/congregations/cfaith/cti_documents/rc_cti_20140610_sensus-fidei_en.html (accessed November 17, 2019).

Johnson, Elizabeth A. *She Who Is: The Mystery of God in Feminist Theological Discourse*. New York: Crossroad, 1992.

Kidd, Ian James, Medina José and Pohlhaus, Gaile Jr. *The Routledge Handbook of Epistemic Injustice*. Routledge, Taylor & Francis Group, 2017.

Kowalewski, Mark. *All Things to All People. The Catholic Church Confronts the AIDS Crisis*. SUNY Press, 1994.

Letter of His Holiness Pope Francis to the People of God, Vatican City, August 20, 2018. http://w2.vatican.va/content/francesco/en/letters/2018/documents/papa-francesco_20180820_lettera-popolo-didio.html (accessed July 28, 2019).

Medina, José. *The Epistemology of Resistance: Gender and Racial Oppression*. Oxford University Press, 2012.

The New American Bible, Revised Edition. Saint Benedict Press, 2010.

Robinson, G.D. "Paul Ricoeur and the Hermeneutics of Suspicion: A Brief Overview and Critique." *Premise* 8 (1995), http://individual.utoronto.ca/bmclean/hermeneutics/ricoeur_suppl/Ricoeur_Herm_of_Suspicion.htm (accessed November 12, 2019).

Ogden, Steven G. *The Church, Authority, and Foucault: Imagining the Church as an Open Space of Freedom*. London: Routledge, 2017.

Scaraffia, Lucetta. *Open Letter to Pope Francis*, https://www.futurechurchnews.org/article/scarrafias-open-letter-to-pope-francis (accessed November 13, 2019).

Schüssler-Fiorenza, Elisabeth. *Discipleship of Equals: A Critical Feminist Ekklēsia-logy of Liberation*. New York, NY: Crossroad, 1993.

———. *Jesus: Myriam's Child, Sophia's Prophet: Critical Issues in Feminist Christology*. The Continuum International Publishing Group, London: 1994.

———. *Rhetoric, and Ethics. The Politics of Biblical Studies*, Minneapolis, Fortress, 1999.

Statutes of the Dicastery for Laity, Family and Life, http://press.vatican.va/content/salastampa/en/bollettino/pubblico/2018/05/08/180508a.html (accessed November 14, 2019).

Stewart, David. "The Hermeneutics of Suspicion." *Journal of Literature and Theology* 3 (1989): 296–307.

The Supreme Sacred Congregation of the Holy Office, *Instruction on the Manner of Proceeding in Causes involving the Crime of Solicitation*. Vatican Polyglot Press, 1962. http://www.vatican.va/resources/resources_crimen-sollicitationis-1962_en.html (accessed September 6, 2019).

Voices of the Faithful, Confronting the Systemic Dysfunction of Clericalism. https://www.futurechurch.org/sites/default/files/Model%204%20A%20-AUSCP%20White%20Paper-Systemic%20Dysfunction%20Clericalism.pdf (accessed August 5, 2019).

Chapter 6

The Archdiocese of Galveston-Houston

The Eye of the Storm

Siobhan Fleming

Similar to how states have boundaries and within those are counties, a diocese is a geographic boundary for Catholic Churches led by one bishop. An archdiocese consists of several dioceses, led by an archbishop who has jurisdiction over each of the dioceses in his archdiocese.[1] In Texas, there are fifteen dioceses and two Archdioceses: San Antonio and Galveston-Houston. Individually on January 31, 2019, the fifteen Catholic dioceses in Texas simultaneously released the names of clergy credibly accused of sexually abusing minors.[2]

As a Catholic, a researcher of clergy sexual abuse, and a Houstonian, I anxiously waited that day, along with the local media outlets, for the list to appear on the website of the Archdiocese of Galveston-Houston (ADGH).[3] I did not have high expectations for a transparent and forthcoming list, and I was right in that regard, but it was an implosion, nonetheless. The disclosure was unprecedented in my home diocese, where for fifty years it managed to control and prevent the dissemination of information about sexual abuse allegations against clergy. The archdiocese gave very little information on the priests other than the parishes to which they were assigned and a few other pieces of data (i.e., ordination and retirement year, etc.). The list had no dates of parish assignments, when the alleged abuse occurred, or when the allegations were received by the archdiocese.

The revelation of the credibly accused clergy had a profound effect on me as a Catholic. The priests were my parish priests growing up. They were my professors in college. They were fellow alumni of the Catholic university I attended. These ordained men had sexually abused boys

I knew in high school. The bishop responsible for the cases prior to 1984 had confirmed me—one of the Catholic Church's seven sacraments meant to unite Catholics more firmly to Christ—when I was in seventh grade.[4] The sacrament of confirmation is a visible rite of passage that the church believes was instituted by Jesus Christ. They are very serious occasions and are typically a very memorable part of childhood.[5] It was a big deal to meet the bishop back in the 1980s. Thus, this list of credibly accused clergy that included some of the most revered men in my life hit me like a brick in January 2019.

When I began researching the priests on the disclosure list, I thought I was an insider in the church. I thought this because of my faithful attendance at mass and Holy Days of Obligation,[6] my sixteen years of Catholic schooling, and my background as someone who grew up with a current bishop and went to school with so many of the priests in the diocese. Quite literally my life revolved around the connections I had to the Church in Houston. My educational, social, spiritual, and professional networks were all intertwined in tangible ways with the ADGH.

As I researched, it did not take me long to realize that I was not anything near an insider at all. The organization to which I belonged as a devout and practicing Catholic had deep hidden corners that were completely unknown to me; namely, ones that prioritized the reputation of the church above victims, ones that used Canon Law to dictate every step when responding to allegations of sexual abuse specifically designed to protect the reputation of the accused—not the victim.[7] I learned that the church is a business that protects its brand, and accusations against its priests pose a viable threat to the brand. I learned that the church does not operate alone in its massive cover-up of sexual abuse by the priests; it is aided and abetted by a vast social and professional network of Catholics. In order to prove this thesis, we will begin by examining this archdiocese and the events leading up to the implosion in Texas that resulted in the list being made public on January 31, 2019.

The ADGH is the fifth largest diocese in the United States.[8] Since 2004, His Eminence Daniel Cardinal DiNardo has led the 1.7 million Catholics in the ten counties that comprise the diocese. In 2016, DiNardo took on the additional role of president of the United States Conference of Catholic Bishops (USCCB) for a three-year term.[9] DiNardo's role as president of the USCCB meant that his archdiocese received an unprecedented amount of media attention and the spring of 2018 began with a series of unfortunate events that forever changed the Catholic Church in the United States. Houston was involved directly or indirectly in each event, thus forming DiNardo's *Annus Horribilis* ("horrible year") 2018.

HORRIBILIS EVENT #1: PENNSYLVANIA (JUNE–AUGUST 2018)

As president of the USCCB, DiNardo was certainly aware that an intensive eighteen-month-long Pennsylvania Grand Jury Investigation had begun in 2016 in which the Pennsylvania Office of Attorney General conducted a grand jury investigation into the sexual abuse by Catholic clergy in six Pennsylvania dioceses. In addition to being the president of the USCCB, DiNardo had served as a former priest of the Diocese of Pittsburgh and was a longtime friend of Cardinal Wuerl, who was central to the grand jury report due to his former role as Bishop of Pittsburgh.[10] For two months during the summer of 2018 the release of the report was held up in court—unnamed parties had requested that Pennsylvania's Supreme Court block its release. The unnamed parties—presumably priests and/or bishops named in the report—claimed they had not been granted due process to protect their reputational rights as guaranteed by the state constitution. On June 20, 2018, the Supreme Court of Pennsylvania did indeed block the release of the report.[11]

Pennsylvania Attorney General, Josh Shapiro, responded to that ruling on June 29 stating that he would be taking legal action to force the report's release.[12] And then on July 6, 2018, nine Pennsylvania news outlets along with victims of clergy sex abuse filed a petition with the Pennsylvania Supreme Court saying that the release of the report was a "matter of extraordinary public importance."[13] Ultimately, on July 27, 2018, the Pennsylvania Supreme Court ordered that a redacted copy of the grand jury report be released. Subsequently, on August 14, 2018, the attorney general of Pennsylvania held a press conference reviewing the highlights of the devastating report.[14] The press conference was live streamed on social media, complete with survivors of sexual abuse on stage with the attorney general who used a video montage to emphasize the abuse and degradation these victims endured. The details of the massive cover-up of their crimes only underscored the horrific nature of the abuse.

I watched the live press conference with my children—two in college and one in middle school. It was important for us as devout Catholics to understand what happened in the church even though it was difficult and beyond sickening. It also clearly spelled out that the cover-up of the abuse was a well-orchestrated, *policy-driven process* with many active co-conspirators.[15] Shapiro, in my opinion, came across as smart, professional, strong, and intent on exposing corruption. Some colleagues of mine thought he was grandstanding with the drama of the video montage. A close friend, who is an apologist for the church, actually refuted the sensationalized information in the report, adding that it was all old news that had been dealt with already. It was a witch hunt, he declared.

When the press conference ended that day, Cardinal Wuerl, archbishop of the Diocese of Washington DC put out a press release saying of the grand jury report, "[it] confirms that I acted with diligence, with concern for the victims and to prevent future acts of abuse."[16] That statement was a very significant turning point for me as a researcher. The grand jury report was emotional and it was disturbing to read evidence of such depraved and coordinated sexual abuse of children and the cover-up by bishops like Wuerl. My reaction was a visceral one to protect my children and mourn for the children who were assaulted. Most people I spoke to about the report had the same reactions of disgust and revulsion. But Wuerl's reaction was almost as if he had read a completely different report. How could it be that he believed he acted with diligence? Children were sexually assaulted. He allowed the abusers to stay on the payroll. There was plenty of irrefutable evidence that the abuse occurred. How could Wuerl think he acted with diligence if those priests weren't put in prison?

I believe it was because Wuerl was referring to his actions with regard to *following the Canon Laws of the church*—not how he dealt with the criminal acts brought to his attention in the report. It was a turning point for me as a researcher because I have noticed this same peculiar doublespeak by the bishops; they answer questions that were not asked. They all *manage the information and control the narrative*.

Wuerl continued his hubris the same day when his archdiocese posted a link on its website to TheWuerlRecord.com—a website specially created to refute the points in the Pennsylvania Grand Jury report and defend the cardinal. It was in shockingly poor taste. The backlash from the public was so swift that the site was taken down within 24 hours, and the communications director for the diocese took the blame for it.[17]

The release of the Pennsylvania Grand Jury Report was important not only in terms of justice for the survivors of sexual abuse, but also because of the link to Houston's own Cardinal DiNardo. The report referenced Wuerl more than 200 times relating to cases of abuse during his tenure as Bishop of the Diocese of Pittsburg from 1988 to 2006. Wuerl's diocese had ninety priests named in the report, the most of the six dioceses examined by the grand jury. DiNardo was not specifically mentioned in the redacted report. Of course, it is possible he was one of the redacted names, but that is not something that can be verified. Wuerl quickly became the subject of scorn and ridicule. An online petition to remove Cardinal Wuerl received more than 60,000 signatures by August 23, 2018.[18] There was no further mention of Wuerl and DiNardo's chummy past.

A recurring question I am asked in discussions about sexual abuse in the church is, *How could the bishops not put these guys in prison?* It is a painful realization as a Catholic to find out that it is an organization that is a closed system. It runs by its own rules and regulations. And for myriad reasons, it does not conform to the commonly accepted societal norms and procedures when it comes to one of their priests sexually abusing a child. It is that simple. They do not have the same standards or abide by the same laws. The church has codified every action and process and the fact is, they don't send their ordained clerics to prison without external intervention by a government agency or law enforcement.

HORRIBILIS EVENT #2: MCCARRICK AND WUERL (JUNE 2018)

As the legal machinations revolved around the release of the Pennsylvania Grand Jury report unfolded during the summer of 2018, another tempest was brewing. On June 20, 2018, breaking news revealed that one of the most powerful Cardinals in the Catholic Church, Theodore McCarrick, had been removed from public ministry after a review board of the Archdiocese of New York found an abuse allegation "credible and substantiated." The board found that he had sexually abused a sixteen-year-old altar boy while a priest in New York.[19] Cardinal McCarrick was the first cardinal in history to step down from the College of Cardinals because of sexual abuse allegations.[20]

I spoke to several colleagues who are Catholic scholars, philosophers, and theologians who were surprised, not because McCarrick was accused of sexually abusing a male, but because the boy was a legal minor. To a person, they all said it was well known that McCarrick had sex with men.

As is the case with most scandals in the church, this revelation formed just the tip of the iceberg. Soon tales of McCarrick's sexual harassment of seminarians and priests came pouring out into the public domain. *The New York Times* reported that two separate lawsuits filed by victims alleged that Archbishop Theodore McCarrick sexually abused them when they were seminarians. *The New York Times* revealed that the church reached financial settlements with the victims.[21] This wasn't the first time McCarrick had been accused of being a predator. The late Richard Sipe wrote about the lawsuits and settlements eight years prior in May 2010.[22] Sipe authored an article for his website titled, "The Cardinal McCarrick Syndrome"[23] in which he discussed the 2006 financial settlement from the dioceses of Metuchen and Newark, New Jersey. McCarrick was the founding Bishop of Metuchen, New Jersey from 1981 to 1986 when he was appointed archbishop of Newark until 2000.

When the McCarrick news engulfed Twitter in June of 2018, I remembered hearing his name repeatedly in Houston years earlier. I discussed it with a relative who already had joked that McCarrick was at Archbishop Joseph A.

Fiorenza's anniversary party in 2004. Fiorenza led the Diocese of Galveston-Houston as bishop from 1984 until his retirement in 2006. The anniversary party celebrating Fiorenza's fiftieth year as a priest was held at Reliant Stadium in Houston—the same stadium where the Super Bowl was held in February 2017. Thousands of people attended the event including Cardinal Theodore McCarrick of Washington DC.[24] In July 2008 Cardinal Theodore E. McCarrick, then archbishop emeritus of Washington DC, graced Houston again with his presence as the archdiocese celebrated the dedication of its new $49 million Co-Cathedral of the Sacred Heart.[25]

It struck me when I read about the anniversary and the dedication parties that the cardinals, archbishops, and bishops who support each other by showing up to significant events all know each other well. There aren't that many of them. In 2004 there were seven cardinals and 182 archbishops/bishops leading U.S. dioceses.[26] Three cardinals and forty-five bishops (25 percent of all U.S. bishops) were in attendance in Houston at Archbishop Fiorenza's fiftieth anniversary party. Thus, it is impossible for any reasonable person to believe the disclaimers that they didn't knew anything about McCarrick's lawsuits or the complaints against him. For months after the McCarrick story broke, Cardinal Wuerl denied having any knowledge of the many credible allegations against McCarrick. Yet on January 15, 2019, Cardinal Wuerl said he forgot that he received a report in 2004 detailing McCarrick's inappropriate conduct from the Pittsburgh Diocesan Review Board.[27] Who among us wouldn't forget a report that the highest ranking American Cardinal was accused of sexually assaulting adult men in the seminary? It's a safe bet that Fiorenza and DiNardo knew.

The year 2004 is significant because the USCCB was still touting the 2002 "zero-tolerance" policy and the Dallas charter that outlined the process for dioceses to handle accusations of clergy sexual abuse of a minor.[28] McCarrick served on the four-person committee that drafted it. There was no mention of a process for sexual abuse accusations against bishops or cardinals.[29] When McCarrick was invited back to Houston for the Co-Cathedral dedication in 2008—it was after two dioceses had paid two men settlements for McCarrick's sexual abuse. There is no chance that the cardinals and bishops didn't know about the settlements. And they all knew he preyed upon young seminarians. And yet, Archbishop Fiorenza had him at the dedication in 2008.

It didn't make sense to me. McCarrick was retired by then. Wuerl took his place as Archbishop of Washington DC in 2006. Why would the bishops voluntarily include McCarrick in their celebrations? I wracked my brain trying to figure it out until I remembered that they operate under a different set of laws and social *mores*—they live in the world of the ordained with their peculiar loyalties to each other over those of God's people.

Maybe the world wasn't ready for the #MeToo movement in 2008. Maybe the media wouldn't have picked up on the significance of the McCarrick story. Maybe the Attorney General in Pennsylvania wouldn't have been interested in pursuing a grand jury. But ten years later, *the world was ready*, the media did pick up the McCarrick story, and the Pennsylvania Attorney General did get a grand jury to investigate six dioceses. All those events laid the foundation for the implosion in Houston.

HORRIBILIS EVENT #3: ARRESTS AND RAIDS (SEPTEMBER 2018)

Just a week before the release of the Pennsylvania Grand Jury report on August 8, 2018,[30] an adult male met with Cardinal DiNardo in Houston to discuss the sexual abuse he experienced as a minor in 1999 at the hands of a priest.[31] Shortly after this meeting with DiNardo, the survivor filed a police report on August 27, 2018. A woman filed a similar complaint with the archdiocese against the same priest in 2001 for abusing her that same year, followed by an official police report on August 29, 2018. In an unprecedented move, the police issued a warrant for the arrest of a priest in the ADGH: Rev. Manuel La Rose-Lopez, formerly of Sacred Heart Catholic Church in Conroe (just north of Houston). The priest reported to the civil authorities on September 11, 2018[32] and was charged with four counts of indecency to children.[33]

The ADGH seemed to have a protective shield around it against negative press—particularly regarding its clergy—for more than fifty years leading up to this notable arrest. This protective shield, however, eroded by 2018. In rapid succession, the Conroe Police Department executed three unprecedented search warrants aimed at the church and its ordained clerics. On September 12, 2018, while LaRosa-Lopez sat in jail, the Conroe Police searched his residence at St. John Fisher Catholic Church, where he had been assigned since 2005. Police reported that they found documentation there indicating LaRosa-Lopez had been a patient at the Shalom Center—a diocesan treatment center for priests[34]—from April 16, 2001 to January 3, 2002.[35] Subsequently, on September 17, 2018, the police searched Sacred Heart Catholic Church in Conroe where LaRosa-Lopez had been assigned when the abuse allegedly occurred. Then, two days later on September 19, 2018, the police descended on the Shalom Center in Splendora, Texas (just north of Houston).[36]

Nothing could stop the tsunami of media attention brought to the ADGH in 2018, made all the more intense because of DiNardo's high profile position in the USCCB. On September 13, 2018—right in the middle of all those raids—Cardinal DiNardo was at the Vatican meeting with the Pope and three other top cardinals. He had requested the meeting August 16 to discuss the sexual abuse scandals in the United States in general and the McCarrick allegations specifically.[37] DiNardo pledged to investigate the McCarrick allegations to "the full extent of the USCCB's authority."[38] On September 14, the Vatican Press Office released an unfortunate photo from this meeting—Pope Francis at his desk across from DiNardo, Cardinal Sean O'Malley, Los Angeles archbishop Jose Horacio Gomez, and Monsignor Brian Bransfield of Philadelphia, and they were all laughing hysterically.[39] The optics were terrible.

HORRIBILIS EVENT #4: ANNOUNCING THEIR PLANS (OCTOBER 2018)

When Cardinal DiNardo returned home to Houston that September, he kept a low profile, but had to return back to Rome from October 3 to 28 for the Synod on Young People, the Faith, and Vocational Discernment.[40] On October 10 seemingly out of the blue, from Rome, DiNardo recorded a video that was published in tandem with a press release. The video was odd, to say the least, emphasizing his nervousness and guilty deportment. His message stated that the fifteen Catholic dioceses in Texas had decided to release names of clergy credibly accused of sexually abusing a minor since 1950 and they would do so by the end of January 2019.

It seemed like a step forward toward transparency to rebuild trust, but there were many reasons to doubt this new transparency. The ADGH would be engaging the services of an outside consultant to conduct an independent review of its records so that the list could be as accurate and complete as possible. And yet the criminal investigation going on at that time after the LaRosa-Lopez arrest seemed to suggest that the archdiocese might not be interested in transparency at all. A high-powered criminal defense attorney had been hired by the archdiocese to defend LaRosa-Lopez. We can only assume that his attorney discussed with the cardinal what actions to take with regard to clergy sexual abuse. The second red flag was the outside consultant. The church has spent centuries keeping their documents hidden, inaccessible, and secret. The ADGH led by the president of the USCCB would never willingly hand over files to any outside entity unless something other than transparency was afoot.

Catholics were skeptical since we had long known that the church controls information and the official narrative. The cardinal's credibility concerning this move took a blow a few weeks later on October 26, 2018, when blogger Rocco Palmo broke the story that on October 9, 2018—one day before DiNardo's announcement—the U.S. Department of Justice (DOJ) issued a letter to Cardinal DiNardo as President of the USCCB[41] ordering all Catholic dioceses and chancery offices in the United States, "to not destroy, discard, dispose of, delete, or alter" any personnel records or records of abuse. William McSwain, U.S. Attorney for the Eastern District of Pennsylvania, signed the letter. Rocco Palmo further reported, "the letter was privately circulated to the nation's hierarchy by the US Conference of Catholic Bishops on Tuesday, 23 October, and has duly spread since among internal counsels and personnel-chiefs across the stateside church's 198 jurisdictions."[42] In light of the DOJ demand to the USCCB, DiNardo's effort at transparency took on an air of panicked crisis response. Of course he had stated that the Texas Conference of Catholic Bishops had decided to release the names during a "recent meeting in Austin"[43] as if to imply the decision took place *before* the DOJ letter.

On November 2, 2018, I attended a gala in Houston that DiNardo also attended. He said the grace before dinner and kept a low profile. In years past I had interacted with him at this yearly event when he was much more jovial. But now in 2018, DiNardo humbly asked us to pray for him and his fellow bishops as they headed to Baltimore for the USCCB Fall General Assembly on November 12. That meeting would prove to be another implosion in DiNardo's *annus horribilis*.

HORRIBILIS EVENT #4: PALACE INTRIGUE (NOVEMBER 2018)

I never paid attention to any of USCCB General Assemblies in my life before 2018, but I was glued to the live stream webcast of the November 2018 meeting. The bishops were set to discuss the abuse crisis. They would vote on processes to address sexual abuse, such as a third-party reporting mechanism, standards of conduct for bishops, and protocols for bishops resigned or removed because of abuse.[44] This would be DiNardo's chance to show Catholics in the United States that the bishops were sincerely going to address the problem. Then the shocking blow came: DiNardo opened the General Assembly with the announcement that the Vatican ordered the bishops to delay all votes on proposed changes regarding how they would handle sexual abuse claims until after a February meeting with the Pope.[45] The audience shown on the live stream looked shocked, except Cardinal Blase Cupich of Chicago. He immediately stood up and said a cringe worthy, obsequious statement, apropos of nothing, "It is clear the Holy See is taking the abuse crisis seriously."[46] Cupich then posed a clearly pandering question to DiNardo asking if the bishops could take nonbinding votes on the policy proposals. DiNardo replied that the bishops could discuss that idea on Tuesday.[47] DiNardo still seemed to be knocked off kilter from the announcement he had to make. Cupich's bizarre statement and penetrating question seemed to be more than just posturing. His passive-aggressive behavior seemed to shatter DiNardo's very core.

Later in the day, at a press conference DiNardo said the request to delay action came from the Vatican's Congregation for Bishops and that he was informed via a letter the night before. Coincidently, two American Cardinals serve on the Congregation for Bishops: Cardinals Blase Cupich and Donald Wuerl. They were both at the assembly in Baltimore. So the whole Cupich drama earlier in the day now appeared to be palace intrigue and maneuvering. Cupich and Wuerl set out to cut DiNardo off at the knees, and they did. The Catholic News Agency reported that Wuerl had advance notice of the decision from Rome.[48] Of course he did. When Cupich asked the inane question about having a pretend nonbinding vote, one could almost visualize the vultures circling around DiNardo. Who could see these men as Christ's representatives on earth anymore; they looked more like senior executives orchestrating a coup.

At the time of the General Assembly, CBS Evening News was investigating the ADGH generally, and more specifically, DiNardo for keeping two accused priests in active ministry. On November 20, 2018, CBS reporter Nikki Battiste interviewed DiNardo while he was in Baltimore, or rather she attempted to do so.[49] The footage showed DiNardo walking away from the reporter with contempt as she was asking him questions. The USCCB had taken steps to keep reporters away from the bishops, cordoning off areas where the media could not enter. The CBS reporter happened upon DiNardo during a break and asked why he kept two priests in ministry, Rev. Terrence Brinkman and Rev. John Keller. DiNardo declared that he did not find the accusations against those priests to be credible. Then he walked in front of the female reporter and got on the escalator and walked into the meeting shutting the door. As a Catholic in the ADGH, I was embarrassed by his boorishness and lack of dignity in dealing with the media. He appeared to be shaken to the core. I wondered how Nikki Battiste had been able to get near DiNardo. No other bishops were spotted or filmed, let alone close enough to the cordoned off reporters for them to get a sound bite. The video clearly showed that DiNardo was down a floor from the meeting rooms. I asked a priest in Houston how it happened. He said that DiNardo had to leave the hotel to have a cigarette. Yes, he was at that time a chain smoker, and when he had to go outside to have a smoke, CBS was lucky enough to spot him coming back in.

We won't ever know the real machinations that went on behind the scenes at that General Assembly, but it was clear that DiNardo's power and authority were disappearing right before our eyes, and that the General Assembly that November was disastrous for the church. Yet, that wasn't the worst thing to happen to DiNardo that November.

HORRIBILIS EVENT #5: POLICE, DAS, TEXAS RANGERS, AND THE FBI (NOVEMBER 28, 2018)

While other U.S. dioceses have had more than their share of lawsuits and negative media coverage in the past three decades, such as Boston, Los Angeles, and San Diego, Galveston-Houston largely avoided them. Even our neighbors in the Diocese of Dallas had gone through the ringer in the late 1990s,[50] settling a lawsuit brought by twelve victims against Rev. Rudy Kos. A jury verdict awarded them $119 million, and Kos was criminally convicted and received four life sentences. Galveston-Houston, however, had been spared a lot of the scandal associated with sexual abuse.

In 2004 then bishop Joseph Fiorenza reported the results of a USCCB commissioned survey by the John Jay College of Criminal Justice, who examined the scope of clergy sexual abuse in the United States.[51] In an astounding show of hubris, Fiorenza announced in the *Texas Catholic Herald* that between the years of 1950 and 2002, only twenty-two priests and four deacons sexually abused forty-six minors in the Roman Catholic Diocese of Galveston-Houston. He added that nearly all of the abuse occurred before 1980.[52] Fiorenza assured everyone that the perpetrators had either died, resigned, or were removed from ministry as of 2004, as he underscored the insignificance of their numbers. The twenty-two priests only represented a small fraction—less than 1 percent—of the 2,285 priests who had served the diocese since 1950. But the data he provided cannot be verified. And of course there was no way to find any accusations against clergy unless there were public records of some sort.

The other piece of Fiorenza's statement that 80 percent of the abuse happened before 1980, but was reported between 1994 and 2004, is also unverifiable. He used the same method of obfuscation we have seen with Wuerl and his answer about how diligent he was as a bishop in Pittsburgh. It is the same convoluted logic used when the bishops were asked a straightforward question and instead answered a question that was not asked. Fiorenza released information and data that are held under lock and key, known only to the archdiocese, that no one can verify. In a discussion about Fiorenza's summary of the clergy sexual abuse, a fellow Catholic who is an avowed apologist for the church told me repeatedly that Fiorenza wouldn't tolerate clerical sex abuse. The flaws in this argument are myriad, and my response is the obvious one: the only difference between the ADGH and Dallas, Boston, Los Angeles, and San Diego is that Houston has not had the external interventions by law enforcement or lawsuits. The Statute of Limitations is one factor for the lack of lawsuits. An examination of other possible reasons for the lack of publicly known sexual abuse accusations warrants a separate study altogether. In any event, by 2018 the long reign of Galveston-Houston's cone of silence was ending.

THE RAID: NOVEMBER 28, 2018

On November 27, 2018, a person involved in the LaRosa-Lopez case tipped me off that the next day there would be a raid on the Chancery Office of the ADGH. The archdiocese has always been immune to these types of humiliating acts. On the off chance it was accurate information, I drove to the chancery office in downtown Houston, right next to the $49 million Co-Cathedral. I arrived at 8 a.m. and sat across from the chancery and waited. I noticed when a local news crew arrived about 30 minutes later and stayed in their van. Then at 9:30 a.m., like a scene out of a movie, the one-square city block the chancery resides on was surrounded all at once, from all directions. Large black SUVs, Conroe police department cars with the sirens blaring and lights rolling ran red lights and blocked intersections giving room for vans and trucks to pull up close to the building. The District Attorney from Montgomery County was there. It was his raid. He held a press conference outside the building.[53] There was an endless procession of Texas Rangers complete with their uniform Stetson cowboy hats. I was told the FBI was there as well. Reports stated that more than sixty-five officers and agents participated that day. It was an impressive feat coordinating so many agencies and officers. I stayed a few hours to watch as the media showed up, slowly at first, then swarmed with helicopters and every reporter, it seemed, in Houston. They stayed well past 10 p.m. that evening.

The media released the official warrant the District Attorney and Conroe Police obtained in order to execute the search.[54] It detailed the abuse by LaRosa-Lopez in excruciating detail. It revealed information about the first victim—a sixth-grade boy in 1992—when LaRosa-Lopez was apparently assisting at St. Thomas More Catholic Church in Houston. The warrant stated that there were only two letters relating to that complaint that the archdiocese turned over to the Conroe Police; hence the need for a search warrant. The peculiar information about those two letters is that one was from a lawyer to Bishop Fiorenza dated October 1992 discussing whether the diocese was legally obligated to report the incident to Children's Protective Services (CPS). Fiorenza's reply letter stated that he would require an additional psychological examination before LaRosa-Lopez was admitted to the seminary.

This was troubling on many levels. Obviously it was troubling because of the sexual abuse of the child by LaRosa-Lopez (known at that time as LaRosa). Also, the shocking letter from Fiorenza asking legal counsel if they were required to report the abuse to CPS was unsettling. I don't know Fiorenza well, but I grew up with him in this diocese and have heard about him my whole life in Houston. He is a close friend with a relative of mine, and I have socialized with him on many occasions in the past decade. Fiorenza comes across as a no-nonsense Texan. The question that vexed me was why on earth would he equivocate on reporting the incident to CPS, let alone the police? LaRosa-Lopez at that time was not even a student at the diocesan-run St. Mary's Seminary. Why was LaRosa-Lopez even assisting at St. Thomas More church when he wasn't yet admitted to the seminary? LaRosa-Lopez didn't enter St. Mary's Seminary until spring 1993. Presumably he passed the psychological evaluation Fiorenza told the lawyer he would require.

The warrant contained more information about the other victims, but the details about the 1992 complaint intrigued me. I knew LaRosa-Lopez was a transfer student from a seminary in Mexico City because it was on his Facebook page that I viewed while he was in jail in September. Seminary students rarely transfer to another seminary unless they are dismissed for cause. This was certainly the case for LaRosa-Lopez. In 1993, he spent only one semester at St. Mary's Seminary in Houston before being transferred to Sacred Heart School of Theology in Hales Corner, Wisconsin after having been credibly accused of molesting a sixth-grade boy. Why did Fiorenza allowed LaRosa-Lopez to enter St. Mary's Seminary to continue his path toward ordination? It only makes sense when we consider that the church doesn't conform to standards and practices of the secular world. The church has an operational manual in the Canon Laws. The bishops function on a different playing field. Society's standards and the local, state or federal laws do not trump their code of laws.

I have learned not to discuss Fiorenza's or DiNardo's actions with my relatives who are apologists. There is no point. They believe Fiorenza did not put up with any sort of sexual abuse in his diocese. The flaw in that argument is that he is portrayed as some sort of deterrent, like the death penalty. It's as if a pedophile would ignore his urges for fear of Fiorenza's reprisals. It is nonsense on all counts, least of which is that there was no reprisal for LaRosa-Lopez. After the first known complaint about him, Fiorenza admitted him to seminary in Houston, and then sent him to Wisconsin to finish his graduate degree. The tuition for that degree was paid for by the Diocese of Galveston-Houston. Thus Fiorenza not only tolerated sexual abuse in his Diocese, he rewarded it. When LaRosa-Lopez was ordained in December 1996, the diocese assigned him to Sacred Heart Church in Conroe where he started molesting boys and girls within two years.

FINALLY MAKING GOOD ON THEIR PROMISE: JANUARY 31, 2019

The clergy disclosure list for the ADGH named forty priests credibly accused of sexual abuse of minors from 1950 to 2018—notably, two other priests were already under investigation. I have researched many of the priests on the disclosure list and have had to face the horrifying realizations that priests I knew personally committed these crimes. Moreover, Bishop Morkovsky, who confirmed me, was instrumental in covering up those crimes. One of the first priests I researched was Rev. Ivan Turic.

Although I had never heard of Turic, the archdiocese listed the parishes to which he was assigned and one was St. Mary Star of the Sea in Freeport, Texas about sixty miles south of Houston. I have a good friend who was from that same parish in Freeport. It was a long shot, but I called him just in case he remembered something about Turic. As fate would have it, my call interrupted a lunch he was having with a friend as they were discussing Rev. Turic, having seen his name on the list. My friend answered the phone and sounded almost scared. He said they did know Turic and they needed to call me to get information on him just when I called.

Rev. Ivan Turic was in active ministry in Houston for less than ten years when a warrant was issued for his arrest for a felony charge of indecency with a child in May 1977. Ordained in May 1968, his career as a priest in Galveston-Houston was a debacle by any standard. He absconded from Houston when the warrant was issued, but the chaos he created manifested in Harris County Courts for the next thirty-six years.

1966–1968: TIME TO ORDINATION

Turic's time in the (then) Diocese of Galveston-Houston began shrouded in mystery. Two former parishioners at St. Mary Star of the Sea Catholic Church in Freeport, who spoke on condition of anonymity, knew Turic before he was ordained in 1968. Both remembered him well when he was in charge of the youth recreational center at the church. A local newspaper at the time ran a feature article on Turic describing his "heavy Austrian accent" and noted that he had been in the United States a little more than a year.[55] According to this account, Turic was a twenty-six-year-old seminary student at St. Mary Star of the Sea in Freeport who had already received his doctorate from the University of Vienna. However, there was no seminary at St. Mary Star of the Sea in Freeport. The seminary in the diocese then, and now, is St. Mary's Seminary (SMS), Houston. The same local newspaper published a front page photo[56] of Turic when he was ordained as transitional deacon, his last step before being ordained a priest in the Catholic Church.[57]

AN UNUSUAL PATH TO ORDINATION

The *Texas Catholic Herald* reported that Bishop John L. Morkovsky ordained Turic to the priesthood on May 18, 1968. Very little detail was given about Turic in the article compared to the other priests whose histories included their elementary schools, high schools, parents' names, and when they entered the seminary. Turic's background was summed up in two sentences: "A native of Zupa, Austria, Father Turic studied at the University of Vienna and St. Mary's Seminary. He spent two years working in parishes of the Galveston-Houston diocese."[58] Although it was reported that Turic studied at St. Mary's Seminary, he is noticeably absent in the St. Mary's Seminary 1968 class photo the newspaper published. The three men in the class photo, Fr. Isidore Rozycki, Fr. Clifton Ransom, and Fr. Leonard Derden, were all ordained the same day as Turic, and were all featured in the same *Texas Catholic Herald* article.

The seminary program at that time required four years of undergraduate work leading to a bachelor's degree, and four years of graduate work for a master's degree, typically in theology.[59] Seminarians could enter the seminary after receiving a bachelor's degree elsewhere, but were required to take undergraduate theology coursework if they hadn't already done so. The St. Mary's Seminary academic catalogs from the 1960s list the Register of Students enrolled, both undergraduate and graduate students. Turic's name does not appear in the published register until the 1967–1968[60] catalog that lists him as a Theology IV Student, meaning he completed the four years of graduate theology work. Turic is not listed anywhere as an alumnus. It is possible he transferred to St. Mary's Seminary in 1966, but he was not listed as a student in any available documentation. Further, he is not included in any alumni lists of SMS and, of course, he is not in the class photo.

Also of note is the time between his ordination to the deaconate, and his ordination to the priesthood. Turic was ordained as a transitional deacon February 10, 1968, and barely three months later on May 18, 1968, he was ordained to the priesthood. A transitional deacon is the last phase of training for the Catholic priesthood. In 1968, the rules governing the time from deaconate to priesthood were defined in the 1917 Code of Canon Law.[61] Formally known as the Codex Iuris Canonici (CIC) (1917), these laws were in place until 1983 when the church instituted a revised version. At the time Turic was ordained, CIC 978 §2 required that a candidate for the priesthood first pass through four steps known as minor orders before the major orders of subdeacon, deacon, and priest were conferred. CIC 978 §2 stipulated that there should be a minimum of three months from subdeacon to deacon, and three months from deacon to ordination as a priest.

There are no published accounts of Turic receiving or progressing through minor orders, or when (or if) he began his time as a subdeacon. We only know that his time from deaconate to priesthood was three months. And regardless of whether there was any irregularity with his timeline, like many laws in the church, there was a backdoor. The 1917 CIC 978 §2 states that diocesan bishops can waive the minimum time requirement in specific cases.[62] Perhaps, Bishop John L. Morkovsky did just that when he ordained Turic on May 18, 1968, so soon after he ordained him a deacon in February.

1968–1971: SHORT-LIVED FIRST ASSIGNMENT FOLLOWED BY TWO YEARS ABSENT ON LEAVE

Turic's first assignment as a priest after ordination was at St. Vincent de Paul Catholic Church in Houston. *The Official Catholic Directory* (OCD)[63] from 1969 shows the following priests assigned to St. Vincent de Paul: Revs. J. D. Connelly, Robert E. Daigle, Ivan Turic, In Residence: Antonio J. Morales. Turic only spent one year at St. Vincent de Paul Church. He was listed in the OCD 1970[64] and 1971[65] as Absent With Leave [with permission]. Turic's first three years as a priest were comprised of only one year at a parish followed by two consecutive years of leave. This is what is known as a bad sign. Not only was Ivan Turic's entry into the priesthood unusual, his activities after his first year as a priest make him stand out from his child molesting peers on the list.

1972–1973: ONE YEAR ON, ONE YEAR OFF

In the OCD 1972,[66] Turic was no longer listed as Absent With Leave. He was assigned to St. Francis of Assisi Church on the opposite side of Houston from St. Vincent's. The parish had an elementary school run by the Sisters of Charity, with 279 students. Like his tenure at St. Vincent's, Turic only lasted one year at St. Francis of Assisi. The 1973 Galveston-Houston Catholic Directory[67] listing for Turic is: Leave of Absence. Curiously, although he was on a leave of absence in both the OCD 1973 and the Diocese of Galveston-Houston Directory, Turic was still active as a priest. In September 1973, Rev. Ivan Turic was the full-time chaplain at the newly established International Seaman Center.[68] Established in January 1973, the International Seaman Center at the Port of Houston (renamed Seafarer's Center) was spearheaded by Bishop John L. Morkovsky, according to his biographer, Dawn Orsak. The Port of Houston describes the center as a "home away from home for seafarers visiting the Port of Houston . . . established to provide a safe and welcoming recreational and spiritual environment on land for those who have chosen the sea as their livelihood."[69] And who better to be full-time chaplain to thousands of international seamen far from home than a priest with only two years of experience who has been on a leave of absence for three years?

CANON LAW ON LEAVES OF ABSENCE

We do not know why Turic was on leave for three of his first five years of active ministry as a priest in Houston. In the "Impact of a Leave of Absence on a Cleric's Right to Remuneration," Canon lawyer Msgr. Jason A. Gray explained different scenarios under which the term "leave of absence" might be applied for a priest. "A cleric may voluntarily request a leave of absence or may be involuntarily placed on a leave of absence. The circumstances of the leave may also vary greatly." Those varied circumstances, Gray wrote, could be that the priest requested a leave of absence, "for personal reasons, to continue some sort pastoral formation . . . because of an illness or some other obstacle that prevents him from fulfilling his ministerial obligations . . . but is temporarily prevented from offering his service."[70] If a priest is put on an involuntary leave of absence, Gray explained that it could be due to an allegation of a crime against Canon Law, or because the bishop didn't give him an assignment for another reason. We don't know the details, but the short assignments and multiple leaves of absence indicate that there was a significant problem.

It was during Turic's third leave of absence in 1973, when he was full-time chaplain at the Seaman Center, that he began building his real estate portfolio. Harris County Clerk property records show that on July 26, 1973, Rev. Ivan Turic was the grantee of a warranty deed for a property he purchased in Houston: Clairmont Place, Section 2, Lot: L0793, Block: B0035. It was the first of seven properties he purchased in Houston.[71]

1974: ANOTHER PARISH, THE SEAMAN CENTER AND REAL ESTATE

In 1974, his sixth year as priest, Turic made it back into a parish, but with a caveat: he was listed as, *In Residence* at Our Lady of Fatima in Galena Park, Texas. There were 152 students at Our Lady of Fatima elementary school. And the OCD 1974[72] noted, for the first time, his role at the Seaman Center, "Turic, Chap., Port of Houston." The term *In Residence* meant that he was not assigned to work at the parish, but was living in the rectory that was conveniently located only a few miles from the International Seaman Center and his job there as the full-time chaplain. The proximity of his residence at Our Lady of Fatima to his assigned chaplaincy at the Seaman Center was apparently not an important factor to Turic because Harris County Clerk property records show that on June 14, 1974, Reverend Ivan Turic purchased properties #2 and #3 in Clairmont Place in Houston and began living in one of them. Harris County Appraisal District records show that the 8157 Laura Koppe home was a 770-square foot single-family home, built in 1946 and remodeled in 1960.[73]

On August 24, 1974 Harris County Clerk property records show that Turic purchased property #4 in Clairmont Place: Sec: 1, Lot: L0331, Block: B0017.[74] Turic had purchased a total of four properties in his name between July 1973 and August 1974, and he wasn't done.

1975: LAST ASSOCIATION WITH A PARISH

In the OCD 1975 Turic was once again listed as *In Residence* at Our Lady of Fatima and Chaplain at the Port of Houston's International Seaman Center.[75] But on November 26, 1975, he purchased property #5 in Clairmont Place: Sec: 1, Lot: L0330, Block: B0017.[76] It was his seventh year as a priest, and his last to be assigned to a church in the Diocese of Galveston-Houston. For Turic, 1976 was the last year he was listed in the OCD with a specific assignment.[77] For reasons we do not know, he was no longer assigned to live at the rectory of Our Lady of Fatima. The OCD shows that he was assigned to the newly created Diocesan Office of Port Ministry, all of which seem highly unusual. Rev. Rivers Patout, who graduated from St. Mary's Seminary Houston the year before Turic in 1967, was listed first in the directory as assigned to Port Ministry. Turic is listed as the, "Co-ordinator" and "Chaplain of the International Seaman Center."[78]

In March 1976, Harris County Clerk property records show that Turic purchased property #6 in Clairmont Place, Section 1, Lot: L0312, Block: B0015.[79] He then immediately took out a loan in the mount of $2,500 with a 10 percent interest rate and monthly installments of $219.79. The deed of trust for the promissory note was in the name of Phillip Johnson. Despite his chaplaincy work at the Seaman Center, Turic managed to expand his side job of flipping properties. On June 16, 1976, while living at his home on Laura Koppe Road, Turic sold the first property he had purchased back in 1973 for $13,950.[80]

1977: FINAL YEAR IN HOUSTON

Significantly, the OCD 1977[81] doesn't list Turic at all. And yet he still qualified for yet another mortgage on January 27, 1977 when Harris

County Clerk property records show he purchased property #7 in the same area: Clairmont Place: Sec: 1, Lot: L0313, Block: B0015.[82] Turic's career in buying and selling personal properties is not typical for a diocesan priest. When these atypical activities are viewed in light of Turic's specious seminary training, his inability to remain at a parish for more than one year, his three yearlong leaves of absence, and the fact that he is named by the archdiocese as a credibly accused sex abuser, what emerges is the profile of a sexual predator who cannot be managed or controlled by his bishop.

We might imagine that Turic's removal from his first assignment at St. Vincent de Paul Church was due to some misconduct because it was followed by two years classified as *Absent with Leave*. If that extended leave of absence was meant to remediate Turic, it is also likely that his bishop's attempt didn't work because Turic was removed after only one year from his next assignment at St. Francis of Assisi, and again placed on a leave of absence. We might infer from his assignment history that the diocese must have been aware that he was a problem because he was not assigned to ministry in a parish after St. Francis of Assisi. He was allowed to live at a parish that included an elementary school, but in 1977 even this residence status appears to have been revoked. When a problem priest can't be managed or controlled by his bishop, it can make it difficult for the bishop to manage the collateral damage created by the priest, especially if external agencies get involved. That is exactly what happened on May 17, 1977 when a boy and his father filed a police report against Turic for indecency with a child—a felony complaint.[83]

On June 16, 1977, a grand jury indicted Turic. And on June 17, 1977, a warrant was issued for his arrest. His home address was indicated on the warrant—he had been living at his Laura Koppe home for three years. Turic must have had an inkling that the grand jury decision would not go his way because on June 9, 1977—only one week before they returned the indictment—he filed with the Harris County Clerk to give his Power of Attorney to a woman named Vida Virginia Dixon.[84] One of the reasons he may have given that Power of Attorney to Vida Dixon was so she could manage the sale of two of his properties after he had fled the jurisdiction. Harris County Clerk property records show that on February 13, 1978, Ivan Turic through authorized agent and attorney in fact, Vida Virginia Dixon, sold property number #6 for $9,500, and again on April 10, 1978 with Vida Dixon acting as his agent, Turic sold property number #7. These two transactions occurred almost a year after the warrant had been issued for his arrest. It was still active, but wouldn't be for long.

CASE DISMISSED

Despite the courage of the boy and his father to go to the police, and the coordinated efforts of the Harris County Sheriff's Department, the District Attorney's Office and the grand jury to indict Turic, the case was dismissed on December 15, 1980.[85] The reason given on the case file at Harris County District Clerk's Office was that they could not locate Turic. That wasn't the last of Turic in Harris County though. Harris County District Courts made several attempts to locate Turic after he absconded in 1977, not for the felony indictment, but for tax delinquencies on the four properties that he still owned. Harris County District Clerk documents show that beginning in 1977 and continuing through 2014, the North Forest Independent School District, the City of Houston, and Harris County attempted to locate, serve, and collect the past due property taxes he owed.[86] Turic's chaos took up Harris County Court resources for almost forty years after he ran out on the warrant for his arrest. In September 2008, the tenacious attorneys representing the Harris County Tax Assessors Office located Turic in Croatia and served him notice of the lawsuit and final judgment for his tax delinquencies. They actually got a signature from Turic confirming that he received the notice in August 2009. Harris County sold Turic's four properties at auction to recover his property tax delinquencies that dated back to 1977.

Turic is still a priest in Croatia and listed as retired at a parish in Župa Biokovska.[87] Croatian journalist Hrvoje Šimičević obtained a document from Turic's file with the Yugoslav Secret Police dated January 5, 1978, stating that Turic had already been sent to work in the Archdiocese of Rosario in Santa Fe, Argentina directly from Houston.[88] The significance of this information is that the bishop at that time, John Morkovsky, would have contacted the bishop in Rosario to ask him to accept Turic as a priest. Morkovsky would have known when he transferred Turic that there was a warrant for his arrest for sexual assaulting a fourteen-year-old boy. So, the Bishop of Galveston-Houston interfered with the execution of justice and aided and abetted Turic to escape despite the warrant for his felony charge.

And what became of the victim who reported Turic to the police? According to public documents from the initial complaint and arrest warrant to criminal proceedings later in his life, he is serving a life sentence for murder at a Texas prison,[89] which is where Turic should be.

IN CONCLUSION

Unpacking the revelations of the past year has been an arduous task. I chose the example of Rev. Ivan Turic for this chapter because it is a microcosm of the church's global conspiracy to cover up the crimes of clerics. This *modus operandi* is more or less the same in every case of credible accusations of sexual abuse by a priest. The Turic case shows the lengths the church will go to in order to protect one of its own, including obstructing justice in the legal system. It contains all the elements of a church cover-up from start to finish. First, there is the mystery surrounding his seminary education. The information I was able to gather from primary sources, such as the first-hand accounts by people who knew him prior to his ordination as well as newspaper articles, all point to a nontraditional education and an ordination that was fast-tracked by Bishop Morkovsky. Second, his spotty intermittent assignments at parishes that never lasted more than a year or two—all bookended by leaves of absence—indicate he caused problems at each parish necessitating his removal from all public ministry ultimately. Third, he was indicted for indecency with a child and evaded arrest. So how did a parish priest from Yugoslavia disappear from Houston in May 1978 when the police were looking for him? Did he just happen to get reassigned at that exact moment? Of course not, the bishop handled the legal problem by moving Turic out of the country so he wouldn't be arrested. The focus was on protecting the perpetrator in the name of protecting the reputation of the church.

As Bishop Morkvosky was busy coordinating the escape of Turic and securing him a parish assignment in Argentina and communicating with the Secret Police in communist Yugoslavia, he was also scheduled to preside over confirmation in the diocese—my confirmation in May 1978. I know now that while I was preparing for confirmation, committing myself to Christ and the Catholic Church and excited to have the bishop confirm me, the bishop was aiding in the escape of the priest who sexually assaulted a fourteen-year-old boy. It dilutes the solemnity of the sacrament of confirmation for me and it adds an air of deceit and disgust for me as I look back on that day. The question that stays with me is: how could the bishop appear so pious and holy to me, and also assist someone evading justice when he knew Turic was a sexual predator?

The salient lesson is twofold. First, the cardinals and bishops do not tell the truth, at least not as the rest of the world defines truth. Second, the ordained clergy are members of a very codified and fiercely guarded fraternity. They protect each other before they protect the faithful. To that end, when the church deals with a priest accused of sexual abuse, the pattern and practice of the church has been to transfer the priest to another parish where his past is not disclosed. And we know from investigations around the country that those priests typically continued sexually abusing minors at their newly assigned parishes. A priest I know casually explained to me that the secrecy is all about protecting *la bella figura*, an Italian phrase that translates to "good image." Protecting the image of the church is the number one tenet above all else when dealing with allegations of sexual abuse by its clergy, not the protection of minors.

The reports from around the country show the consistent pattern and practice of indiscriminate transfers of the sex offender priests. There is no single city that is a dumping ground because every city has been a potential dumping ground. I have spent countless hours trying to discern a pattern to the transfers of credibly accused priests and cannot identify one.

The revelations of the last eighteen months have irrevocably changed the image of the church when the world learned conclusively that the church has lied about the sexual abuse problem for decades. Many Catholics describe an erosion of trust in the church across the board, not just about sexual abuse. If the bishops lied to protect child rapists, what else have they lied about? Did they teach us something in catechism that is a lie?

The motive of the bishops might have been to protect *la bella figura* of the church, but the unintended result is that many Catholics now question their faith after the public disclosures of the sexual abuse and the cover-ups. It is an institutional betrayal and it is not just an American phenomenon. The church has betrayed all Catholics.

NOTES

1. "Catholic Glossary." The Archdiocese of Saint Paul Minnesota. Accessed January 18, 2019, https://www.archspm.org/catholic-glossary.
2. "Preventing the Sexual Abuse of Minors: A Statement of the Texas Catholic Conference of Bishops." Texas Catholic Bishops Conference, Accessed January 31, 2019, https://txcatholic.org/pastoral-resources/preventing-the-sexual-abuse-of-minors.
3. "Archdiocese of Galveston-Houston Clergy Disclosure List." The Archdiocese of Galveston-Houston. Accessed January 31, 2019, https://www.archgh.org/clergylist.
4. "The Sacrament of Confirmation: Grace for Fullness of Faith and Life." BeginningCatholic.com, Accessed May 14, 2019, http://www.beginningcatholic.com/confirmation
5. "Sacraments of the Catholic Church." Catholic Online. Accessed May 14, 2019, https://www.catholic.org/prayers/sacrament.php
6. "Canon 1246, §2 – Holy Days of Obligation." The United States Conference of Catholic Bishops. Accessed May 14, 2019, http://www.usccb.org/beliefs-and-teachings/what-we-believe/canon-law/complementary-norms/canon-1246.cfm.
7. Canon Law is the code of laws that govern the Catholic Church, "Canon Law." The United States Conference of Catholic Bishops. Accessed May 14, 2019, http://www.usccb.org/beliefs-and-teachings/what-we-believe/canon-law/index.cfm.

8. "About Us." The Archdiocese of Galveston-Houston. Accessed May 14, 2019, https://www.archgh.org/about/about-us.

9. "USCCB Officers." The United States Conference of Catholic Bishops. Accessed May 14, 2019, http://www.usccb.org/about/leadership/usccb-officers.cfm.

10. "Newly Named Cardinal to Speak in Houston." Archdiocese of Galveston-Houston. Accessed September 13, 2017, https://www.archgh.org/news-data/latest-news/newly-named-cardinal-to-speak-in-houston.

11. Deb Erdley, "Supreme Court Blocks Release of Grand Jury Report on Sexual Abuse in Catholic Dioceses." Trib Live. Accessed June 20, 2018, https://archive.triblive.com/news/pennsylvania/supreme-court-blocks-release-of-grand-jury-report-on-sexual-abuse-in-catholic-dioceses.

12. "Newspapers, Victims Sue for Release of Pa. Grand Jury's Clergy Sex Abuse Report." *Catholic News Agency*. Accessed July 9, 2018, https://www.catholicnewsagency.com/news/newspapers-victims-sue-for-release-of-pa-grand-jurys-clergy-sex-abuse-report-56094.

13. Michelle Boorstein, "Pennsylvania Supreme Court Approves Release of 900-page Grand Jury Report about Catholic Clergy Sex Abuse." *The Washington Post*. Accessed July 27, 2018, https://www.washingtonpost.com/news/acts-of-faith/wp/2018/07/27/pennsylvania-supreme-court-oks-release-of-900-page-grand-jury-report-about-catholic-clergy-sex-abuse.

14. "Pennsylvania Dioceses Victims Report." Office of the Attorney General Commonwealth of Pennsylvania. Accessed August 14, 2018, https://www.attorneygeneral.gov/report.

15. Laurie Goodstein and Sharon Otterman, "They Hid It All: Catholic Priests Abused 1,000 Children in Pennsylvania, Report Says." *The New York Times*, 2018. Accessed August 14, 2018, https://www.nytimes.com/2018/08/14/us/catholic-church-sex-abuse-pennsylvania.html.

16. Michelle Boorstein, "Cardinal Wuerl Target of Rising Anger After Pa. Grand Jury Report." *The Washington Post*. Accessed August 20, 2018, https://www.washingtonpost.com/local/social-issues/2018/08/20/0a6ae810-a49f-11e8-97ce-cc9042272f07_story.html.

17. "Archdiocese Creates, Takes Down Website Defending Cardinal Wuerl's Record on Abuse." Catholic Culture.org. Accessed August 16, 2018, https://www.catholicculture.org/news/headlines/index.cfm?storyid=38162.

18. Tom Fitzgerald, "Online Petition to Remove Cardinal Wuerl has More than 60,000 Signatures." *Fox5 Washington, D.C.* Accessed August 24, 2018, https://www.fox5dc.com/news/online-petition-to-remove-cardinal-wuerl-has-more-than-60000-signatures.

19. Elisabetta Povoledo and Sharon Otterman, "Cardinal Theodore McCarrick Resigns Amid Sexual Abuse Scandal." *The New York Times*. Accessed July 28, 2018, https://www.nytimes.com/2018/07/28/world/europe/cardinal-theodore-mccarrick-resigns.html.

20. Povoledo and Otterman, "Cardinal Theodore McCarrick Resigns Amid Sexual Abuse Scandal."

21. Ibid.

22. Kathy Schiffer, "Richard Sipe Tried to Warn Us – But No One Was Listening." *National Catholic Register* (August 16, 2018). Accessed August 20, 2018, http://www.ncregister.com/blog/kschiffer/richard-sipe-tried-to-warn-us-but-no-one-was-listening.

23. Richard Sipe, "The Cardinal McCarrick Syndrome." *Priests, Celibacy, and Sexuality* (May 12, 2010). Accessed September 20, 2018, http://www.awrsipe.com/Comments/2008-04-21-McCarrick_Syndrome.html.

24. Richard Vara, "Fiorenza Looks Back on 50 years in Priesthood, 25 Years as Bishop." *Houston Chronicle* (October 30, 2004). Accessed July 2, 2018, https://www.chron.com/life/houston-belief/article/Fiorenza-looks-back-on-50-years-of-ministry-1524162.php.

25. Tara Dooley, "Catholics Celebrate Dedication of Houston's Co-cathedral, Clergy, VIPs Join Laborate Ritual." *Houston Chronicle* (April 2, 2008). Accessed July 20, 2018, https://www.chron.com/life/houston-belief/article/Dedication-of-Houston-s-co-cathedral-celebrated-1632899.php.

26. *The Official Catholic Directory 2004* (New Providence, NJ: P.J. Kenedy & Sons, 2004).

27. Rhina Guidos, "Cardinal Wuerl Says He 'forgot' He Knew about Sexual Abuse Accusation against McCarrick." *America The Jesuit Review* (January 16, 2019). Accessed January 20, 2019, https://www.americamagazine.org/faith/2019/01/16/cardinal-wuerl-says-he-forgot-he-knew-about-sexual-abuse-accusation-against.

28. "Charter for the Protection of Children and Young People." The United States Conference of Catholic Bishops. Accessed May 14, 2019, http://www.usccb.org/issues-and-action/child-and-youth-protection/charter.cfm.

29. John L. Allen JR, "Cardinals Promise Tough Policy On Abuse." *National Catholic Reporter* (May 3, 2002). Accessed January 20, 2019, http://www.natcath.org/crisis/050302d.htm.

30. Goodstein and Otterman, "They Hid It All."

31. J.R. vs. Sacred Heart Catholic Church and the Roman Catholic Archdiocese of Galveston-Houston [2019]. 201924564, Plaintiff's Original Petition. (District Court 234), https://www.hcdistrictclerk.com.

32. "Texas Priest Arrested for Alleged Child Sex Abuse." *Catholic News Agency*. Accessed September 12, 2018, https://www.catholicnewsagency.com/news/texas-priest-arrested-for-alleged-child-sex-abuse-99832.

33. "Texas Priest Arrested for Alleged Child Sex Abuse."

34. Ibid.

35. Jessica Borg, "Investigators Raid Splendora Facility Where Priest Was Treated After Sex Abuse Allegation." *KHOU11 Houston* (September 19, 2018). Accessed September 19, 2018, https://www.khou.com/article/news/crime/investigators-raid-splendora-facility-where-priest-was-treated-after-sex-abuse-allegation/285-596206468.

36. "Montgomery County Serves Search Warrants on Catholic Archdiocese in Houston." *Montgomery County Police Reporter* (November 28, 2018). Accessed November 28, 2018, https://montgomerycountypolicereporter.com.

37. Daniel Burke and Hada Messia, "Pope to Meet Thursday with Leaders of Besieged United States Catholic Church." *CNN* (September 11, 2018). Accessed September 12, 2018, https://www.cnn.com/2018/09/11/us/pope-francis-dinardo-omalley-meeting/index.html.

38. "Cardinal DiNardo Calls Meeting with Pope Lengthy, Fruitful." *The Catholic World Report* (September 13, 2018). Accessed September 14, 2018, https://www.catholicworldreport.com/2018/09/13/cardinal-dinardo-calls-meeting-with-pope-lengthy-fruitful.

39. Gerard du Cann, "SOMETHING FUNNY? Vatican Releases 'shockingly inappropriate' Photo of Pope Francis and Cardinals Laughing during Sex Abuse Scandal Meeting." *The Sun* (September 14, 2018). Accessed September 15, 2018, https://www.thesun.co.uk/news/7260306/vatican-photo-pope-francis-cardinals-laughing-sex-abuse-scandal-meeting.

40. "Archdiocese of Galveston-Houston among Texas Catholic Dioceses to Release Names of Clergy Credibly Accused of Sexual Abuse." *Archdiocese of Galveston-Houston* (October 10, 2018). Accessed October 10, 2018, https://www.archgh.org/news-data/cardinals-corner/archdiocese-of-galveston-houston-among-texas-catholic-dioceses-to-release-names-of-clergy-credibly-accused-of-sexual-abuse.

41. Rocco Palmo, "Expanding PA Probe, Feds Warn United States Church: 'All Your Files Are Belong To Us.'" *Whispers in the Loggia* (October 26, 2018). Accessed October 26, 2018, http://whispersintheloggia.blogspot.com/2018/10/expanding-pa-probe-feds-warn-us-church.html.

42. Palmo, "Expanding PA Probe, Feds Warn United States Church."

43. "Archdiocese of Galveston-Houston among Texas Catholic Dioceses to Release Names of Clergy Credibly Accused of Sexual Abuse."

44. "United States Bishops To Meet Nov. 12–14 in Baltimore; Will Address Abuse Crisis and Action Items; Assembly to be Live Streamed, Live Tweeted, Carried Via Satellite." *The United States Conference of Catholic Bishops* (October 30, 2018). Accessed November 8, 2018, http://www.usccb.org/news/2018/18-172.cfm.

45. Dennis Sadowski, "Vatican Asks USCCB to Delay Vote on Sex Abuse Response Proposals." *Catholic News Service* (November 12, 2018), https://www.catholicnews.com/services/englishnews/2018/vatican-asks-usccb-to-delay-vote-on-sex-abuse-response-proposals.cfm.

46. Ed Condon and JD Flynn, "USCCB Meeting: What Just Happened, and What Might Happen Next?" *Catholic News Agency* (November 12, 2018). Accessed November 14, 2018, https://www.catholicnewsagency.com/news/usccb-meeting-what-just-happened-and-what-might-happen-next-30605.

47. Condon and Flynn, "USCCB Meeting: What Just Happened, and What Might Happen Next?"

48. Ibid.

49. Nikki Battiste, "Head of U.S. Catholic Bishops Kept 2 Priests Accused of Abuse in Active Ministry." *CBS Evening News with Norah O'Donnell* (November 20, 2018). Accessed November 20, 2018, https://www.cbsnews.com/news/cardinal-daniel-dinardo-head-of-u-s-catholic-bishops-kept-2-priests-accused-of-abuse-in-active-ministry.

50. "Rev. Rudolph Kos." Assignment History. Bishop Accountability (Accessed July 10, 2019), http://www.bishopaccountability.org/assign/Kos_Rudolph.htm.

51. "The Nature and Scope of Sexual Abuse of Minors by Catholic Priests and Deacons in the United States 1950–2002. USCCB." (February 2004). (Accessed November 18, 2018), http://www.usccb.org/issues-and-action/child-and-youth-protection/upload/The-Nature-and-Scope-of-Sexual-Abuse-of-Minors-by-Catholic-Priests-and-Deacons-in-the-United-States-1950-2002.pdf.

52. Tara Dooley, "Houston Area Diocese Reports 46 Abuse Victims, 22 Priests, 4 Deacons Blamed." *Houston Chronicle* (January 27, 2004). Accessed December 5, 2018, https://www.chron.com/life/houston-belief/article/Houston-area-diocese-reports-46-abuse-victims-1519590.php.

53. Jeremy Rogalski, "Sources: More Clergy Abuse Files Found During Search of Archdiocese 'secret archives.'" *KHOU11 News* (November 28, 2018). Accessed November 28, 2018, https://www.khou.com/article/news/local/sources-more-clergy-abuse-files-found-during-search-of-archdiocese-secret-archives/285-618390274.

54. Rogalski, "Sources: More Clergy Abuse Files Found During Search of Archdiocese 'secret archives.'"

55. Pat Bean, "FP Teen Center Attracts Crowds, But Leader Leaving." *Brazosport Facts* (January 3, 1968).

56. *The Brazosport Facts* (February 12, 1968).

57. "Diaconate." *The United States Conference of Catholic Bishops*. Accessed May 14, 2019, http://www.usccb.org/beliefs-and-teachings/vocations/diaconate/index.cfm.

58. Diane Schade, "Priesthood Ordinations Set in Houston, Baytown." *Texas Catholic Herald* (May 17, 1968).

59. St. Mary's Seminary Academic Catalogue 1967.

60. St. Mary's Seminary Academic Catalogue 1968.

61. 1917 Codex Iuris Canonicis, Libreria Editrice Vaticana, can. 978 §2.

62. Ibid.

63. The Official Catholic Directory for the Year of Our Lord 1969. New York: P.J. Kenedy New Providence, New Jersey: P.J. Kenedy & Sons.

64. The Official Catholic Directory for the Year of Our Lord 1970. New York: P.J. Kenedy New Providence, New Jersey: P.J. Kenedy & Sons.

65. The Official Catholic Directory for the Year of Our Lord 1971. New York: P.J. Kenedy New Providence, New Jersey: P.J. Kenedy & Sons.

66. The Official Catholic Directory for the Year of Our Lord 1972. New York: P.J. Kenedy New Providence, New Jersey: P.J. Kenedy & Sons.

67. *1973 Edition Galveston-Houston Catholic Directory*. Texas Catholic Herald Publisher.

68. *Port of Houston Magazine*, Vol. 17, No. 9. (September 1973).

69. "Welcome to the Houston International Seafarers' Centers." Houston International Seafarers' Center. Accessed May 14, 2019, https://houstonseafarers.com.

70. See also, Jason A. Gray, "The Impact of a "Leave of Absence" on a Cleric's Right to Remuneration." Accessed January 1, 2006, http://www.jgray.org/docs/remuneration.html.

71. Harris County Clerk, "Property Records." Digital images, General Property Records entry for Ivan Turic, Harris County, Texas.

72. The Official Catholic Directory for the Year of Our Lord 1974. New York: P.J. Kenedy New Providence, New Jersey: P.J. Kenedy & Sons.

73. Harris County Clerk, "Property Records."

74. Ibid.

75. The Official Catholic Directory for the Year of Our Lord 1975. New York: P.J. Kenedy New Providence, New Jersey: P.J. Kenedy & Sons.

76. Harris County Clerk, "Property Records.".

77. The Official Catholic Directory for the Year of Our Lord 1976. New York: P.J. Kenedy New Providence, New Jersey: P.J. Kenedy & Sons.

78. The Official Catholic Directory for the Year of Our Lord 1976. New York: P.J. Kenedy New Providence, New Jersey: P.J. Kenedy & Sons.

79. Harris County Clerk, "Property Records."

80. Ibid.

81. The Official Catholic Directory for the Year of Our Lord 1977. New York: P.J. Kenedy New Providence, New Jersey: P.J. Kenedy & Sons.

82. Harris County Clerk, "Property Records."

83. The State of Texas vs. Ivan Turic, 228th District Court, May 17, 1977.

84. Harris County Clerk, "Personal Records." Digital images, General Records entry for Ivan Turic, Harris County, Texas.

85. Harris County District Clerk, "Criminal Records." Digital images, entry for Ivan Turic, Harris County, Texas.

86. Harris County District Clerk, "Civil Records." Digital images, entry for Ivan Turic, Harris County, Texas.

87. "Parish Parishioners." Parish of Biokovska. Accessed May 15, 2019, https://www.bijakova.com/crkva-sv-ivana/zupski-zupnici

88. Hrvoje Šimičević, "Crkveno lice s potjernice." *Novosti Weekly*. (March 16, 2019). Accessed August 7, 2019, https://www.portalnovosti.com/crkveno-lice-s-potjernice.

89. Harris County District Clerk, "Criminal Records."

BIBLIOGRAPHY

Allen, John L. JR. 2002. "Cardinals Promise Tough Policy on Abuse." *National Catholic Reporter*. Accessed January 20, 2019. http://www.natcath.org/crisis/050302d.htm.

Archdiocese of Galveston-Houston. "Archdiocese of Galveston-Houston among Texas Catholic Dioceses to Release Names of Clergy Credibly Accused of Sexual Abuse." Accessed October 10, 2018. https://www.archgh.org/news-data/cardinals-corner/archdiocese-of-galveston-houston-among-texas-catholic-dioceses-to-release-names-of-clergy-credibly-accused-of-sexual-abuse.

Archdiocese of Galveston-Houston. "Newly Named Cardinal to Speak in Houston." Accessed September 13, 2017. https://www.archgh.org/news-data/latest-news/newly-named-cardinal-to-speak-in-houston.

Bean, Pat. "FP Teen Center Attracts Crowds, But Leader Leaving." *Brazosport Facts*. January 3, 1968.

BeginningCatholic.com. "The Sacrament of Confirmation: Grace for Fullness of Faith and Life" Accessed May 14, 2019. http://www.beginningcatholic.com/co nfirmation

Bishop Accountability. "Rev. Rudolph Kos Assignment History." Accessed July 10, 2019. http://www.bishopaccountability.org/assign/Kos_Rudolph.htm.

Boorstein, Michelle. 2018. "Pennsylvania Supreme Court Approves Release of 900-page Grand Jury Report about Catholic Clergy Sex Abuse." *The Washington Post*. Accessed July 27, 2018. https://www.washingtonpost.com/news/acts-of-faith/wp/2018/07/27/pennsylvania-supreme-court-oks-release-of-900-page-grand-jury -report-about-catholic-clergy-sex-abuse.

Burke, Daniel and Messia, Hada. 2018. "Pope to Meet Thursday with Leaders of Besieged United States Catholic Church." *CNN*. Accessed September 12, 2018. https ://www.cnn.com/2018/09/11/us/pope-francis-dinardo-omalley-meeting/index.html.

Catholic Culture.org. "Archdiocese Creates, Takes Down Website Defending Cardinal Wuerl's Record on Abuse." Accessed August 16, 2018. https://www.catholic culture.org/news/headlines/index.cfm?storyid=38162.

Catholic News Agency. "Newspapers, Victims Sue for Release of Pa. Grand Jury's Clergy Sex Abuse Report." Accessed July 9, 2018. https://www.catholicnewsa gency.com/news/newspapers-victims-sue-for-release-of-pa-grand-jurys-clergy-sex-abuse-report-56094.

Catholic News Agency. "Texas Priest Arrested for Alleged Child Sex Abuse." Accessed September 12, 2018. https://www.catholicnewsagency.com/news/texas -priest-arrested-for-alleged-child-sex-abuse-99832.

Catholic Online. "Sacraments of the Catholic Church." Accessed May 14, 2019. https ://www.catholic.org/prayers/sacrament.php

Codex Iuris Canonicis. 1917. Libreria Editrice Vaticana, can. 978 §2.

Condon, Ed and Flynn, J. D. 2018. "USCCB Meeting: What Just Happened, and What Might Happen Next? *Catholic News Agency*. Accessed November 14, 2018. https://www.catholicnewsagency.com/news/usccb-meeting-what-just-happen ed-and-what-might-happen-next-30605.

Dooley, Tara. 2004. "Houston Area Diocese Reports 46 Abuse Victims, 22 Priests, 4 Deacons Blamed." *Houston Chronicle*. Accessed December 5, 2018. https://ww w.chron.com/life/houston-belief/article/Houston-area-diocese-reports-46-abuse-vi ctims-1519590.php.

Dooley, Tara. 2008. "Catholics Celebrate Dedication of Houston's Co-cathedral, Clergy, VIPs Join Elaborate Ritual." *Houston Chronicle*. Accessed July 20, 2018. https://www.chron.com/life/houston-belief/article/Dedication-of-Houston-s-co-cat hedral-celebrated-1632899.php.

du Cann, Gerard. 2018. "SOMETHING FUNNY? Vatican Releases 'shockingly inappropriate' Photo of Pope Francis and Cardinals Laughing During Sex Abuse Scandal Meeting" *The Sun*. Accessed September 15, 2018. https://www.thesun. co.uk/news/7260306/vatican-photo-pope-francis-cardinals-laughing-sex-abuse-s candal-meeting.

Erdley, Deb. "Supreme Court Blocks Release of Grand Jury Report on Sexual Abuse in Catholic Dioceses." *Trib Live*. Accessed June 20, 2018. https://archive.triblive.com/news/pennsylvania/supreme-court-blocks-release-of-grand-jury-report-on-sexual-abuse-in-catholic-dioceses.

Galveston-Houston Catholic Directory, 1973 Edition. Texas Catholic Herald Publisher.

Goodstein, Laurie and Otterman Sharon. 2018. "They Hid It All: Catholic Priests Abused 1,000 Children in Pennsylvania, Report Says." *The New York Times*. Accessed August 14, 2018. https://www.nytimes.com/2018/08/14/us/catholic-church-sex-abuse-pennsylvania.html.

Gray, Jason. 2006. "The Impact of a Leave of Absence on a Cleric's Right to Remuneration." Accessed 1 January 2018. http://www.jgray.org/docs/remuneration.html.

Guidos, Rhina. "Cardinal Wuerl says He 'forgot' He Knew about Sexual Abuse Accusation against McCarrick." *America The Jesuit Review*. Accessed January 20, 2019. https://www.americamagazine.org/faith/2019/01/16/cardinal-wuerl-says-he-forgot-he-knew-about-sexual-abuse-accusation-against.

Houston International Seafarers' Center. "Welcome to the Houston International Seafarers' Centers" Accessed May 14, 2019. https://houstonseafarers.com.

Montgomery County Police Reporter. "Montgomery County Serves Search Warrants on Catholic Archdiocese in Houston." Accessed November 28, 2018. https://montgomerycountypolicereporter.com.

Office of the Attorney General Commonwealth of Pennsylvania. "Pennsylvania Dioceses Victims Report." Accessed August 14, 2018. https://www.attorneygeneral.gov/report.

Palmo, Rocco. "Expanding PA Probe, Feds Warn United States Church: 'All Your Files Are Belong To Us'." *Whispers in the Loggia*. Accessed October 26, 2018. http://whispersintheloggia.blogspot.com/2018/10/expanding-pa-probe-feds-warn-us-church.html.

Port of Houston Magazine, Vol. 17, No. 9. September 1973.

Povoledo, Elisabetta and Otterman, Sharon. 2018. "Cardinal Theodore McCarrick Resigns Amid Sexual Abuse Scandal." *The New York Times*. Accessed July 28, 2018. https://www.nytimes.com/2018/07/28/world/europe/cardinal-theodore-mccarrick-resigns.html.

Sadowski, Dennis. 2018. "Vatican Asks USCCB to Delay Vote on Sex Abuse Response Proposals." *Catholic News Agency*. Accessed November 12, 2018. https://www.catholicnews.com/services/englishnews/2018/vatican-asks-usccb-to-delay-vote-on-sex-abuse-response-proposals.cfm.

Schade, Diane. 1968. "Priesthood Ordinations Set in Houston, Baytown." *Texas Catholic Herald*, May 17, 1968.

Schiffer, Kathy. 2018. "Richard Sipe Tried to Warn Us – But No One Was Listening." *National Catholic Register*. Accessed August 20, 2018. http://www.ncregister.com/blog/kschiffer/richard-sipe-tried-to-warn-us-but-no-one-was-listening.

Šimičević, Hrvoje. 2019. "Crkveno lice s potjernice." *Novosti Weekly*. Accessed August 7, 2019. https://www.portalnovosti.com/crkveno-lice-s-potjernice.

Sipe, Richard. 2010. "The Cardinal McCarrick Syndrome." *Priests, Celibacy, and Sexuality*. Accessed September 20, 2018. http://www.awrsipe.com/Comments/2008-04-21-McCarrick_Syndrome.html.

Texas Catholic Bishops Conference. "Preventing the Sexual Abuse of Minors: A Statement of the Texas Catholic Conference of Bishops." Accessed January 31, 2019. https://txcatholic.org/pastoral-resources/preventing-the-sexual-abuse-of-minors.

The Archdiocese of Galveston-Houston. "About Us." Accessed May 14, 2019. https://www.archgh.org/about/about-us.

The Archdiocese of Galveston-Houston. "Archdiocese of Galveston-Houston Clergy Disclosure List." Accessed January 31, 2019. https://www.archgh.org/clergylist.

The Archdiocese of Saint Paul Minnesota. "Catholic Glossary." Accessed January 18, 2019. https://www.archspm.org/catholic-glossary.

The Brazosport Facts. February 12, 1968.

The Catholic World Report. "Cardinal DiNardo Calls Meeting with Pope Lengthy, Fruitful." Accessed September 14, 2018. https://www.catholicworldreport.com/2018/09/13/cardinal-dinardo-calls-meeting-with-pope-lengthy-fruitful.

The Official Catholic Directory 2004. New Providence, NJ: P.J. Kenedy & Sons, 2004.

The Official Catholic Directory for the Year of Our Lord 1969. New York: P.J. Kenedy New Providence, New Jersey: P.J. Kenedy & Sons.

The Official Catholic Directory for the Year of Our Lord 1970. New York: P.J. Kenedy New Providence, New Jersey: P.J. Kenedy & Sons.

The Official Catholic Directory for the Year of Our Lord 1971. New York: P.J. Kenedy New Providence, New Jersey: P.J. Kenedy & Sons.

The Official Catholic Directory for the Year of Our Lord 1972. New York: P.J. Kenedy New Providence, New Jersey: P.J. Kenedy & Sons.

The Official Catholic Directory for the Year of Our Lord 1974. New York: P.J. Kenedy New Providence, New Jersey: P.J. Kenedy & Sons.

The Official Catholic Directory for the Year of Our Lord 1975. New York: P.J. Kenedy New Providence, New Jersey: P.J. Kenedy & Sons.

The Official Catholic Directory for the Year of Our Lord 1976. New York: P.J. Kenedy New Providence, New Jersey: P.J. Kenedy & Sons.

The Official Catholic Directory for the Year of Our Lord 1977. New York: P.J. Kenedy New Providence, New Jersey: P.J. Kenedy & Sons.

The United States Conference of Catholic Bishops. "Canon 1246, §2 – Holy Days of Obligation." Accessed May 14, 2019. http://www.usccb.org/beliefs-and-teachings/what-we-believe/canon-law/complementary-norms/canon-1246.cfm.

The United States Conference of Catholic Bishops. "Canon Law." Accessed May 14, 2019. http://www.usccb.org/beliefs-and-teachings/what-we-believe/canon-law/index.cfm.

The United States Conference of Catholic Bishops. "Charter for the Protection of Children and Young People." Accessed May 14, 2019. http://www.usccb.org/issues-and-action/child-and-youth-protection/charter.cfm.

The United States Conference of Catholic Bishops. “Diaconate.” Accessed May 14, 2019. http://www.usccb.org/beliefs-and-teachings/vocations/diaconate/index.cfm.

The United States Conference of Catholic Bishops. “United States Bishops To Meet Nov. 12–14 in Baltimore; Will Address Abuse Crisis and Action Items; Assembly to be Live Streamed, Live Tweeted, Carried Via Satellite.” Accessed November 8, 2018. http://www.usccb.org/news/2018/18-172.cfm.

The United States Conference of Catholic Bishops. “USCCB Officers.” Accessed May 14, 2019. http://www.usccb.org/about/leadership/usccb-officers.cfm.

The United States Conference of Catholic Bishops. 2004. “The Nature and Scope of Sexual Abuse of Minors by Catholic Priests and Deacons in the United States 1950-2002.” Accessed November 18, 2018. http://www.usccb.org/issues-and-action/child-and-youth-protection/upload/The-Nature-and-Scope-of-Sexual-Abuse-of-Minors-by-Catholic-Priests-and-Deacons-in-the-United-States-1950-2002.pdf.

Vara, Richard. “Fiorenza Looks Back on 50 Years in Priesthood, 25 Years as Bishop.” *Houston Chronicle*. Accessed July 2, 2018. https://www.chron.com/life/houston-belief/article/Fiorenza-looks-back-on-50-years-of-ministry-1524162.php.

Chapter 7

#NunsToo

Media Coverage of Sexual Violence against Nuns and Sisters after #MeToo

Tara M. Tuttle

The first tweet using #NunsToo was posted in 2013, but it did not reference sexual misconduct. The use of the hashtag in connection to #MeToo originated with a tweet by Twitter user @lamarquesina, or Lulu Marquez,[1] on March 1, 2018, linking to a *New York Times* story "In Vatican Magazine *Exposé*, Nuns Reveal Their Economic Exploitation" by Elisabetta Povoledo.[2] Marquez used the hashtag to link to the broader movement and its hashtag in response to sexual violence. #MeToo is the moniker given to the movement and social media phenomenon begun by activist Tarana Burke in 2006 on MySpace to promote solidarity among survivors of sexual violence and to raise awareness of the extent of the problem.[3] Following news coverage of several allegations of sexual assault by American film producer Harvey Weinstein, the hashtag was popularized over a decade later in October 2017 by a tweet[4] from actress and activist Alyssa Milano who asked those affected by harassment and violence to reply to her tweet with "#MeToo" to demonstrate the scale of the problem of sexual misconduct and to ensure victims of such mistreatment did not feel alone. The effect was staggering. Within three days, more than 800,000 tweets included the hashtag, and another social media platform, Facebook, tracked more than 12 million posts, comments, and reactions to the hashtag within 24 hours of Milano's tweet.[5] Many of the victims of sexual misconduct suffered abuse at the hands of religious authorities. This part of the story—that a sexual abuse crisis involving clergy existed—was not a breaking news. As more information from ongoing investigations into perpetrator priests given institutional cover continues to be released a staggering eighteen years after

The Boston Globe's Spotlight team broke the story of an epidemic of sexual abuse by priests, this paper considers the impact of the 2017 emergence of the #MeToo movement on the media coverage of the sexual abuse of women religious. Many victims of abuse are themselves members of religious orders. As #MeToo gained widespread attention, subsequent hashtags emerged highlighting the problem of sexual violence among different populations, including #NunsToo. This work builds on Dr. Mary Marcel's earlier analysis of the lack of media coverage of the sexual assaults of nuns in reports on the Catholic Church sexual abuse crisis from 2001 and considers whether the U.S. media's prior neglect of female victims in light of widespread media coverage of #MeToo has improved the coverage of crimes against women religious.

Many victims of sexual assault experience interrogations of their sexual histories and personal lives following their accusations against sexual perpetrators. The unique positions of nuns and sisters[6] whose profession of vows of chastity with an expectation of modesty makes them unlikely targets for journalists to treat them in the usual manner. This media analysis of coverage of "#NunsToo" stories examines whether coverage of violence against nuns and sisters included the shaming of survivors of sexual violence, diminishment or upholding of credibility of survivor claims, cultivation of sympathy for perpetrators and/or survivors, and contextualization of the violence within the patriarchal structure of the church and of society. Finally, I analyze how mainstream media narratives of #NunsToo consider the future of the church in light of these scandals.

BEFORE #METOO: VIOLENCE AGAINST WOMEN AND GIRLS "ISN'T NEWS"

The sexual assaults of women religious is, of course, not a new story. The 1998 "A National Survey of the Sexual Trauma Experiences of Catholic Nuns" by John T. Chibnall, Ann Wolf, and Paul N. Duckro provided data suggesting as many as 40 percent of women religious had experienced sexual assault,[7] but readers of print and online media reports of the Catholic Church sexual abuse crisis might never consider women religious among the victims given the media erasure of their stories. The results of this study, for example, did not break into mainstream media coverage until six years after its initial publication, not until after *The Boston Globe* Spotlight team broke open the story of the Catholic Church sexual abuse crisis and cover-ups in 2002.[8] Finally, in 2003, as part of media coverage of the Catholic sexual abuse crisis, *St. Louis Dispatch* reporter Bill Smith included their findings.[9] Still, Professor Mary Marcel's media analyses of the coverage of the crisis in the early 2000s found that almost no attention was paid to female victims. She points out that even "*The Globe* did not cover the story."[10] They eventually did, but minimally and not until almost a year after their initial report.[11]

Given that this violence against women religious had been studied in 1998, that many victims came forward after the *Globe's* coverage in 2001, and that researchers at St. Louis University followed with a study completed in 2006 that found nearly 10 percent of women religious in 123 orders in the United States "have been 'sexually exploited' in adulthood by a male or female clergy member,"[12] why was the abuse of nuns and sisters by clergy still considered a breaking news story in 2018? The media's disinterest in news affecting women and girls, often attributed to the public's disinterest, has devastating effects upon women and girls. Victims feel alone and suffer in silence and shame. Potential jurors, law enforcement officers, school officials, coaches, counselors, family members, and others routinely disbelieve victims when they have been exposed to no or faulty media representations of sexual violence. Survivors may not know where to seek help. Representation matters, and the media erased or distorted the violence girls and women experienced at the hands of clergy. Violence against women and girls was deemed something not worth talking about. "We expect it, it happens, and so it isn't news," explains Marcel.[13] She continues, "The question has been raised as to whether, in the eyes of the Church hierarchy, there was no scandal if the victims were female."[14] She observes this was compounded because "some evidence suggests the *Globe* had decided that female cases were not of interest" back in 2002. Furthermore, "this underreporting thus made it more difficult for female victims to come forward and win the credibility of group reinforcement, which so often preceded the award of financial restitution in or out of court."[15] When a Boston-area SNAP (Survivors Network of Those Abused by Priests)[16] member contacted the very *Globe* reporters investigating the church crisis and "offered details of her own story, she was told stories of the abuse of girls were not of interest."[17] This makes it unsurprising then that in 2007, Marcel wrote, "The U.S. press never succeeded in covering the full magnitude the crisis as it emerged worldwide: that it involved adult women as well as girls and boys; that it involved clerical as well as lay victims; that it involved accusations of both physical abuse, even unto death, as well as sexual abuse and rape."[18] The prior framing of this story of the Catholic Church sexual abuse crisis persists in ways that continue to contribute to the silencing of female victims of this crisis, even as it has become attached to the larger #MeToo narrative.

BEFORE #METOO: HOMOPHOBIC AND PEDOPHILIC FRAMING OF THE CATHOLIC CHURCH SEXUAL ABUSE CRISIS

Refusing attention to women's stories, a skewed interpretation of the Catholic Church sexual abuse crisis emerged from the media coverage of the early 2000s. The story of sexual abuse by priests has been framed as if "this universal crisis was a problem only of a few liberal, 'gay,' American priests—thereby (1) conflating a gay (male) sexual orientation with child sexual abusing and (b) implying that the victims were all male."[19] In the 2018 panel discussion at "Overcoming Silence—Women's Voices in the Catholic Abuse Crisis," a symposium hosted by Voices of Faith, an international initiative to empower women in the Catholic Church, former SNAP Outreach Director Barbara Dorris stated, "At SNAP the victims we helped were about 40 percent girls," to which Robert Mickens responded, "We don't hear that often, I think, in the United States. The picture we've been given by a lot of people in the church, especially bishops, and most recently by the former Prefect of the Congregation for the Doctorate of Faith, Cardinal Gerhard Müller, says that these are mostly teenage boys."[20] Dorris explains, "But that's part of the smokescreen, because if you say that the victims are teenage boys, then it's a homosexual problem [. . .] And it's not. Homosexuals are less likely to sexually assault a child than a heterosexual, but now they've got everybody talking about homosexuality and all of a sudden, we've missed the real topic, which is children—boys *and* girls are being sexually assaulted."[21] Not only did this framing render invisible little girls as victims, it obscured the abuse against nuns and sisters by clergy.

However, Marcel points out that this benefitted the Vatican and shaped their strategy to the reports of sexual violence. "One could conclude that the U.S. press, in a strange alignment with the Vatican's position, characterized almost the entire crisis as a matter of abuses within the U.S., and overwhelmingly involving boys," she explains.[22] This was "the framing they wanted" through which they were able "to argue that the problem was limited to already sinful people" given that church doctrine considers homosexual sex acts sinful.[23] Ignoring and suppressing the violence against girls and women, and women religious in particular, allowed them to contain the story and save potentially millions of dollars in reparations. The media, by deciding violence against girls and women wasn't newsworthy and by creating or at least accepting this homosexual and pedophilic framing, became complicit in the ongoing suppression and enduring abuse of other victims. "The cases involving priests raping nuns provide one of the clearest conditions for rebutting the claim made by both the Vatican and many in the U.S. Catholic hierarchy: that the current sex abuse crisis is rooted in a homosexual minority of

U.S. priests,"[24] Marcel explains, but "the studies of abuse of nuns by priests has never been offered as a refutation of the Vatican's homosexual claim."[25]

This erasure was exacerbated by rape myths about female victims and male perpetrators. Rape myths are "attitudes and beliefs that are generally false but are widely and persistently held, and that serve to deny and justify male sexual aggression against women."[26] Marcel points out that cultural rape myths that appear frequently in reporting "corroborate the logic of men's violence against women by construing their victims as inferior and even disposable because of their gender, race, and class."[27] Rape myths "consistently follow a pattern whereby they blame the victim for their rape, express a disbelief in claims of rape, exonerate the perpetrator, and allude that only certain types of women are raped."[28] One might expect nuns and sisters, given their vows of chastity and expectations of modesty, to be exempted from some rape myths that result in blaming female victims for their own assaults. However, Sue Archibald, then president of Linkup, a support group for sexual abuse victims of clergy, asserted in 2002, "Women are treated more as seductresses who tempted priests into sin than as people who were victimized."[29] Marcel concurs: "Vatican spokesmen and *Globe* journalists often seemed to agree, prior to 2002, that a priest raping any woman or girl was not rape at all."[30] At the time, when victims reported, some were told by their supervisors that the crimes against them were less important than the reputations or work of the perpetrators of the crimes. For example, Dr. Rocio Figueroa Alvear, a theologian at Good Shepherd College in Auckland who is also survivor of clerical violence, was asked to help in the cause of beatification of Herman Doyle who had assaulted her as a young woman in the lay movement Sodalicio. When she reported his abuse to deter this beatification, she was blamed and blackmailed. She was told by the priest to whom she reported Doyle's crimes, "What happened to you was nothing. It doesn't matter. I'm sure that you seduced him, and it doesn't matter because we need a saint."[31] Following this dismissal of her trauma, like many other victims, Figueroa Alvear did not go public for years.

Framing the crisis as one of homosexuality and pedophilia meant that the media silence on the abuse of women religious and lay women and girls has had damaging effects. Marcel writes that the "focus on one class of victims to the exclusion or erasure of all others" leads to "high-level protection for the class of male perpetrators who, by virtue of taking opposite-sex victims, are less vulnerable to the categorical denunciation to which any same-sex perpetrator becomes sensationally liable."[32] Despite widespread abuse and a pattern of victimizing sisters and nuns, many victims of sexual assault by clergy believed they were alone in their experiences. As a novitiate, Doris Wagner was raped by a priest and left her community in 2011. The priest who raped her remains among that community. She says, "It is ridiculous to say this now, but at that time I still thought I was the only nun that had ever been raped by a priest because, you see, I had never heard of similar instances. I didn't know other stories. I thought I was the only one."[33] Lacking solidarity with other survivors, Wagner and others were left vulnerable after their assaults when supervisors failed to help them and heaped upon them further trauma. Some were shamed by their superiors and others threatened into silence. For example, Dr. Figueroa Alvear was told that if she went public about Doyle's abuse, two men would identify her as an abuser and spread rumors about her sanity. A cardinal gave her two painful options: "You leave the community or you become a silent soldier."[34]

Failures of the supervisors in the institution to respond in just or victim-centered ways meant that many survivors of sexual violence at the hands of clergy became not silent soldiers but silent carriers of trauma. They were treated in their organizations in ways other victims of sexual assault had been treated by the press. This problem in crime reporting, which Marcel calls the "good girl/bad girl dichotomy," presents the good girl as someone who "adheres to rigidly defined gendered behaviors and whose sexual behavior is considered 'respectable,' making her an 'innocent victim.'"[35] Nuns and sisters, in obvious ways, fit the good girl paradigm. Their own vows of celibacy position them safely within the confines of the concept of sexual purity.[36] Marcel's 2005 study, however, found that nuns and novitiates did not receive "the universally positive coverage their exemplary characters should otherwise have earned them," which, she says, "suggests the ultimate irrelevance of female sexual virtue in the reportage of sexual assault."[37] Sadly, "It would appear in the cases of nuns that, no matter how 'good' they are, journalists sometimes chose to preferentially defend the respectability of *male* clergy and the Vatican's repeated injunction to avoid scandal to the Church above reporting on the scandal of violating the human rights and dignity of these ordained and faithful women," Marcel argues.[38] This makes the fight of women perceived to have less sexual "purity" feel hopeless. If violence against women who have devoted their lives to God and who have practiced chastity is not deemed newsworthy, what does this mean for other victims? If even nuns did not receive assumptions of innocence in the media, would any others? Marcel affirms, "It bears witness to the most striking abuse of power that even a woman who is celibate becomes blameworthy or punished for her own rape. The very most continent and nonsexualized persons, living out their celibacy by choice, did not succeed in gaining sympathetic coverage by *Globe* reporters."[39] This national conversation around sexual violence has changed significantly in the years since, however, and social media have helped circulate information dispelling rape myths and highlighting rape culture, information that has influenced public perceptions about sexual assault and victims of sexual violence.

AFTER #METOO: HOW THE MEDIA TALKS ABOUT SEXUAL VIOLENCE

By framing the clergy sexual abuse crisis as pedophilic and homosexual, journalists obfuscated the impact upon girls and women, including women religious. Yet even when the media cover sexual violence against women and girls, their language and framing may still undermine the victims. Previous studies have examined how media framing shapes public perception.[40] Victim credibility may be undermined by references to clothing, social activities, and prior sexual histories, as well as through valorization of perpetrators by enumerating their accomplishments and contributions to the community and through expressions of sympathy for what a conviction or loss of reputation following allegations might cost them. Considering the vows of chastity and expected modesty of women religious as well as the celebrated role priests occupy in communities, I investigated several highly circulated online print media stories of sexual violence against nuns and sisters by priests. In my analyses, I considered the following points of inquiry: Does the language serve to obfuscate the most frequently identified agents of the violence against women religious, priests? Are nuns and sisters subject to the same rape myths that affect perceptions of other victims? What happens when modesty and chastity are assumed of the victims? Do the stories offer biographical or contextual information about the victims' or perpetrators' lives? Does the language lead readers to doubt the credibility of the nuns and sisters? Who is blamed?

Researchers Ashlie Siefkes-Andrew and Cassandra Alexopoulos point out that in many media reports of sexual violence, the "use of nominalizations (e.g., 'battery' or 'violence') serves to obfuscate the agent of such violence."[41] They explain, "Specifically, the use of words such as 'claim' or 'admit' can elicit disbelief among readers [. . .] compared with the words 'state' or 'report.'"[42] Verbs that implied that the writer did not believe that what the original speaker said was true were also noted and are referred to as language of doubt. These words included "*admit, allege, claim, concede, confess, lie, misinform, purport,* and *make out.*"[43] Language of support, on the other hand, employs verbs and adverbs which imply "that the writer endorsed, supported, or believed that what the original speaker said was true," such as "*acknowledge, disclose, divulge, foretell, forewarn, indicate, mention, not, recall, reveal, let on, let slip, make clear,* and *point out.*"[44] In my review of nineteen reports on the sexual abuse of nuns following #MeToo, I was pleasantly surprised to discover that these articles contain almost none of the verbs Siefkes-Andrew and Alexopoulos list as indicative of doubt.[45] When sexual violence against women religious was finally covered, victims were treated as credible.

Imp

Since #MeToo and #NunsToo began as Twitter hashtag phenomena, I start by examining the most widely retweeted news items on the sexual abuse of nuns. Many of these articles include language of support, but they vary widely in their framing. *The New York Times* article "Pope Acknowledges Nuns Were Sexually Abused by Priests and Bishops" by Jason Horowitz and Elizabeth Dias[46] possesses both a headline and opening sentence that include one of the verbs Siefkes-Andrew and Alexopoulos assert constitute language of support. However, by mid-article, their failure to center victims of abuse or even to center the crime of the abuse itself becomes clear. Horowitz and Dias give Pope Francis quite a bit of space in the article, quoting his defenses of the Vatican's response to the crimes. In the third paragraph, they quote Pope Francis: "It's true, Francis said. 'There are priests and bishops who have done that.'" They write in paragraphs 9–12:

> Asked about these developments on Tuesday, Francis said that it was a continuing problem and that the Vatican was working on the issue. Some priests, he said, have been suspended. "Should more be done? Yes," Francis said. "Do we have the will? Yes. But it is a path that we have already begun." Francis recalled that his predecessor, Benedict XVI, had been "a strong man" who he said had sought to remove priests who committed sexual abuse and even "sexual slavery." Francis spoke about a case in which Benedict dissolved an order of nuns "because a certain slavery of women" had crept in, slavery to the point of sexual slavery on the part of clergy or the founder.[47]

As the head of the church, their inclusion of Pope Francis's remarks makes journalistic sense, but what they omit could significantly affect public understanding of the scope of the Vatican's inaction on this issue.

What the authors of this article fail to acknowledge or put into context is that Francis's words do not include the language of support but instead shield perpetrators' names and use passive constructions. Horowitz and Dias offer no commentary nor quote any reaction to the decision to dissolve an order of nuns rather than oust the perpetrator. They do not inform readers of the aftermath of this response. What happened to these nuns? Where did they go? Were they given treatment for the abuse they received at the hands of the priest? The authors fail to address these questions, allowing Francis's words to do the work of undermining support and perpetuating problematic aspects of media responses to sexual violence even as they may be striving to support the nuns who have experienced abuse themselves. This article centers on the Pope and decenters the victims in the story. It offers more context on the Pope than on the lives of those affected by the crimes and leaves the perpetrators mostly invisible. Even when they offer example anecdotes of abuse, they omit the names of those responsible for further traumatizing the victims of sexual abuse in their responses to learning of those crimes. Of the case in Chile they cite, Horowitz and Dias write, "Current and former nuns said the women had been removed from the order when they reported the abuse."[48] Removed by whom? What happened after they were removed? Where did they go? Were they relocated? What happened to the perpetrator? These details remain unaddressed. Citing a case in Malawi in which "priests impregnated thirty sisters in one congregation,"[49] though they do identify the pregnancies as the results of priests' actions, they simply offer as the outcome of their reporting to the archbishop that the sisters "were replaced." Again, by whom? Where did they go? What happened with the pregnancies? Were they carried to term? If so, what happened to these babies, the children of the priests? Were the women thrust into poverty, single parenthood, or shame? These omissions reflect similar diminishment of violence against women that Marcel observed in her earlier analysis.

One of the article's most devastating quotes is from Sister Rose Pacatte's presentation on how to prevent abuse: "Don't report to bishop or priest as the first step to deal with the situation [. . .] They may be the abusers or may protect them." The anecdotal evidence they offer and this instruction from Sister Pacatte illustrate the lack of support sisters and nuns have received in response to reporting the abuse they experienced, Horowitz and Dias offer little context on institutional failures. Furthermore, what is most telling in this article is the structure; none of the last eight paragraphs of this article purportedly on the acknowledgment of sexual abuse of nuns by priests address that topic at all. The article shifts into a discussion of the Pope's travels and work on interreligious dialogue with Muslim communities in the Middle East. He is the story, not the victims of sexual violence. #MeToo may have helped this story make the news, but the victims in this story still struggle for attention in its text.

Other journalists treat female victims of abuse with greater regard. In "After Years of Abuse by Priests, #NunsToo Are Speaking Out," *NPR's* Sylvia Poggioli's opening sentence also uses the word "acknowledged," lending support to the victims' narratives from the start.[50] In contrast with the aforementioned article in *The New York Times*, Poggioli's reporting takes a more victim-centered approach. She writes, "In February, Pope Francis acknowledged a longstanding dirty secret in the Roman Catholic Church—the sexual abuse of nuns by priests." Poggioli offers greater analysis; she makes clear that the poverty of nuns contributes to their exploitation. She quotes editor of *Women Church World* Lucetta Scaraffia in describing the nuns as "poor women" who have at times been "forced to have abortions—paid by the priest because nuns have no money." Moreover, she includes perspectives that reflect upon the role patriarchy plays in the sexual abuse crisis. Poggioli includes the observation that "the abuse is the result of male domination in church leadership" from Sister Catherine Aubin, a French Dominican nun and theology professor at Pontifical University of St. Thomas in Rome. Poggioli also provides historical context of the suppression of the news of this epidemic of abuse, citing the 1994 report by Sister Maura O'Donohue "shelved" by the Vatican and made public only in 2001 by *National Catholic Reporter.*[51] Poggioli also indicts institutional failures, noting that a recent AP investigation "found the Vatican had not punished offenders for abuse of nuns in Europe, Asia, Africa, and Latin America."[52]

Poggioli's article includes personal anecdotes that reveal the lack of support some nuns have received when reporting crimes against them to their superiors, describing how nuns who have reported assault have been mistreated and expelled. Her writing shows an assumption that victims are telling the truth, and her language casts no doubt upon their allegations. She does not fall into habits of victim-blaming or "both-sidesisms" that can inadvertently benefit perpetrators or perpetuate rape myths and rape culture.

Despite the strengths of Poggioli's analysis for *NPR*, the news outlet that offered the most thorough coverage of #NunsToo was *The Washington Post.* Their careful and contextual reporting offers a victim-centered model for journalists covering sexual assault. Two articles from *The Washington Post* invoke Pope Francis as did the aforementioned *New York Times* piece. In "Pope Francis Confirms Catholic Clergy Members Abused Nuns," Max J. Rosenthal and Michelle Boorstein[53] similarly offer much of the space of their article to quotes from Pope Francis's acknowledgment of the abuse and intention to respond to it. However, they also point out that the Vatican has been criticized for its failure to respond adequately to the abuse and mention Francis's previous dismissal of accusations of one cover-up in particular. They also provide crucial context for understanding Vatican procedures that help suppress public knowledge and criminal convictions in cases of sexual abuse by clergy, and close the article with two specific cases involving nuns harmed by clergy and a quote from lawyer Indulekha Joseph who states, "Once a nun speaks, she is thrown out of the convent and may find herself on the street, because often her family is not willing to accommodate her. A campaign of character assassination starts. The nun will be portrayed as a prostitute." These survivors have little recourse given their lower positions in church hierarchy and their poverty. Marcel explains, "Obviously legal counsel retained by the church would not undertake to support litigation by nuns against Catholic male clergy whilst those nuns were still members of holy orders."[54] In what they have chosen to include and in the structure of their article, Rosenthal and Boorstein also cultivate sympathy for the nuns without forfeiting neutrality, illustrating the difficulties they face in reporting abuse up a hierarchy with a history of victim-blaming, suppression, and cover-ups.

Ruby Mellen's report, "Pope Francis is holding the Vatican's first summit on sexual abuse. Recent scandals suggest it is long overdue" is far more damaging to the reputation of the once immensely popular Pope. It opens with remarks about the "historically bad year for the Catholic Church" and reports of abuse "that are threatening Francis's legacy." Then she recounts Francis's warning to accusers that "they could find themselves guilty of slander if they made such accusations without evidence." She includes the information that a Vatican official claimed Francis covered up the assaults perpetrated by Cardinal Theodore McCarrick and notes "the inner dissatisfaction among some in the Catholic Church with how Francis is handling abuse scandals." Following Mellen's discussion of Francis's acknowledgment of the abuse of nuns, she quotes former nun Mary Dispenza: "I'm really angered by the words of the pope just now [. . .] I am angered by the pope not standing up and really speaking out about the tragedy, and actions he will take." However, the end of Mellen's article shifts in tone. Though she notes "little was done in response" to cases of abuse against deaf children in Italy and Argentina, she quotes Bishop Angelo Becciu's remarks that the Pope "wishes to remind you of what the Holy See has done and keeps on doing with unwavering commitment on clerical sexual abuses, operating in support of the victims' tragedies and to prevent the sad phenomenon."[55] But she cites no examples to support this, perhaps because few seem to exist.

Emily Tamkin's brief article "How Women Raised Their Voices at the Vatican" follows this article in *The Washington Post* coverage and brings women's voices into the discussion of the Vatican's sexual abuse summit, a summit still dominated by men.[56] Tamkin quotes from the remarks of Nigerian nun Sister Veronica Openibo and Mexican journalist Valentina Alazraki (who has covered five papacies), both of whom admonished Vatican officials. This is crucial inclusion. Dr. Figeuroa Alvear insists, "This organization that is a club of men, that the church is breathing just with one masculine lung, so suffocating."[57] While feminists including this author maintain patriarchy is unhealthy for everyone, this church structure is likely more suffocating for the women, particularly female victims of sexual violence by their superiors. While male priests were often simply relocated upon discovery of their crimes, nuns and sisters who had been victims were sometimes expelled or left of their own volition. This is a loss of community, home, and livelihood. This disproportionate harm to women is further illustrated in "Founder and Staff of Vatican Women's Magazine Step Down, Citing Pressure over Nun Abuse Stories" by Chico Harlan and Stefano Pitrelli for *The Washington Post*.[58] This report explained that it was because of the women's magazine *Women Church World's* February 2019 report on the abuse of nuns that Pope Francis was asked about the violence they faced and that the founder Lucetta Scaraffia and all-female staff of the magazine "stepped down en masse citing what they call a newly difficult work environment and a Vatican attempt to undercut the women's voices on sensitive issues, including the sexual abuse of nuns." Harlan and Pitrelli describe the Vatican as "a male-dominated world" and note that the magazine only "recently captured global attention" after its report on the abuse of nuns by clerics and of forced abortions. They not only include the response from *L'Osservatore Romano* (the Vatican newspaper) editor Andrea Monda, who maintained that *Women Church World* was not being "disempowered" or interfered with, but they also note Scaraffia felt *L'Osservatore Romano* "had been publishing pieces that contradicted the *Women Church World* editorial line" and that an attempt to replace her with Monda had occurred.[59] This article shows the pressure women face following the voicing of allegations, even women employed by the Vatican.

In "#NunsToo: How the Catholic Church has worked to silence women challenging abuse," Lila Rice Goldenberg[60] offers historical perspective that provides a fuller understanding for readers following the stories of sexual abuse of nuns by clergy. Her reporting in *The Washington Post's* "Made in History" series presents the nuns as credible and shows the pattern of silencing that has allowed the abuse to continue relatively unchecked. Goldenberg offers examples that date back hundreds of years, damning evidence that bolsters the credibility of contemporary nuns and sisters and their harrowing stories of intimidation, blackmail, and expulsion following reporting abuse by clergy. By including this article tracing the historical legacy of suppression, *The Washington Post* not only provides readers a deeper understanding of the long story of sexual abuse of women religious but also illuminates why the Vatican has felt safe in its perpetrations of injustices against these victims and others.

Another article from *The Washington Post's* "Made by History" series illuminates the suppression of women's voices and survivor testimonies by the Catholic Church. In "When the Catholic Church's Prohibition on Scandal Helped Women," Sara McDougall explains that "causing scandal was considered a sin not just for the perpetrator of the sin, but also for anyone who made that sin public." This understanding "has tragically justified the quiet transfer of pedophile priests from one diocese to another," she writes. However, much of the article illuminates how pregnant nuns in medieval Europe received care as a result of this policy. Nevertheless, McDougall offers this story as an example of an alternative mode of response. "What is needed [. . .] is another version of scandal theology: the notion that public confession, restitution and rehabilitation can forge a more authentic community of the faithful, and ultimately, a more authentic experience of faith."[61] Her call for reform and revitalization offers optimism for the future of the church and women's places within it.

Disappointingly, though, *The Washington Post,* despite its careful attention to the topic, did not cover the symposium held by Voices of Faith, an international initiative to empower women in the Catholic Church, on

November 27, 2018, in Rome. During the symposium entitled "Overcoming Silence—Women's Voices in the Catholic Abuse Crisis," several survivors of abuse by priests told their stories. Unlike the mainstream news articles on the abuse, the survivors indict the patriarchal and hierarchical structure of the church that devalues women. In the opening address, Professor Cettina Militello asserts, "behind violence, there is always the delusion of omnipotence [. . .] behind this kind of violence is the very special presumption that they have as churchmen to feel and be recognized as holders of a sacred power. Precisely for this reason, they place themselves above the rules."[62] Other participants at the symposium agreed. Former nun Doris Wagner states, "The reason why they don't act, it's the monarchical power of the church [. . .] It's the fact that there is no proper separation of powers inside the Church."[63] Furthermore, Wagner insists, "Their lack of action makes it very clear that they are not acting in the interest of the Church."[64] Wagner here reminds listeners and readers that the church is not merely the empowered hierarchy but also the women religious and the body of believers. The incredible accounts offered in the symposium could have yielded significant news reports and insight into ways the patriarchal structure of the church contribute to its very own rape culture, but this symposium organized by women and dominated by survivors' voices did not garner the same media attention as the Vatican's summit.

WHAT #NUNSTOO MEANS FOR FUTURE RESPONSES OF THE CHURCH

The harrowing reports in the "Overcoming Silence" symposium give voice to despair at the pattern of exploitation, abuse, concealment, and corruption in the church, but their call to action inspires hope. The dearth of coverage on this symposium is disheartening. Helpful to the cause of justice and reform, though, is the fact that in none of the aforementioned articles by *The Washington Post*, *The New York Times*, and *NPR* reporters do the claims of women religious come under suspicion. Their reporters do not explicitly side with the nuns and sisters or against alleged perpetrators, but they break from media practices that made it harder for victims of sexual assault to achieve perceptions of credibility by providing contextual information on the pattern of suppression of disclosures of abuse, the history of relocations rather than removals of offender priests, and discussions of patriarchal structures that contribute to the disempowerment of women religious and dismissals of crimes against them. By avoiding the homophobic and pedophilic framing of the past, by including women's voices, and by refusing to engage in common patterns of sexual assault reporting that paint sympathetic portraits of accused perpetrators, recent mainstream media coverage of #NunsToo, particularly that of *The Washington Post,* has not been complicit in propping up rape culture in the ways some media outlets have done in the past. Joseph Adebayo, NRF Innovation Postdoctoral Fellow in Africa Studies at the University of Cape Town, insists, "It is callous, inconceivable and insensitive for journalists to remain aloof and disconnected in the face of social injustice and tyranny."[65] Though the reporters of *The Washington Post* and *NPR* preserve neutrality in their coverage of the sexual abuse of nuns by clergy, they do not remain aloof but offer enough consideration of the Vatican hegemony and inclusion of women's perspectives to connect the plight of women religious experiencing sexual assault at the hands of clergy to the larger cultural conversations about the epidemic of sexual assault disproportionately affecting women and girls.

Journalists are crucial in the fight to transform rape culture and the efforts to reduce violence against women and girls. Media mistreatment of victims has kept victims from coming forward and has allowed harmful institutional practices to continue. Yet careful, balanced, and victim-centered reporting can have the opposite effect. Following the emergence of #MeToo, the media are less likely to ignore violence against women and girls or sexual violence against victims of all genders. But how they cover it will make dramatic differences in the lives of survivors. The media can sensationalize violence against women and girls to gain clicks and sell ads, or they can help violence prevention activists by framing narratives and disseminating information in socially responsible ways. In "The Task of Peace Journalism," founder of Peace Studies Johan Galtung says, "To say that violence is the only thing that sells is to insult humanity [. . .] People are demanding something else and it's not that difficult. So, the opposite is much more complicated: it consists of all those who have a stake in the conflict, to whom the outcome matters."[66] #MeToo activists and participants demanded something else—attention, recognition, and respectful considerations of the problem of sexual violence, as well as deeper understandings of rape culture. Much work remains, but the effects of this social movement are already evident in the ways in which the media is responding to reports of sexual assault. Will the Vatican change course as well?

The women religious who have come forward, as well as others assaulted by clergy and even members of the church who have not experienced abuse, have expressed their dismay at what it has taken to get the Vatican to respond. "We feel a little disappointed that it has to be the media who has to press the church and the Pope to comment," says Zuzanna Flisowska, the general manager of Voices of Faith.[67] Their disappointment is surely justified. The Vatican should have responded of its own volition from the very first report of abuse. The Vatican should have responded in ways that prevented further violence and protected victims rather than perpetrators. Still, church reform activists have harnessed the power of media pressure to address injustices long concealed and unaddressed. Members of the media, too, have realized the role they can play in reform. The aforementioned Mexican journalist who has reported on five papacies, Valentine Alazraki, warned the Vatican at its summit on sexual abuse, "If you do not decide in a radical way to be on the side of the children, mothers, families, civil society, you are right to be afraid of us, because we journalists, who seek the common good, will be your worst enemies."[68] The church leadership seems finally to realize the reputation, if not the future, of the church is at stake. According to Lila Rice Goldenberg, "In the #MeToo era, the Vatican's attempts to discredit those women who speak out against sexual abuse and harassment by members of the clergy may seem like a desperate ploy to preserve its own fast-eroding moral authority."[69] Victims, activists, church members, and others have long hoped for a compassionate, trauma-informed Vatican response stemming from concern for the victims of violence, but many see only a too-late reaction motivated by self-preservation.

This onslaught of media coverage did yield admission of the horrific pattern of violence and promise of reform. Not only have many victims come forward to share their stories and to demand change in the church, in *Vos Estis Lux Mundi*, a papal decree that went into effect June 1, 2019, Pope Francis acknowledged "The crimes of sexual abuse offend Our Lord, cause physical, psychological and spiritual damage to the victims and harm the community of the faithful" and issued new regulations requiring the reporting of sexual abuse. He also stated, "An obligation to keep silent may not be imposed on any person with regard to the contents of his or her report."[70] This is a step in the right direction.

The leadership of activists and survivors should steer these efforts. Activists and this author hope the Vatican solicits their guidance. Dr. Figueroa Alvear asserts, "I am convinced that the victims themselves are the prophetic voices that will help in the renewal of the Church." Those harmed by prior policy failures and cover-ups have crucial insight to offer, insight sorely needed by those whose failures allowed such abuse to continue unchecked. Chantal Götz, Managing Director of Voices of Faith, says, "I refuse to live in a world where abuse of power by leaders in this church remains unchallenged. I refuse to live in a world where women's voices are drowned out, unheard or silenced. I refuse to live in a world where the scales of equality are tipped to favour one gender over the other."[71] Though prior media framing of sexual assault and the Catholic Church sexual abuse crisis had been tipped toward men and boys in initial reports and responses, the transformative effects of #MeToo on media practices are evident in the recent coverage of the longstanding, centuries-old problem of violence against women religious by clergy. This better balance wrought by #MeToo and #NunsToo has finally forced Pope Francis and Vatican officials to address violence against women and girls. When an institution will not hold itself accountable, the media can help by shedding light on its injustices. The effects of this on church reform remain to be seen, but the change in reporting offers hope that change in the Vatican response to the violence against its own women religious might follow.

NOTES

1. @lamarquesina (Lulu Marquez), "#nunstoo," *Twitter* (March 1, 2018). https://twitter.com/lamarquesina/status/969420961555632140.

2. Elisabetta Povoledo, "In Vatican Magazine *Exposé*, Nuns Reveal Their Economic Exploitation." *New York Times* (March 1, 2018). Accessed July 31, 2019. https://www.nytimes.com/2018/03/01/world/europe/vatican-catholic-church-nuns-work.html. The first tweet using #nunstoo was posted in 2013, but it did not reference sexual misconduct. View the English-language tweets including #nunstoo here: https://twitter.com/hashtag/nunstoo?lang=en.

3. "History and Vision." *MeToo Movement.* Accessed July 31, 2019. https://metoomvmt.org/about/#history.

4. Alyssa Milano, #MeToo tweet (October 17, 2017). https://twitter.com/Alyssa_Milano/status/919659438700670976.

5. Cassandra Santiago and Doug Criss, "An Activist, a Little Girl, and the Heartbreaking Origin of 'Me too,'" *CNN* (October 17, 2017). Accessed October 27, 2019. https://www.cnn.com/2017/10/17/us/me-too-tarana-burke-origin-trnd/index.html.

6. Though the terms "nuns" and "sisters" are often used interchangeably, nuns are those women who typically reside in cloistered or semi-cloistered monasteries as contemplatives whereas sisters are apostolic and participate in ministries that take them outside of their residences into work in fields such as education, healthcare, or social work, and for causes such as environmental protections, immigration reform, reducing homelessness, and eliminating sex trafficking. Both nuns and sisters take vows of poverty, chastity, and obedience. The term "women religious" includes both groups.

7. John T. Chinball, Ann Wold, and Paul N. Duckro, "A National Survey of the Sexual Trauma Experiences of Catholic Nuns." *Review of Religious Research* 40, no. 2 (Dec. 1998): 142–167.

8. Globe Spotlight Team reporters Matt Carroll, Sacha Pfeiffer, and Michael Rezendes; and editor Walter V. Robinson, "Church Allowed Abuse by Priest for Years (Part 1 of 2)," and "A Revered Guest: A Family Left in Shreds." *The Boston Globe* (January 6, 2002). Accessed July 31, 2019, https://www.bostonglobe.com/news/special-reports/2002/01/06/church-allowed-abuse-priest-for-years/cSHfGkTIrAT25qKGvBuDNM/story.html. Also, "Geoghan Preferred Preying on Poorer Children (Part 2 of 2)." *The Boston Globe* (January 7, 2002). Accessed July 31, 2019. https://www3.bostonglobe.com/news/special-reports/2002/01/07/geoghan-prefer

red-preying-poorer-children/69DE1kOuETjphwmIBcgzCM/story.html?arc404=true. The Globe Spotlight team published ten additional reports on this topic from January 31 to December 14, 2002.

9. Bill Smith, "Nuns as Sexual Victims Get Little Notice; An Estimated 40 pct. Were Victimized, Some by Priests, Other Nuns, Survey Found." *St. Louis Post-Dispatch*, (2003, January 5), A1. Reprinted on *SNAP Network*. Accessed July 31, 2019. https://www.snapnetwork.org/female_victims/nuns_as_victims.htm.

10. Mary Marcel, "Incommensurable Data, Procrustean Paradigms: Why News of Sexual Abuse of Nuns by Priests Never Made your Hometown Newspaper." *Proceedings of the Alta Biennial Conference on Argumentation* (August 2007), 508.

11. Sascha Pfeiffer, "Women Face Stigma of Clergy Abuse." *The Boston Globe* (December 27, 2002). Accessed July 31, 2019. https://archive.boston.com/globe/spotlight/abuse/stories4/122702_women.htm.

12. Mary Marcel, "Victim Gender in News Coverage of the Priest Sex Crisis by the Boston Globe." *Women's Studies in Communication* 36 (2013), 298.

13. Marcel, "Incommensurable Data," 510.

14. Marcel, "Victim Gender," 290.

15. Ibid., 291.

16. SNAP, the Survivors Network of Those Abused by Priests, was founded by Barbara Blaine in 1988 and is a support group for women and men wounded by religious and institutional authorities. Following the publication of abuse stories by *The Boston Globe*, SNAP opened a national office in Chicago in 2003 following a surge in requests for support. For more on the history and activism of SNAP, visit their "About" webpage at https://www.snapnetwork.org/about.

17. Marcel, "Incommensurable Data," 509.

18. Ibid., 511.

19. Marcel, "Victim Gender," 289.

20. *Overcoming Silence: Women's Voices in the Catholic Abuse Crisis.* Rome: Voices of Faith (November 27, 2018), 49. Accessed July 31, 2019. https://xn--vulnerabilittsdiskurs-h2b.de/wp-content/uploads/Breaking_the_Silence-VoicesofFaithMagazine2019.pdf.

21. *Overcoming Silence.*

22. Marcel, "Incommensurable Data," 511.

23. Ibid., 512.

24. Marcel, "Victim Gender," 296.

25. Marcel, "Incommensurable Data," 509.

26. Kimberly A. Lonsway and Louise F. Fitzgerald, "Rape Myths: In Review." *Psychology of Women Quarterly* 18, no. 2 (June 1994), 134.

27. Marcel, "Victim Gender," 292.

28. Amy Grubb and Emily Turner, "Attribution of Blame in Rape Cases: A Review of the Impact of Rape Myth Acceptance, Gender Role Conformity and Substance Use on Victim Blaming." *Aggression and Violent Behavior* 17, no. 5 (2012), 445.

29. Sascha Pfeiffer, "Women Face Stigma of Clergy Abuse." *The Boston Globe* (December 27, 2002). Accessed July 31, 2019. https://archive.boston.com/globe/spotlight/abuse/stories4/122702_women.htm.

30. Marcel, "Victim Gender," 294.
31. *Overcoming Silence*, 26.
32. Marcel, "Victim Gender," 291.
33. *Overcoming Silence*, 19.
34. Ibid., 26.
35. Marcel, "Victim Gender," 293.
36. See Jessica Valenti's *The Purity Myth* (New York: Seal Press, 2009).
37. Marcel, "Victim Gender," 293.
38. Ibid.
39. Ibid., 305.
40. See M. Baum and P. Gussin, "Issue Bias: How Issue Coverage and Media Bias Affect Voter Perceptions of Elections." Paper presented at 2005 Meeting of the American Political Science Association, Washington DC. Retrieved from https://www.hks.harvard.edu/fs/mbaum/documents/IssueBias_APSA05.pdf. Accessed July 31, 2019. See also S. Knoblock-Westerwick and L. D. Taylor, "The Blame Game: Elements of Causal Attribution and Its Impact on Siding with Agents in the News." *Communication Research*, 35 (2008): 723–744.
41. Ashlie J. Siefkes-Andrew and Cassandra Alexopoulos, "Framing Blame in Sexual Assault: An Analysis of Attributions in News Stories About Sexual Assault on College Campuses." *Violence Against Women* 25, no. 6 (2019): 747.
42. Siefkes-Andrew and Alexopoulos, "Framing Blame in Sexual Assault," 748.
43. Ibid., 752.
44. Ibid.
45. In addition to the articles cited in the body of this paper, I also examined Jason Horowitz, "Sexual Abuse of Nuns: Longstanding Church Scandal Emerges From Shadows." *The New York Times* (February 6, 2019); Megan Specia, "Gay Priests, Secret Rules and the Abuse of Nuns: Some of the Vatican Controversies as Bishops Meet." *The New York Times* (February 21, 2019); Nicole Winfield and Rodney Muhumuza, "After Decades of Silence, Nuns Talk About Abuse by Priests." *AP* (July 27, 2018); Amy Wang, "Vatican Chief Who Handled Sexual Abuse Cases Resigns After Accusations of Sexual Abuse." *The Independent* (January 30, 2019); Farrah Tomazin, "Forgotten Victims of Priest Sexual Abuse. They Were Not Children But Could they Consent?." *The Sydney Morning Herald* (December 9, 2018); Patsy McGarry, "The Irish Woman Who Exposed Abuse of Nun by Priests 25 Years Ago." *The Irish Times* (February 10, 2019); Ann Wolf Hodges and John T. Chibnall, "Breaking the Culture of Silence and Secrecy." *The St. Louis Post Dispatch* (February 28, 2019); Susan Shaw, "In the Wake of #NunsToo, It's Time for Repentance and Conversion." *Ms. Magazine* (February 7, 2019); Kathleen McPhillips, "Catholic Church Headed for Another Sex Abuse Scandal as #NunsToo Speak Up." *Christianity Today* (February 15, 2019); and Melissa Bell, Saskya Vandoorne and Laura Smith-Spark, CNN, "They Say they were Sexually Abused by Priests, then Silenced. Now they're Speaking Out." *The St. Louis Post Dispatch* (February 20, 2019).
46. Jason Horowitz and Elizabeth Dias, "Pope Acknowledges Nuns Were Sexually Abused by Priests and Bishops." *The New York Times* (February 5, 2019). Accessed

July 31, 2019. https://www.nytimes.com/2019/02/05/world/europe/pope-nuns-sexual-abuse.html.

47. Horowitz and Dias, "Pope Acknowledges Nuns Were Sexually Abused by Priests and Bishops."

48. Ibid.

49. Ibid.

50. Sylvia Poggioli, "After Years of Abuse by Priests, #NunsToo Are Speaking Out." *NPR. Morning Edition* (March 18, 2019). Accessed July 31, 2019. https://www.npr.org/2019/03/18/703067602/after-years-of-abuse-by-priests-nunstoo-are-speaking-out.

51. See John L. Allen, Jr. and Pamela Schaeffer, "Reports of Abuse: AIDS Exacerbates Sexual Exploitation of Nuns, Reports Allege." *National Catholic Reporter* (March 16, 2001). Accessed July 31, 2019. https://natcath.org/NCR_Online/archives2/2001a/031601/031601a.htm.

52. Poggioli, "After Years of Abuse."

53. Max J. Rosenthal and Michelle Boorstein, "Pope Francis Confirms Catholic Clergy Members Abused Nuns." *The Washington Post* (February 6, 2019). Accessed July 31, 2019. https://www.washingtonpost.com/world/2019/02/05/pope-francis-confirms-catholic-clergy-members-abused-nuns/.

54. Marcel, "Incommensurable Data," 510.

55. Ruby Mellen, "Pope Francis Is Holding the Vatican's First Summit on Sexual Abuse. Recent Scandals Suggest It Is Long Overdue." *The Washington Post* (February 21, 2019). Accessed July 31, 2019. https://www.washingtonpost.com/world/2019/02/21/pope-francis-is-holding-vaticans-first-summit-sexual-abuse-recent-scandals-suggest-its-long-overdue/.

56. See Jamie Manson's, "Why the Sex Abuse Summit Accomplished Nothing." *National Catholic Reporter* (March 6, 2019). Accessed September 7, 2019. https://www.ncronline.org/news/accountability/grace-margins/why-sex-abuse-summit-accomplished-nothing.

57. *Overcoming Silence*, 48.

58. Chico Harlan and Stefano Pitrelli, "Founder and Staff of Vatican Women's Magazine Step Down, Citing Pressure over Nun Abuse Stories." *The Washington Post* (March 26, 2019). Accessed July 31, 2019. https://www.washingtonpost.com/world/europe/founder-and-staff-of-vatican-womens-magazine-step-down-citing-pressure-over-nun-abuse-stories/2019/03/26/c32c591c-4fb0-11e9-88a1-ed346f0ec94f_story.html.

59. Ibid.

60. Lila Rice Goldenberg, "#NunsToo: How the Catholic Church Has Worked to Silence Women Challenging Abuse." *The Washington Post* (April 17, 2019). Accessed July 31, 2019. https://www.washingtonpost.com/outlook/2019/04/17/nunstoo-how-catholic-church-has-worked-silence-women-challenging-abuse/.

61. Sara McDougall, "When the Catholic Church's Prohibition on Scandal Helped Women." *The Washington Post* (February 2, 2019). Accessed July 31, 2019. https://www.washingtonpost.com/outlook/2019/02/13/when-catholic-churchs-prohibition-scandal-helped-women/.

62. *Overcoming Silence*, 7.
63. Ibid., 20.
64. Ibid.
65. Joseph Olusegun Adebayo, "The Role of Peace Journalism in the Deconstruction of Elections and the 'national question' in Nigeria." *International Journal of African Renaissance Studies*, 12, no. 1 (May 2017), 150.
66. Johan Galtung, "The Task of Peace Journalism." *Ethical Perspectives*, 7, nos. 2–3 (2000), 163.
67. Jason Horowitz, "Sexual Abuse of Nuns: Longstanding Church Scandal Emerges from Shadows." *The New York Times* (February 6, 2019). Accessed July 31, 2019. https://www.nytimes.com/2019/02/06/world/europe/pope-francis-sexual-abuse-nuns.html?module=inline.
68. Emily Tamkin, "How Women Raised Their Voices at the Vatican." *The Washington Post* (February 23, 2019). Accessed July 31, 2019. https://www.washingtonpost.com/world/2019/02/23/how-women-raised-their-voices-vatican/.
69. Lila Rice Goldenberg, "#NunsToo: How the Catholic Church Has Worked to Silence Women Challenging Abuse." *The Washington Post* (April 17, 2019). Accessed July 31, 2019. https://www.washingtonpost.com/outlook/2019/04/17/nunstoo-how-catholic-church-has-worked-silence-women-challenging-abuse/.
70. Francis. "VOS ESTIS LUX MUNDI." The Holy See (May 7, 2019). Accessed July 31, 2019. http://w2.vatican.va/content/francesco/en/motu_proprio/documents/papa-francesco-motu-proprio-20190507_vos-estis-lux-mundi.html
71. *Overcoming Silence,* 61.

BIBLIOGRAPHY

Adebayo, Joseph Olusegun. "The Role of Peace Journalism in the Deconstruction of Elections and the "national question" in Nigeria." *International Journal of African Renaissance Studies* 12, no.1 (May 2017): 140–156.

Baum, M., and Gussin, P. "Issue Bias: How Issue Coverage and Media Bias Affect Voter Perceptions of Elections." (2005, September). Paper Presented at 2005 Meeting of the American Political Science Association, Washington DC. https://www.hks.harvard.edu/fs/mbaum/documents/IssueBias_APSA05.pdf.

Chibnall, John T., Ann Wold and Paul N. Duckro. "A National Survey of the Sexual Trauma Experiences of Catholic Nuns." *Review of Religious Research* 40, no. 2 (Dec. 1998): 142–167.

Duggan, Paul. "Girl Testifies She Was Repeatedly Kissed and Groped by D.C. Catholic Priest." *The Washington Post,* August 7, 2019. https://www.washingtonpost.com/local/public-safety/girl-testifies-she-was-repeatedly-kissed-and-groped-by-dc-catholic-priest/2019/08/07/4199dabc-b952-11e9-b3b4-2bb69e8c4e39_story.html.

Duggan, Paul. "Girl Testifies that Priest Caressed Her Knee During Confession." *The Washington Post,* August 8, 2019. https://www.washingtonpost.com/local/public-safety/priest-caressed-girls-knee-during-confession-she-testifies-as-child-s ex-abuse-case-continues/2019/08/08/588a6b16-ba23-11e9-a091-6a96e67d9cce_story.html.

Francis. "VOS ESTIS LUX MUNDI." *The Holy See,* May 7, 2019. http://w2.vatican.va/content/francesco/en/motu_proprio/documents/papa-francesco-motu-proprio-20190507_vos-estis-lux-mundi.html

Galtung, Johan. "The Task of Peace Journalism." *Ethical Perspectives* 7, no. 2–3 (2000): 162–167.

Goldenberg, Lila Rice. "#NunsToo: How the Catholic Church Has Worked to Silence Women Challenging Abuse." *The Washington Post,* April 17, 2019. https://www.washingtonpost.com/outlook/2019/04/17/nunstoo-how-catholic-church-has-worked-silence-women-challenging-abuse/.

Grubb, Amy and Emily Turner. "Attribution of Blame in Rape Cases: A Review of the Impact of Rape Myth Acceptance, Gender Role Conformity and Substance Use on Victim Blaming." *Aggression and Violent Behavior* 17, no. 5 (2012): 443–452.

Harlan, Chico and Stefano Pitrelli. "Founder and Staff of Vatican Women's Magazine Step Down, Citing Pressure Over Nun Abuse Stories." *The Washington Post,* March 26, 2019. https://www.washingtonpost.com/world/europe/founder-and-staff-of-vatican-womens-magazine-step-down-citing-pressure-over-nun-abuse-stories/2019/03/26/c32c591c-4fb0-11e9-88a1-ed346f0ec94f_story.html.

Horowitz, Jason and Elizabeth Dias. "Pope Acknowledges Nuns Were Sexually Abused by Priests and Bishops." *The New York Times,* February 5, 2019. https://www.nytimes.com/2019/02/05/world/europe/pope-nuns-sexual-abuse.html.

Horowitz, Jason. "Sexual Abuse of Nuns: Longstanding Church Scandal Emerges from Shadows." *The New York Times,* February 6, 2019. https://www.nytimes.com/2019/02/06/world/europe/pope-francis-sexual-abuse-nuns.html?module=inline.

Knoblock-Westerwick, S. and L. D. Taylor. "The Blame Game: Elements of Causal Attribution and Its Impact on Siding with Agents in the News." *Communication Research* 35 (2008): 723–744.

Lonsway, Kimberly A. and Louise F. Fitzgerald. "Rape Myths: In Review." *Psychology of Women Quarterly* 18, no. 2 (June 1994): 133–164.

Marcel, Mary. "Incommensurable Data, Procrustean Paradigms: Why News of Sexual Abuse of Nuns by Priests Never Made Your Hometown Newspaper." *Proceedings of the Alta Biennial Conference on Argumentation* (August 2007), 506–514.

Marcel, Mary. "Victim Gender in News Coverage of the Priest Sex Crisis by the Boston Globe." *Women's Studies in Communication* 36 (2013): 288–311.

McDougall, Sara. "When the Catholic Church's Prohibition on Scandal Helped Women." *The Washington Post,* February 2, 2019. https://www.washingtonpost.com/outlook/2019/02/13/when-catholic-churchs-prohibition-scandal-helped-women/.

Mellen, Ruby. "Pope Francis Is Holding the Vatican's First Summit on Sexual Abuse. Recent Scandals Suggest It Is Long Overdue." *The Washington Post,* February 21, 2019. https://www.washingtonpost.com/world/2019/02/21/pope-francis-is-holding-vaticans-first-summit-sexual-abuse-recent-scandals-suggest-its-long-overdue/.

Overcoming Silence: Women's Voices in the Catholic Abuse Crisis. Rome: Voices of Faith. November 27, 2018. https://xn--vulnerabilittsdiskursh2b.de/wpcontent/uploads/Breaking_the_Silence-VoicesofFaithMagazine2019.pdf.

Pfeiffer, Sascha. "Women Face Stigma of Clergy Abuse." *The Boston Globe,* December 27, 2002. https://archive.boston.com/globe/spotlight/abuse/stories4/122702_women.htm.

Poggioli, Sylvia. "After Years of Abuse by Priests, #NunsToo Are Speaking Out." *NPR. Morning Edition,* March 18, 2019. https://www.npr.org/2019/03/18/703067602/after-years-of-abuse-by-priests-nunstoo-are-speaking-out.

"Report on Nuns Draws Large Response." *LA Times.* Times Wire Reports, January 12, 2003. https://www.latimes.com/archives/la-xpm-2003-jan-12-na-briefs12.1-story.html.

Rosenthal, Max J., and Michelle Boorstein. "Pope Francis Confirms Catholic Clergy Members Abused Nuns." *The Washington Post,* February 6, 2019. https://www.washingtonpost.com/world/2019/02/05/pope-francis-confirms-catholic-clergy - members-abused-nuns/.

Siefkes-Andrew, Ashlie J. and Cassandra Alexopoulos. "Framing Blame in Sexual Assault: An Analysis of Attributions in News Stories About Sexual Assault on College Campuses. *Violence against Women* 25, no. 6 (2019): 743–762.

Smith, Bill. "Nuns as Sexual Victims Get Little Notice; An Estimated 40 pct. Were Victimized, Some by Priests, Other Nuns, Survey Found." *St. Louis Post-Dispatch* (Missouri), January 5, 2003, p. A1. Reprinted on *SNAP Network* https://www.snapnetwork.org/female_victims/nuns_as_victims.htm.

"Study Details Abuse, Harassment of Nuns." *The St. Louis Post Dispatch,* January 5, 2003. Reprinted at *The Baltimore Sun* https://www.baltimoresun.com/news/bs-xpm-2003-01-05-0301050301-story.html.

Tamkin, Emily. "How Women Raised their Voices at the Vatican." *The Washington Post,* February 23, 2019. https://www.washingtonpost.com/world/2019/02/23/how-women-raised-their-voices-vatican/.

Thompson, G. *Guide to Reporting.* London, UK: HarperCollins, 1994.

Valenti, Jessica. *The Purity Myth.* New York: Seal Press, 2009.

Chapter 8

The Perfect Victim

Childhood Sexual Trauma and Gendered Catholic Identity

Jo Scott-Coe

OPENING A WOUND OF UNDERSTANDING: METHOD AND APPROACH

My first sexual experiences with another person were not consensual—a reality that took me nearly four decades to understand, a reality I am only beginning to articulate. These experiences were violating and traumatizing, but not violent. The consequences in my life were chronic over time, compounded by my earliest social circumstances and engagement with religious ritual. I do not seek, nor would I be entitled to, legal remedies, nor do I intend here to overstate or understate what happened. Finding the words to name my reality has been challenging, and part of me still believes strongly that there is no one to hear. Many adults never disclose to anyone.[1]

I come to this essay as an outgrowth of a six-year period of research for a book exploring Catholicism, gender, and abuse of multiple kinds (domestic, sexual, clerical, and institutional). In *MASS: A Sniper, a Father, and a Priest*,[2] I documented new threads of information in the 1966 University of Texas at Austin tower massacre. I was the first researcher to examine the influence of the white, mid-century American Catholic milieu on the shooter, Charles Whitman, whose scoutmaster and confidante from approximately nine years old until seven days before the shooting was a problem priest—a now-deceased priest who, nine months after publication of my book, was named by his archdiocese as "credibly accused" of abusing children.[3] I have written extensively about Whitman's abusive family of origin, his own abusive marriage, his superficial expressions of morality, and his objectification of women, including his wife and his devout Catholic mother, both of whom he brutally stabbed in private before committing his public massacre.[4]

In many ways, my most recent writing and research process—combined with ongoing and intense therapy over the last ten years—gradually helped me to adjust the lens on very grainy "mini-movies" that have replayed over and over in my head as long as I can remember, at times more intensely and anxiously than others. I realize also that those mini movies are precisely what drew me toward the subjects I have been studying and writing about for most of my academic and professional career. In order to recompose my story, I first have to take it apart and reassemble, creating what Rachel Josefowitz Siegel terms "bibliotherapy."[5] I also seek to employ Michel Foucault's "genealogical" method to trace my idiosyncratic experience of Catholic ritual.[6] Because I am trained in the disciplines of rhetoric and literary criticism, with an emphasis in gender studies, composition theory, and education, I will approach my own narrative of damage by "reading" and interpreting it, reasonably applying terms and concepts from psychology, theology, and literature without a posture of final professional diagnosis or doctrinal argument.

As personal context, I offer several elements of my background. My mother was devout, a pre-Vatican II convert at around the age of fifteen, whereas my father "kind of" converted prior to their marriage at a university Newman Center in 1965.[7] My father never fully and comfortably embraced the tradition. He took us to mass and attended with us sometimes, but he never knelt in church, crossed himself, or went to confession. Sometimes he played organ at mass. Both my parents seemed to admire religious figures generally, including Archbishop Fulton Sheen, who had been on television and radio during their childhoods. My father seemed to like the structure the church provided for his family, though he did not seem to think that the rules for us applied to him. Both of my parents were survivors of childhood trauma, about which they spoke very little. My father's mother died when he was sixteen years old; my mother's father had abandoned the family when she was a child, the youngest of five children.

I recall very little supervision during my own childhood, both before and after the birth of my younger sister. Between 1969 and 1983, we moved five times because my father entered the military. My sister and I never went hungry, but my father was largely uninvolved in our lives, except to lay down angry or sudden discipline, jags of enthusiasm, or arbitrary critiques. He freely commented on my body—my ankles, my thighs; my weight (too heavy or too skinny)—in a way that communicated that I was not "right" and that my body did not fully belong to me. My mother did her best to fend for herself and for us, but she too was deeply wounded and self-involved, mostly deferring to our father's judgment and temperament. There were palpable swings of mood in the house, and my sister and I were emotionally neglected. On the outside, I imagine we looked like the model family, but I was disoriented and anxious much of the time, eager for models of any adult, friend, or stranger, who could show me alternative ways of being in the world. I look back and am stunned by my own desperation as much as I am stunned by my native instincts for survival. Some of my most vivid memories prior to my sister's birth involve confusing experiences of discipline and punishment, not knowing whether a rule, or a task, or a reprieve offered by my mother was a trick or a test destined to land me in trouble again. I adapted by becoming externally amenable, deferential, and compliant, hiding any discomfort or turmoil I did not understand, and suppressing any rebellions that I intuited would only be doomed within our family system.

My troubling incidents took place at a female friend's house in a working-class Midwest town, between 1976 and 1977. I was between seven and eight years old, a brand new "Air Force brat" attending a neighborhood public school, terrified of being alone at lunch or on the playground, desperate for protection if not friendship. Over a period of several months, perhaps a year, this girl "played with" me, the most upsetting and abrupt occasions taking place with another boy from our school. I remember not wanting to enter the room one afternoon when I could see that something was already happening: the boy seated at the edge of a bed, his pants off, and my friend waving me toward them. I remember not wanting to touch the boy's penis with my hand and mouth just because she showed me how. I remember feeling scared as I "stood watch" the way I was told, outside the closet where she and the boy were doing something I could not see ("It feels good," I heard her say). I remember not wanting to go into the closet with him even though I did so, while my friend said she would guard the door. I remember him standing there with his genitals exposed, and my not pulling down my pants far enough in the dim space even though the boy said "pull them lower" as he reached and grabbed to pull them further anyway. I remember the fear and humiliation and also relief when my friend's sister yanked open the closet door and yelled something. The camera stops there.

I returned to that house on many occasions because I saw the girl as my only friend and because, in my childlike perception, I decided that I had nowhere else to go. I do not know if that day was my last visit. I recall that my friend and the boy were around the same age as I, but even at the time I thought each of them looked gray and strangely tired and shriveled, like much older people. I remember that the incidents made me feel ashamed, confused, and scared. I now wonder how my friend's disordered behavior indicated that she was herself sexually disturbed or traumatized, perhaps because she had experienced physical boundary violations, abuse, and/or had prematurely witnessed sexual activity.

Prior to these incidents, there had been several stages of disordered sexual interactions that I found confusing. I remember not wanting to follow my friend into the bathroom when she used the toilet, but that when she called me to come, I did. I did not understand why, when I told her how I "liked" a boy in our second or third grade class, she presented me with a cartoonish crayon drawing of a naked boy and a naked girl, complete with our names and exaggerated genitals. I remember not liking it when she lifted up my shirt and kissed my chest, and how I froze, staring awkwardly at the wall and the ceiling while she did it. I remember not resisting her kisses in a sad playhouse she and her sister had created in the yard out of giant cardboard boxes, and also out in a back shed that was like a converted garage. Most vividly, in the pit of my belly, I remember that saying "no" or "don't do that" or "I am not comfortable" never felt like an option.

For a brief time overlapping this period, I engaged in sexually precocious activities—which I can now distinguish as being consensual—with other children my age, in situations where there was talking and sexual touching but no nudity. I remember one boy that I saw fairly often telling me that I was too "ugly" to have sex with. I vaguely recall suggesting to a much older neighborhood boy that we could "play around" in the basement, a memory that deeply alarms me as an adult—as much as I am both sad and relieved to remember how he dismissed the idea with a vulgar gesture toward to a poster on his wall, a naked woman brandishing a sword, as the standard by which I was being measured ("Later," he said, "when you look like that").

I remember the swarms of much older unsupervised teens around our block, mostly white boys prowling on bikes, blasting KISS from car stereos, and seeming to be perpetually leering and laughing—a laughter I interpreted at the time with deep vigilance, as if it meant toxic indifference or, worse, foreshadowed harm. I have vivid memories of feeling chronically exposed and afraid. If my mother was late to pick me up from somewhere, I panicked. If I came home from school for lunch and found the front door locked, I was terrified. Throughout my life, I have managed (or not managed) dueling states of low-grade, chronic anxiety and flares of panic and outrage that can, in part, be traced to this very confusing period.

As an adult forty years later, I see now how isolated and emotionally neglected I was inside my family system at the time, an understanding that I have denied most of my life, and which I offer here as a statement of simple recognition rather than blame. It was never an option to talk to my parents about what had happened, how I actually felt about it, or what I could do. The extent of my sexual education up to this point had been quiet admonitions not to touch myself in bed at night. Writing even now, I still feel the familiar, fierce clutch of tension, self-protection, and self-blame that plagued my child self. Those wary, tight sensations in stomach and throat, curling into shoulder muscles and across my chest, feel as fresh as they did when I stepped into those confusing scenes as a child whose identity had already been shaped to accommodate and please others.

While these early experiences were disturbing and violating, the deeper emotional and psychological wounds emerged in the months and years that followed, as I sought to compensate for the lack of a family confidante, counselor, or advocate by employing the Catholic rituals and practices that were available to me. While on the one hand I compartmentalized my feelings about these sexual events, I also took inappropriate ownership and responsibility, repeating and relitigating particular summaries or details that troubled me for many years afterward in the confessional, with proxy fathers who were priests. To a compulsive degree, I acted out a cycle that only compounded anxieties and further warped my self-image.

Different elements of Catholic teaching, ritual, imagery, and practice simultaneously damaged me and provided raw materials that are finally enabling me to understand what it means to parent one's self, to recognize the same vulnerability in others, and to mentor when possible—all work that remains very much in progress.

CHILD-ON-CHILD SEXUAL ABUSE (COCSA) DEFINED AND AVOIDED, IN SECULAR AND ROMAN CATHOLIC CONTEXT

Although it is a common phenomenon, COCSA is a relatively new area of inquiry and study. This fact should not be surprising given that the most significant strides in research and public policy related to supposedly "obvious crimes" of domestic violence, sexual assault, and other forms of abuse (within families or institutions) have their origins in the 1960s and 1970s.[8] Even the term "abuse" in itself is problematic when referring to disordered sexual activity perpetrated by a child prior to age twelve, the approximate onset of puberty.[9]

On the one hand, minimization or avoidance of COCSA seems tied to an adult unwillingness, or fear, to acknowledge or understand the sexuality of children. On the other hand, adults have few tools to address the subject without criminalizing behavior that falls within a broad spectrum of disordered actions requiring nuanced and caring therapeutic interventions rather than legal punishment. Discussion of COCSA also requires a degree of self-awareness that might well bring up uncomfortable personal histories for which there will be no ready forum or resolution. Discussion would also require adults to reflect on the subtle and overt messages they communicate to children about sexual behavior and expression, gender roles, and consent.

As a result of such complex dynamics, survivors of COCSA do not often merit attention or understanding, rendering them as "'victimological others'—persons whose experiences are discarded because they do not conform to accepted discourses of victimization."[10] From a practical point of view, unless such cases are referred to social workers or family court, there is no formal system to engage these situations, leaving children—and their families—to avoid, ignore, deny, or fend for themselves. If sexually disordered activity is acknowledged at all, a child may be simply stigmatized as "deviant" rather than treated.[11] If our approaches and categorizations do not evolve, we will continue to replicate dynamics that have historically enabled, perpetuated, and denied abuse of all kinds. Research demonstrates that the psychological consequences of COCSA (including anxiety, depression, and posttraumatic stress) are no less significant than in more commonly agreed-upon forms of abuse or assault.[12]

As James Kincaid points out in *Erotic Innocence: The Culture of Child Molesting*, a significant influence is our mass appetite for sensational, demonizing stories of extreme cases involving violence or sexual harm of children, whether as participants or victims. Most compelling is Kincaid's analysis that "this operatic spectacle" betrays a broader cultural problem: "a blank indifference to the fate of children."[13] Our collective emphasis on shame, blame, and criminalization displaces understanding, shared accountability, and thoughtful solutions. Whether through romanticizing or monster-making, these habits allow adults to pretend "that, after all, it's the child himself who is the source of pain that is visited on him."[14] Thus a secondary—and arguably more damaging—abuse occurs as children are left to bear the brunt of the blame, with no language, outlet, or social support to validate or resolve the original conflict or distress. Until very recently, most child victims carried this burden entirely alone.

Thankfully, experts across a spectrum of disciplines and professions are developing new research and educational tools, although notably much of this work originates in the United Kingdom. Stop it NOW! has produced a brochure to help adults distinguish between "'common' and 'uncommon', 'age-appropriate' and 'developmentally expected' sexual behavior" and "sexually harmful behavior" in children and minors up to sixteen years of age.[15] Parent resources include suggestions for open conversations about physical boundaries, self-respect, the right to say and accept "no." The materials also emphasize that parents need to stay aware of children's interactions and listen to what kids say.[16] Similarly, the webpage for the UK's National Society for the Prevention of Cruelty to Children (NSPCC) includes resources to help parents recognize not only signs that their child is a victim of abuse by another person, but may have harmed someone else as well.[17]

As with many other forms of sexual trauma, a common aspect of COCSA is that the child "is uncomfortable or confused . . . but may feel that he or she is willingly involved or to blame for being in the situation" or "enjoyed the sexual interaction and wanted it to happen."[18] Feelings of guilt, blame, and embarrassment are cited. Self-blame is particularly harmful when reinforced by silence, denial, and/or specific religious teachings and social training within the family. Redmond emphasizes how traditionally structured Christian households can make child victims "particularly vulnerable to an incomplete resolution" of any abuse, especially when it is so common for children not to confide or report an assault to parents. When children do tell, they are assumed to be "enjoying or willingly participating" in the abuse, which may be also brushed aside as easily forgotten, with "no long-lasting effects."[19]

Slowly, the discourse is beginning to evolve beyond avoidant and extreme or decontextualized notions of "good" and "evil," and toward more humanistic, sociological, and psychological frameworks. Some agencies in the United States have been awakening to these realities. A white paper published by the Florida Department of Children and Families documented the need for more systemic and national study of COCSA in the United States.[20] The paper provides "an overview of COCSA cases in the State of Florida" with "an emphasis on sexual abuse and sexual behavior problems among children under the age of twelve."[21] The authors emphasize the need for recognition and treatment rather than criminalization or labeling of juveniles as "sex offenders," and they call for more comprehensive training for state departments and agencies, including "community members, schools, daycare centers, and parents" in distinguishing between inappropriate and appropriate sexual behaviors in children.[22] The document includes a thorough literature review, as well as highlighting distinct traits, characteristics, and risk factors of COCSA or "sexual behavior problems."[23] Unfortunately though not surprisingly, there is no reference to the training of religious ministers.

The pattern of avoidance and denial of COCSA is acutely ironic as it intersects in lives shaped by traditional Catholic practices, especially in the most recent century of church history. Pope Pius X, head of the church from 1903 to 1914 and known for his opposition to modern interpretations of church teaching, decreed in 1910 that children as young as age seven should be trained to examine their consciences and articulate their "bad" behaviors as sins in the confessional.[24] When I was a child in the 1970s, reception of First Holy Communion remained contingent on making a First Confession, a very powerful message to children about the conditions necessary for divine acceptance at an age where nuances of morality are not likely to be comprehended. In many ways, the traditional moral instruction favored by my parents—in the vein of *Modern Youth and Chastity* (1941) and *The New St. Joseph Baltimore Catechism* (1962)[25]—was not only litigious but fundamentally sexualizing for young children, who were urged to "train" their consciences to avoid occasions of temptation as well as action. The timing for these messages in my own life—as in the life of any child who had already experienced a sexual violation of any kind—could not have been worse.

The paradox of the Catholic penitential ritual is that it simultaneously *demands* and *enables* children to articulate sexual thoughts, desires, behavior, or perceived violations in order to receive absolution from a priest and "reconciliation" with the church family—yet without any promise of full intellectual understanding, psychological integration, or emotional resolution for the child penitent. Secrecy, intended to enable full-disclosure, may instead simply reinscribe silencing. As a result, any sexual and emotional problems may be further ingrained, complicated, and compartmentalized through this ritual.

The damage redoubles for girls and women who are already culturally socialized to internalize sexual violations with hyper-responsibility and self-judgment.[26] Such internalized damage may result in suicidal ideation as well.[27] Furthermore, the Catholic "purity ethic," emphasizing sexual sins as grave, grievous acts—committed "against God" rather than against people with bodies—only repeats identity-effacing messages for girls who learn about sacramental forgiveness by subjecting themselves to all-male adult confessors, men whose formal and informal education is explicitly gendered.[28] As Keenan puts it, Catholic priests of the mid-century were instructed in "this ethic of purity and property rather than an ethic of love, justice, or goodness . . . [a] theology of sexuality [which] contribute[d] to a deep-seated suspicion and distrust of women [as well as] a distrust of the body that has marred Christian ethics for far too long."[29]

Catholic canon law goes so far as to acknowledge the vulnerability of children (and all penitents) within the confessional rite, insofar as a series of delicts formally criminalizes solicitation by priests who abuse their privileged position to exploit what they hear for predatory sexual purposes.[30] Cornwell argues that the document expressly denouncing such acts, titled *Crimens Solicitationis,* was a direct response to Pope Pius X's decree lowering the age of first confession. The emphasis on priests avoiding "crime" during this sacrament suggests that standards for respectful and thoughtful interaction with children specifically, and laity generally, were already far too low. The catechism identifying all sexual matters outside marriage as potential "mortal sins" certainly contributed to widespread compulsions of "fear and shame" that could be resolved *exclusively* through confession.[31] Maya Mayblin notes a "sudden renewed spike in disciplinary fervor" among lay Catholics encouraged to confess their sins weekly during the mid-twentieth century,[32] raising a question about whether such frequency reflected spiritual and emotional health, compliance with rules, repetition of spiritual and emotional damage, and/or compulsive behaviors in certain personalities.

How even a non-abusing priest would handle a child's intimate confidences "properly" was left to his individual education, seminary formation, personality, and personal history. As Georges Bernanos explores in his novel, *The Diary of a Country Priest*, only a sensitive cleric could speak empathetically of "lust" in young penitents while being even more deeply troubled by the "general silent conspiracy" among grownups to ignore the sexual troubles of children: "I knew sorrow, also, too early in my life to feel no disgust with the blind injustice we all are guilty of towards children, whose sorrows are so profound and mysterious."[33] The reader must wonder to what early "sorrows" the narrator alludes. Quoting Bernanos more than fifty years later, Cornwell notes how separation from women, lack of domestic responsibilities, and limited knowledge of children or stages of emotional development rendered priests like children "to the very end of [their] lives."[34]

For those without access to counseling or therapy, confession may still appear as the available and "holy" remedy for internalized disturbances, at the same time only perpetuating broader social silences. Routine violence against women and girls remains such a significant crisis globally that the World Health Organization has composed a "Global Plan of Action" to educate health care professionals about the scope of incidents, short and long-term health consequences, and best practices of education and intervention, across national borders, cultural practices, and religion.[35] What about spiritual health providers? Given the gender-power dynamics outside the confessional in the broader male-centered milieu of church and society, it is not surprising that "the documentation reveals that most victims [of solicitation] were women (including young girls)."[36] In other words, girls and women became likely, and therefore understandable, targets of predatory behavior. A recent case in the Archdiocese of Galveston-Houston, where a devout Catholic—a grown, married woman, also white—was allegedly solicited for sex as well as hundreds of thousands of dollars in church donations, provides one contemporary example of exploitation under the pretense of confessional "counsel."[37] In a more extreme and historic example, a young Latina in McCallen Texas went to confession and was sexually assaulted and then murdered by her confessor. This unholy murder took place in 1960 and was not adjudicated until fifty-seven years later, when the priest finally was brought to trial and convicted.[38]

But in systems where women and girls are already seen as lower than men, a less extreme but still pervasive result can be a gendered revictimization during the sacrament, even without exploitative physical contact. Catholic clericalism, a global system of priesthood, exists within theological and secular systems of "hegemonic masculinity"[39]—that is, systems that legitimize men's dominance and women's submission—and thus reinforces the position of a penitent as subordinate when she is already at her most vulnerable. A penitent may easily feel in a sense "molested" by dismissive, insensitive, shaming, or prejudiced interaction. Even when clerical absolution is provided essentially as a rubber stamp, women and girls who already have a profound sense of sexual contamination may not be able to accept such reconciliation as believable, finding it "harder to accept God's grace and love" and generally "feeling less sure of God as loving."[40]

Even as adults inside and outside Catholic tradition may deny, ignore, pathologize, or minimize the realities of COCSA, research suggests that survivors are no less likely to suffer posttraumatic responses than victims of assaults by adults. In her dissertation study, Janelle C. Brown found that "victims of juvenile and adult perpetrators did not present with significantly different levels of anxiety, depression, or posttraumatic stress . . . 83 percent of the sample met clinical threshold criteria on at least one emotional or behavioral outcome." The violated self-image in some COCSA survivors can also lead to a belief also held among rape victims who, following an assault, come to associate any sexual desire with sexual assault, thus choosing to "disown [their] sexuality" or "renounce their own sexual agency" in order to moderate feelings of hyper-responsibility.[41] In my case, an admixture of American conservatism and blend of pre- and post-Vatican II Catholic practice—perceptions absorbed and adopted within my environment from a very young age—intersected to magnify similar results.

HEALING AND RE-WOUNDING WITHIN A COMPULSIVE CATHOLIC CHILDHOOD

My relationship with the girl who engaged me in disordered sexual activities ended at some point after the third grade. At around this time, when my younger sister was to start Kindergarten, our parents decided to enroll both of us in the school of our Catholic parish. After I was enrolled there, I never saw the girl again.

During this time, both of our parents were highly involved in conservative political activism against the alleged influence of secular humanism in public-school curriculum and textbooks, against the possible ratification of the Equal Rights Amendment (ERA), and against legalized abortion.[42] I had attended public school through the milestones of my first Confession and First Holy Communion, during which time my religious instruction had been rather hit-and-miss, confined to Saturday CCD classes, and overlapping with the period where I experienced unwanted sexual contact.[43] In some ways, the righteous and very explicit stridency of my parents' social and political conservatism provided a primary framework within which I would fit my compulsive child's reading of Catholic teachings about women, sin, the body, and personal responsibility.

The switch of schools was a calming relief from what I perceived as the erratic and simply more crowded public-school environment. I loved the teachers and my uniform. I enjoyed the religious art in classrooms, the fusion of the liturgical calendar with the ebb and flow of the school year. My almost-daily feelings of dread abated fairly quickly at first, and I made normal friends. The rhythms of student and family life in a working-class parochial school community were a sharp contrast with the dim daytime shadows and sad basements of the previous three years. Now there were parties and sleepovers, swimming in the public park, donut sales and pancake breakfasts, spelling bees, music lessons, the State Fair, carnivals at the Catholic high school (including a cake walk), and ice-skating. I organized a Catholic girls' club with my classmates and planned variety shows in the yard.

I was a good student at this time, eager to please (I should also say, paranoid about "causing trouble"), and I was an avid, sponge-like reader. As my religious instruction became more thorough, I began to recognize gaps I had missed at a younger age. Our parish was moderately conservative in its transition from Vatican II, slower to resolve disagreements about whether the kneeling rail should be used for communion and whether communion should be taken in the hand rather than on the tongue.[44] I would not consider the religious instruction I received as Draconian by any means, yet I desperately latched onto any and all information about rules, which I now more broadly interpret as "boundaries." I was seeking guidelines that had been unavailable to me—and because I had no means of calibrating interpretations, the rules I fixated upon fit too easily into the other forms of social conservatism with which I was already very familiar. I turned all of these rules against myself.

Confession became an increasingly anxious and compulsive sacrament, especially as I prepared for confirmation in sixth grade. I became obsessed with the distinctions between venial and mortal sin, as well as perfect and imperfect contrition. In my mind, any and all sexual feelings and memories became bound together indistinguishably as grievous, soul-jeopardizing offenses against the sixth and ninth commandments. At the time, I had no terminology other than "sin," "shame," and "offending God," and absolutely zero vocabulary for personal boundaries, consent, pleasure, or desire. It was simpler to understand that anything sexual was sinful, period. And if sins were bad, I must have wanted to *do* bad, which meant that I was myself already deeply in need of redemption. I continued to be incredibly self-conscious and protective about my body and was terrified—even among the friends that I now liked and trusted—to remove my clothes or to shower in the locker room after gym.

Between ages ten and eleven, taking deeply to heart the language from the Act of Contrition of "my past life" and "heartily sorry," I chose Maria Goretti to be the patron saint of my "reformation." As a martyr to purity in 1902, at just eleven years old, Maria had resisted a young male attacker who stabbed her to death. It still stuns and pains me how easily and zealously I attached myself to Maria's story, how deeply its messages fit into a narrative I had already internalized at a young age, with girls and women elevated as victims. Feminist writers have long-explored how damaging this story is for abuse survivors, particularly for those within the Christian, and specifically Catholic, tradition.[45]

Over and over again, I mentally revisited those moments in my friend's house, thinking not that I had been manipulated or hurt, but that my soul and body had been accidentally "saved" by my friend's older sister—saved from imagined defloration, possible pregnancy, and venereal disease—despite what must have been my own most impure intentions that had led me to the brink. The story of Maria's resistance to a sexual assault, proving her virtue even as she was stabbed fourteen times with an awl, became a standard I applied to myself in a way that simultaneously protected and damaged me through my teenage years. It was virginity to the death.

As I entered puberty in an increasingly grown-up looking body, at nearly six feet tall, normal transitional milestones for other girls my age (first bra, pantyhose, simple sex education) were denied or delayed within my family system. My period was not fully explained to me, but its onset was marked with the arrival of a white rose on my bed-stand from the same father who on occasion verbalized profoundly disorienting criticisms of my body. On confirmation day, as I stood for a photograph with friends shoulder to shoulder in our white robes and red beanies, we looked the same. But at the bottom of the picture, I was wearing white nylon knee socks with sandals when all my friends were wearing ladies' stockings.

My family moved to California at this moment of transition and buoyed by my mostly positive experience in Catholic school, I looked forward to the change. But the socioeconomic environment and culture of religious education was much different in Southern California than in a Midwestern town, and as I entered junior high school with anachronistic and age-inappropriate habits and devotional compulsions, determined to protect myself against unwanted contact from peers at all costs, I became an unwary target of bullying that was reminiscent of my pre-parochial school experience, minus the disordered sexual expression.

As before, I felt unable to speak to my parents about the bullying, which occurred almost daily in private school. The reversal this time came when I transferred to a public high school, where the bullying subsided. I continued some of my private religious compulsions, including confession, though I also began obsessing about calorie intake in order to lose and to control my weight, for a few years suffering from what would now likely be considered anorexia. My parents signed a paper to exclude me from ninth grade sex education materials in biology class, and my father culled through my summer reading lists for an Honors English class, requesting different assignments from the teacher. One summer, in what I thought was an unusually encouraging gesture, my father asked me to smile for photos on the back porch while I was reading in my bathing suit. He later presented the images to me as evidence that my body was unhealthy because my bones were poking out. My father's "helpful" shaming only reinforced a belief I had already deeply internalized: that no matter what I did, my body and my self were unacceptable.

Carole R. Bohn emphasizes how a "theology of ownership" as practiced within families can "block positive identity formation," going on to point out that it is all too common for girls with a history of sexual violation to feel that "they do not own their bodies."[46]

CATHOLICISM AND SCRUPULOSITY: A GENEALOGY OF MY EXPERIENCE

The relationship between psychology and religion is well-explored within literary theory and philosophy, but it is less common territory for exploration in therapeutic training, treatment, and practice. More clinical understanding of Catholicism's specific impact upon survivor coping and response to psychotherapy is much needed.[47] Interestingly, the unhealthy preoccupation with sin, internal thoughts, and compulsive ritual was identified within Catholicism as "scrupulosity" mostly by religious clerics long before it was acknowledged more broadly within secular psychological or psychiatric research. The condition is now identified by professionals and religious counselors alike as a specific form of obsessive compulsive disorder (OCD), called Scrupulosity/OCD or simply Scrup/OCD.[48] Emerging research indicates that childhood sexual abuse has a positive association with OCD as well as panic disorder, connections that require further study.[49]

The religious order of Redemptorists founded Scrupulous Anonymous in 1964 and the order still publishes a webpage of resources for those who suffer, along with a monthly newsletter.[50] In his book *A Thousand Frightening Fantasies*, William Van Ornum cites saints traditionally identified as afflicted with the disorder, including Julian of Norwich and St. Ignatius Loyola.[51] Van Ornum's book lacks an official imprimatur, but the author includes a foreword by John Cardinal O'Connor, who is quoted throughout the text, offering the equivalent to an ecclesiastical blessing for the work. Van Ornum's book focuses exclusively on scrupulosity among Catholics and the role of specific elements of religious practice in "compounding" the condition, yet the author emphasizes the need for religious knowledge alongside all possible therapeutic treatments as well as medications to facilitate healing.[52]

Both Cobb and Deacon and Nelson document the ways that scrupulosity manifests in Catholic case studies, with individuals engaging in compulsive religious rituals as well as nonreligious habits.[53] I was never diagnosed with this condition, but I can now "read" the patterns in my behavior and reasonably hypothesize that such a diagnosis would have been likely. I first displayed habits coinciding with the period after my disturbed sexual experiences and continuing through puberty. Between the ages 8–12, my rituals involved counting and repetition, as well as obsessive thoughts related and unrelated to religion. For a time, I had a habit of starting down the staircase from the second floor in our home, and if I did not keep track of my steps "properly," I would return to the top of the stairs and start down again. I also had a copy of the blue Pieta Prayer Book, given to me by a good friend's mother, which I wore smooth from constant use. When praying from the book, I would force myself to start over if my mind wandered or if I missed any words. I also obsessed about the difference between reading and saying a prayer, at times forcing myself to start over if I felt I had not been distinguishing properly. I took comfort in statuary and other sacramentals (holy water, holy cards, rosaries) but worried often about whether praying while looking at a devotional object was the same as praying *to* it—thus another reason to start a prayer over again.[54] I had an impossible time distinguishing between emotions, physical sensations, intentions, and acts, and lived in a near constant panic about committing and/or dying in a state of mortal sin. I always assumed the greatest possible amount of responsibility, gravity, and likely condemnation for myself.

While I had crushes on boys, I kept all fantasies abstract and romanticized, a mindset that continued into early adulthood and into college. For a time, I was almost entirely asexual. I began hoarding food—mostly candy—that I did not eat or consumed only through stingy and well-planned nibbles. I counted calorie intake obsessively. Guilt over childhood sexual memories would overwhelm me when I returned to confession, as I worried whether I had expressed enough detail of all my past sins in the proper words and with the proper kind of contrition. I never felt sure that I had been forgiven. To make matters worse, I anticipated serious sin in ordinary areas of daily life all the time. For a while, I truly believed that it was a mortal sin to eat when I was not hungry.

Throughout my teenage years, vigilance enabled me to avoid taking risks where I anticipated that assault might be possible. I built an emotional wall around all things, physical and sexual feeling that I had barely avoided ruining my virginity and needed to prove my virtue. COCSA became indistinguishable in my mind from other moments of consensual play or exploration, even indistinguishable from masturbation. "Standing up for myself" consisted mostly of urgent pleas to my parents to be driven to confession in the middle of a Saturday evening or on a weeknight. From my very first confession well into my teens, the feedback I received from priests in confession could be characterized as avoidant, dismissive, awkward, or fixated/scandalized. No priest solicited me for sexual activity, but neither did any of them perceive the traumatized young person on the other side of the screen.

However, during a period when I was seeking out confession sometimes more than once a week, I had an encounter with one priest who broke, at least temporarily, the compulsive spell. As I listed my sins, I started to confess a physical sensation that might have been impure, and the priest interrupted me. He told me to leave—not unkindly, but firmly. It was a jolt that did not completely arrest my scrupulosity—in fact, it triggered immediate shame and doubt, a sense of something else to be sorry for. The priest didn't offer any explanation, but the message was direct: *You do not have any sins here.*

I can see now how my confessions for years manifest as a kind of repetition compulsion. Each time I entered the confessional, I was returning to the closet where I believed I had first participated in a sinful violation of my soul, unaware of physical and emotional boundaries to which I was entitled. In the sacramental context, naming details again and again as sins, I was taking ownership and exercising agency because I had neither the language nor the audience to do otherwise. I was seeking to be kicked out of the dark place where I had been pressured, scared, and humiliated at a very young and vulnerable age—because I did not yet know that I could choose to leave. With rare exceptions such as the one described earlier, the confession ritual only reinscribed my original feelings of unworthiness, humiliation, and contamination.

Over time the priest's words re-centered my attention, allowing me permission not to obsess about what was wrong with me. It was the first time I had heard such a message in my life from any man, at a time when I was trying to fit a plaster model of the "good Catholic girl." It makes sense that the priest who kicked me out of the confessional openly identified as a recovering alcoholic: he was coming to terms with his own compulsive behaviors.

CONFESSION AND COMPULSION IN CATHOLIC WOMEN'S EXPERIENCES: CATHOLIC MESSAGES ABOUT WOMEN, GENDER, AND SEXUALITY

One of the oldest known autobiographies in the English language tells the story of a woman who seeks not only to reform her soul and connect with Christ, but, more subversively, desires to choose her experiences of religious ritual and practice. In *The Book of Margery Kempe*, a late medieval text, the inciting incident concerns a married young mother's traumatizing experience with a confessor. At the age of twenty, after a difficult pregnancy and delivery, Margery decides to return to the sacrament to be reconciled in case she might die. She is particularly motivated to confess "that thing which she had so long concealed,"[55] likely an experience of a sexual nature.

The priest's hasty response, however, sends Margery into a deep emotional and spiritual turmoil: "[B]ecause of the dread she had of damnation on the one hand, and his sharp reproving of her on the other, this creature went out of her mind and was amazingly disturbed and tormented with spirits for half a year, eight weeks and odd days."[56] She becomes suicidal, "bit[ing] her own hand so violently that the mark could be seen for the rest of her life" and "pitilessly [tearing] the skin on her body near her heart with her nails."[57] The distress abates only when Christ appears privately to comfort Margery, establishing her as a kind of visionary pilgrim.

Margery Kempe's story, which scholars agree was transcribed and edited by a priest ally, does much more than offer a harbinger of early Protestantism. The opening scene, which emphasizes Margery's age, her role as a wife and mother (she had fourteen children), and her position as a traumatized daughter of the church, importantly underscores the power of the male priest to completely derail her desire for spiritual healing. While we do not know the nature of the sin she tried to articulate after holding it secret for so long—whether in fact it truly was a sin or was something *done to* her—the priest's abrupt condemnation communicates a drastic theological message and social/gender judgment rather than relief or reprieve. At the hands of the male cleric, Margery receives what we could call now a "punitive diagnosis" for "having a normal reaction to trauma."[58] The betrayal drives her temporarily mad not because she is "fallen," but because she is so orthodox.

Fortunately, Margery Kempe becomes the idiosyncratic heroine in her story, bargaining for an end to sex with her husband (curtailing almost-yearly pregnancies), making religious pilgrimages alone, and even tousling publicly with religious leaders. Her personal faults, emotional struggles, and visions are presented within the milieu of a visible male church and social structure that sidelines and judges her when she does not conform. The autobiography moves from a woman "confessing" within the narrow confines of a sacrament where men wield authority and power, to a larger "confession" of personal experience that ultimately transcends the male clerical tradition.

Far from simply dramatizing rigid, harmful, messages about sexuality and gender roles in medieval, Eurocentric Catholicism, the conflicts in Margery Kempe's autobiography provide a compelling portrait of one woman's rebellion. Her example prefigures the work of other women writers across a rich spectrum of formative Catholic cultural origins and practice in this century—from Mary Daly to Gloria Anzaldua, from Angela Bonavoglia to Roxane Gay and Chimamanda Adichie—all who have responded directly and indirectly to the damaging, brittle frameworks of gender and sexuality offered by the male-centered church.[59]

Underlying the distress of my own scrupulosity were the deeply mixed messages in Catholicism about gender roles and the body. I took these very seriously at a young age. When I first asked my mother how married people could avoid pregnancy without contraception, she explained how couples could abstain from sex periodically, emphasizing that this abstinence had to be "by mutual consent," quoting Paul's explanation of marital duty in Corinthians 7:2–5.[60] What troubled me most was that mutual consent was required for a *refusal* of sex rather than for engagement in sexual activity. This concept seemed clearly biased in favor of whoever wanted sex more, undermining reciprocity and negotiation in a tradition that had also taught me how a woman's body was sacred as a vessel. The words attributed to Mary in the Book of Luke when the angel announced her pregnancy, "be it done to me according to thy word," always struck me as ominous. The message appeared to be consistent with what I had absorbed before I ever entered catechism or understood the readings at mass: it was my duty, as a girl, to comply.

Sheila A. Redmond describes how symbols in Christianity broadly, and Catholicism specifically, "can have an overwhelming impact on the developing ego of Christian children and cause subsequent difficulty in their functioning as adults."[61] Redmond inquires about how rigid, systemic thinking can make it difficult for children to identify, process, and recover from sexual abuse, and she identifies several categories of Christian virtue that can cause excruciating damage for children within the Christian family structure: the value of suffering; the virtue of forgiveness; sexual purity; the need for redemption, and obedience to authority.[62]

Similarly, Elizabeth Jordan, quoting Bernard Haring, delves more deeply into the gendered power dynamics inherent in Catholic theology and sacraments, particularly the ritual of confession: "Moral theology became an ethics of obedience and also an ethics of control through the confessor,"[63] who by definition must always be an ordained man. Within this framework,

Jordan argues, teachings about deadly sins and virtuous ideals have disparate impacts on penitents based on their gender socialization:

> [Valerie] Saiving claimed that pride, the first of the seven deadly sins, may well be a problem for males who enjoy status and power in society, and it is appropriate to encourage them to cultivate humility and self-sacrifice. For women, however, the chief danger is not pride, but rather its opposite, the failure to have a centered self.[64]

Jordan here recognizes that one cannot simply detach a virtuous concept from the social context within which it will be practiced and monitored. For girls who are already treated as "lesser than," a sacrifice of ego will not be morally corrective but existentially catastrophic. Within Catholicism, women's veiled bodies are everywhere, celebrated at side altars and in shrines as plaster and marble and wood-carved women often for purposes of veneration. But thus Catholic iconography serves as a kind of gas-lighting for the ecclesiastical realpolitik that fundamentally excludes women from religious authority and renders their testimony as extraneous.

What is a child to make of all this? Particularly a girl child, who will not be entitled to casual (as opposed to formal, ritualized) contact with male clergy, who model self-assurance, flexibility, and male entitlement for boys? Stories of saints (also called hagiographies) become a powerful tool for normalization of male social power and control. At an early age, I paged through the beautiful red leather-bound volumes of our Butler's *Lives of the Saints,* and learned that virginity and martyrdom go hand in hand for many female saints, a sure pathway to holiness. I absorbed the lesson I thought I needed: "If you were assaulted as a child and you did not fight off the attacker to the death, you must be guilty of some sin, some inherent weakness; it must be your fault."[65] With no clear identity in place, I developed instead "a sense of guilt and responsibility disproportionate to my actions"[66] extending far beyond the COCSA incidents that so troubled me in the first place, and predisposing me to "believe that [I] was at fault for others' actions."[67] I saw a need to convert myself in order to atone, to be repaired.

Rita Nakashima Brock, summarizing psychologist Alice Miller, notes that "the tendency to accept blame for being wrong is characteristic of an abused child."[68] In male-dominated families where parents do not see children as separate individuals with distinct needs and feelings, a "fusion of selves" develops.[69] Rather than rebel, I remained largely enmeshed with my mother well into adulthood. This result is typical, according to Miller's view, in family systems where "children learn to bury their own feelings and needs, to rely on false selves that mirror their parents' feelings and needs, and to respect the powers of authority and dominance, rather than their own feelings and needs."[70]

Gravitating toward the "alternative family" I experienced in church, I tried on some level to locate new influences. But the alternatives were not so different, unfortunately, from what I was trying to transcend. In adopting an 11-year-old sexual martyr for my patron saint, and in compulsively engaging confession as a mode of articulation and redress given my ignorance of therapeutic alternatives, I simply was "maintain[ing] [my] ability to be validated as a person by collecting evidence of [my] own inadequacy."[71] Confession only reimposed a medieval power structure rather than inviting equal participation or creating a partnership for healing. The Catholic ritual of Confession further normalized my submissive behavior, which Jordan calls "a repressive technology for women."[72] On the surface, for a significant period of time, I was deeply invested in cooperation with that technology. Even after I stopped engaging regularly in the sacrament, its impact was internalized into other areas of my adjustment as an adult. Until I entered therapy ten years ago, I believed that the easiest way to resolve any conflict was to take the blame.

The most serious internal consequence of this external "cooperation" for myself and for others is the evasion or sublimation of authentic emotions. True feelings are undermined or sequestered away, as in the confessional, bound by its aura of mystery, secrecy, and silence, all which are "problematic for the survivor."[73] Miller, applying Winnicott's idea, notes how individuals will pay a steep price, namely "depression and a sense of emptiness,"[74] realities with which I have only begun to grapple.

CONCLUSIONS AND AREAS FOR FURTHER STUDY

Roland Summit refers to the "secondary trauma" experienced by children in sexual crisis, emphasizing the dilemma for a female victim who may speak up: "[W]hether the child who complains is angry, evasive, or serene, the immediate affect and the adjustment pattern of the child will be interpreted by adults to invalidate the child's complaint."[75] Chesler underscores how cultural influences can deeply undermine the internal assessment of a violation within the mind of a girl child, when sexual offenses (such as rape) become fused with sex generally, as activity "culturally forbidden to [women] outside of marriage, but not to men."[76] As a result of this fusion, girls and women may never be able to connect negative emotional consequences to the original violation at all.[77] For me, one temporary coping mechanism was a retreat from physicality and sexuality, a "renunciation of sexuality altogether."[78]

Experiences of abuse, recovery, and treatment need to be studied across various "social identity perspectives" in Catholic upbringing.[79] Survivors of COCSA, especially within conservative religious contexts, may not only blame themselves but may also take inappropriate responsibility for what occurred. We need more genealogies of survivor-victims across demographics of race, gender identification, sexual orientation, and socioeconomic class for individuals who employed traditional technologies (e.g., the confessional and/or pastoral counseling), whether in strategic or obsessive-compulsive ways, when no therapeutic alternative or adult advocate was available.

We must also take a closer look at how misogyny and homophobia in Catholic teaching simultaneously prescribe outrage over sexual violations against boys as not only pedophiliac/criminal, but as homosexual and therefore "fundamentally disordered." Stereotypical responses to boys' abuse reflect a general prejudice that male-on-male sexual activity, abusive or not, is "bad" and should never happen. I think often about how the Brett Kavenaugh hearings would have been covered by conservative media (secular and Catholic) if an alleged male rather than female victim had come forward to testify.[80]

The sad yet often tepid response when girls are harmed—by other girls, by boys their age, or by adults of either sex—betrays not only a flawed belief in women's more "natural" status as victims but also an unconscionable acceptance of men and boys as expected predators against girls and women. Even now, research documents an outrageous, astonishing "epidemic of disbelief" faced by women who report assaults of any kind to authorities.[81] Sexism and misogyny within clerical structures and law enforcement are certainly entrenched and obvious. A more nuanced yet fixable problem can manifest in the latent sexism of religious abuse recovery and advocacy movements, which may unconsciously replicate the male-centered and narcissistic structures of the church authorities they challenge.

Leaders and organizers—particularly men reclaiming dignity to which they likely felt entitled as males—may need more education about complex barriers faced by survivor-victims unlike themselves, who do not feel intrinsically welcomed to share their stories. Hierarchies of victimization can create unhealthy dynamics of competition among victims, who must "perform" their narratives for gatekeepers—whether parents, priests or bishops, lawyers, reporters/editors, or activist leaders—individuals with a great deal of power to validate or invalidate not only the story, but also the person telling it. Serious self-reflection must take place when advocacy groups do not reflect the demographics of the wounded communities they seek to serve. Those who are ostensibly working for justice and healing must become conscious of the roles that race, gender, sexual identity, language, socioeconomics, and even age will play in outreach, messaging, events, and the elevation of public voices. With the stakes of damage and recovery so high, thoughtless approaches cannot be acceptable.

It is not nostalgia that leads adults to place themselves in positions to advocate for those children that we were. I wonder a great deal about why the girl

I called my friend acted out in a sexually disordered way at such a very young age. I wonder what resources would have enabled my parents to address and heal from their own pain had they not been so suspicious of "outsider" influences beyond family and church. I wonder what it would have felt like to be so assured of acceptance in my family that I could have addressed my experience much sooner, in a healthier way. I wonder what it would have felt like as a child to know without question that I had the right to say "no" and to ask for help when I was hurt.

Unwanted sexual contact in a juvenile relationship "forced or enabled [me] to see, in a clearer light, what has been there all along"[82]—that is, the milieu of objectifying and sexualizing messages children can replicate before they even understand what they are doing. The experience deeply sensitized me to interpersonal subtleties and cues of dysfunction or danger, a sensitivity that has served me well in my research, as well as in my adult relationships and my work as a teacher. My writing for nearly twenty years has been committed to witnessing what goes unacknowledged in histories of violence, abuse, and trauma. Because it can be overwhelming and disorienting, I am also learning to moderate this sensitivity through psychotherapy.

Reorienting my Catholic identity has also been part of my recovery. I go to mass rarely, but I never hesitate to pray. I keep small altars in corners of my home. I identify now as a "stray" (not "strayed," "lapsed," or "fallen away") Catholic, a woman who claims a space that is a product of my faith tradition and exists along a chosen, shifting margin. On a bookshelf in my office stands a very old statue I rescued several years ago from eBay: Maria Goretti with her peasant shawl and long brown hair, the lilies of purity in her crossed arms and the sword of martyrdom at her feet. I no longer see Maria as a metaphor or a moral message, but as a girl whose life and future were stolen. It is not a coincidence that much of my new work related to the UT Austin shooting is now committed to preserving the voice of Kathy Leissner Whitman, the sniper's wife, who was stabbed to death in private in her own bed by the damaged man who claimed to love her. Like Maria, like the millions of women and girls victimized every day by abuse and violence, by disbelief and erasure, Kathy does not need to be canonized as a saint in order for her life and experience to matter.

All too often, vulnerability is weaponized against female victims, who are blamed for being violated, blamed for speaking up, blamed for keeping silent. Such damage will never be adjudicated through any court system, so we must "mother" ourselves and each other out of the darkness "where conflictual experiences remain hidden."[83] As Brock writes, "It is essential that our religious ideas and images function to heal and empower us, rather than reinforce the dynamics of self-denial, self-hate, child abuse, and oppression."[84] A reclaiming of religious identity, Brock emphasizes, can be transformative:

"In understanding the divine spirit as Child incarnate in us, we can see the need to remain connected to the original grace of our playful, feeling self and to seek that self in others as divine incarnation."[85]

Through writing and reading, asking and listening as alternatives to sacramental confession—cognitive-affective processes rather than cycles of compulsion or self-punishment—women can "retrieve suppressed and dangerous memories," not to be absolved but to "chart new maps" for "practices of subjectivity which are self-defined and affirmative."[86] I am so grateful now to locate hope in a catechesis of experience rather than dogma, in expressive rather than repentant modes of interpreting childhood sexual trauma.

NOTES

1. Beverly Engel, "Why Adult Victims of Childhood Sexual Abuse Don't Disclose." *Psychology Today*, March 6, 2019, https://www.psychologytoday.com/us/blog/the-compassion-chronicles/201903/why-adult-victims-childhood-sexual-abuse-dont-disclose. Also see E. J. Dickinson's discussion of the *Journal of the American Medical Association* (JAMA) finding that 6 percent of U.S. women surveyed from 2011 to 2017 reported that their first sexual encounter was "forced sexual initiation." https://www.rollingstone.com/culture/culture-news/rape-first-time-sex-885874/

2. Jo Scott-Coe, *MASS: A Sniper, a Father, and a Priest* (Claremont: Pelekinesis, 2018).

3. Scott Butki, "Before the Violence, and After." *Cultural Weekly*, May 1, 2019, https://www.culturalweekly.com/jo-scott-coe-violence. I also explore the process of excavating Rev. Joseph Leduc's buried narrative in an article I wrote after his name was revealed on the list of "credibly accused" priests in the Archdiocese of Galveston-Houston: Jo Scott-Coe, "Priest Named on Molestation List Was Texas Sniper's Scoutmaster, Friend, and Confidant." *The Press-Enterprise,* February 16, 2019, https://www.pe.com/2019/02/16/priest-named-on-molestation-list-was-texas-snipers-scoutmaster-friend-and-confidant/

4. Jo Scott-Coe, "Invisible Women, Fairy Tale Death: How Stories of Public Murder Minimize Terror at Home." *American Studies Journal* no. 26 (2017), DOI 10.18422/62-05; Jo Scott-Coe, "But What Would She Say? Reframing 'Domestic Terror' in the 1966 UT Austin Shooting." *Pacific Coast Philology* 52, no. 2 (2017); Jo Scott-Coe, "More than the Sniper's Wife: Kathy Leissner Whitman and the Mad Men Milieu," in *Critical Perspectives on Wives: Roles, Representations, Identities, and Work*, ed. Lynn O'Brien Hallstein and Rebecca Jaremko Bromwich (Ontario: Demeter Press).

5. Quoted in Phyllis Chelser, *Women and Madness* (Chicago: Lawrence Hill Press, 2018), 34.

6. Elizabeth Jordan, "Reconciling Women: A Feminist Reading of the History of Confession in the Roman Catholic Tradition." *Australian Feminist Studies* 14, no. 30, 305-306.

7. Newman Centers are Catholic centers of faith community on secular university campuses throughout the world.

8. Leslye E. Orloff and Paige Feldman, "Domestic Violence and Sexual Assault Public Policy Timeline." American University, Washington College of Law, February 12, 2017, http://library.niwap.org/wp-content/uploads/Herstory-2016.pdf.

9. Marie Keenan, *Child Sexual Abuse & the Catholic Church: Gender, Power, and Organizational Culture* (Oxford: Oxford University Press, 2012), 104.

10. Quoted in Konstantin Petoukov, "Violence, Compensation, and Settler Colonialism: Adjudicating Claims of Indian Residential Abuse through the Independent Assessment" (PhD diss., Carleton University, 2018), https://curve.carleton.ca/system/files/etd/fd2669b8-3bd5-45ec-a2f0-a15d20681fb4/etd_pdf/a95af26bb69fb27c009156bac8e78bdb/petoukhov-violencecompensationandsettlercolonialism.pdfPetoukov, 71.

11. Keenan, *Child Sexual Abuse & the Catholic Church*, 104.

12. Janelle C. Brown, "Child-on-Child Sexual Abuse: An Investigation of Behavioral and Emotional Sequelae" (PhD diss. Abstract, University of Pennsylvania, 2004), https://repository.upenn.edu/dissertations/AAI3125791.

13. James Kincaid, *Erotic Innocence: The Culture of Child Molesting* (Durham: Duke University Press, 1998), 160.

14. Kincaid, *Erotic Innocence*, 154.

15. Joan Tabachnick, *Do Children Sexually Abuse Other Children? Preventing Sexual Abuse among Children and Youth*, Stop it Now!, 2016, https://www.stopitnow.org/sites/default/files/documents/files/do_children_sexually_abuse_other_children_0.pdf, 6.

16. Tabachnick, *Do Children Sexually Abuse Other Children?*, 13–14.

17. National Society for the Prevention of Cruelty to Children (NSPCC), https://www.nspcc.org.uk, 2019.

18. Tabachnick, *Do Children Sexually Abuse Other Children?*, 6, 10.

19. Sheila A. Redmond, "Christian 'Virtues' and Recovery from Child Sexual Abuse," in *Christianity, Patriarchy, and Abuse: A Feminist Critique*, ed. Joanne Carlson Brown and Carole R. Bohn (New York: The Pilgrim Press, 1989), 72–73.

20. Kristin Parsons Winokur, Lindsey N. Devers, Gregory A. Hand, and Julia L. Blankenship, "Child on Child Sexual Abuse Needs Assessment." Florida Department of Children and Families, Justice Research Center, Inc., February 2010, http://thejrc.com/docs/Child%20on%20Child%20Sexual%20Abuse%20Needs%20Assessment%20-%20White%20Paper.pdf.

21. Winokur, Devers, Hand, and Blankenship, "Child on Child Sexual Abuse Needs Assessment," 4.

22. Ibid., 10.

23. Ibid., 11–29, 30–32.

24. John Cornwell, *The Dark Box: A Secret History of Confession* (New York: Basic Books, 2014), 83–88.

25. Gerald Kelly, S. J., *Modern Youth and Chastity* (St Louis, The Queen's Work, 1941); Bennet Kelley, C. P., *The New St. Joseph Baltimore Catechism* (Totowa, NJ: Catholic Book Publishing Corporation, 1962).

26. Leslie Lebowitz and Susan Roth, "'I Felt Like a Slut': The Cultural Context and Women's Response to Being Raped." *Journal of Traumatic Stress* 7, no. 3 (1994); Christi M. Collins, Margarita R. O'Neill-Arana, Lisa Aronson Fontes, and Jennifer M. Ossege, "Catholicism and Childhood Sexual Abuse: Women's Coping and Psychotherapy." *Journal of Child Sexual Abuse* 23 (2014), DOI: 10.1080/10538712.2014.918071.

27. David Kealy, Alicia Spidel, and John S. Ogrodniczuk, "Self-Conscious Emotions and Suicidal Ideation among Women with and without a History of Childhood Sexual Abuse." *Counselling and Psychotherapy Research*, December 2017, 269.

28. In Roman Catholic tradition, there are seven sacraments: baptism, confession (also called the sacrament of reconciliation or penance), holy communion (also called the Eucharist), confirmation, marriage, holy orders, and the anointing of the sick.

29. Keenan, *Child Sexual Abuse & the Catholic Church*, 139.

30. Ibid., 209–214; Thomas P. Doyle, A. W. R. Sipe, and Patrick J. Wall, *Sex, Priests, and Secret Codes: The Catholic Church's 2,000-year Paper Trail of Sexual Abuse* (Los Angeles: Volt Press, 2006), 37–47.

31. Keenan, *Child Sexual Abuse & the Catholic Church*, 134.

32. Maya Mayblin, "The Lapsed and the Laity: Discipline and Lenience in the Study of Religion." *Journal of the Royal Anthropological Institute* 23 (2017), 510.

33. Georges Bernanos, *The Diary of a Country Priest* (New York, DaCapo Press, 2001 [1937]), 97–98.

34. Cornwell, *The Dark Box*, 88.

35. World Health Organization (WHO), "Global Plan of Action to Strengthen the Role of the Health System within a National Multisectoral Response to Address Interpersonal Violence, in Particular against Women and Girls, and against Children," 2016, https://apps.who.int/iris/bitstream/handle/10665/252276/9789241511537-eng.pdf;jsessionid=3204109EEC16CFE563C2EB335D62C177?sequence=1.

36. Doyle, Sipe, and Wall, *Sex, Priests, and Secret Codes*, 40.

37. Nicole Winfield, "Top US Cardinal Accused of Mishandling Aide's Sex Abuse Case." *Associated Press*, June 5, 2019, https://www.apnews.com/8a80c0c1276f4cc485e0599e922759c2.

38. Samantha Schmidt, "In 1960, She Went to Confession and Vanished. Now We Know the Priest Who Murdered Her." *The Washington Post*, December 8, 2017, https://www.washingtonpost.com/news/morning-mix/wp/2017/12/08/in-1960-she-went-to-confession-and-vanished-now-we-know-the-priest-murdered-her.

39. Keenan, *Child Sexual Abuse & the Catholic Church*, 120.

40. Collins, O'Neill-Arana, Fontes, and Ossege, "Catholicism and Childhood Sexual Abuse," 521.

41. Lebowitz and Roth, "'I Felt Like a Slut,'" 376.

42. The ERA (Equal Rights Amendment) is a proposed Amendment to the U.S. Constitution designed to guarantee legal rights for all American citizens regardless of sex.

43. CCD stands for "Confraternity of Christian Doctrine." This acronym refers to the Roman Catholic equivalent of catechism or Sunday school classes directed at students who are not attending religious schools.

44. Vatican II, also referred to as the Second Vatican Council of the Roman Catholic Church, was convened by Pope John XXIII in 1962 to renew the place of the church in the modern world. The Council concluded under Pope Paul VI, in 1965.

45. Redmond, "Christian 'Virtues' and Recovery from Child Sexual Abuse"; Rebecca Hamilton, "Many Rape Victims Have a Problem with Maria Goretti: Here's Why." *Patheos: Public Catholic*, July 7, 2015, https://www.patheos.com/blogs/publiccatholic/2015/07/many-rape-victims-have-a-bit-of-trouble-with-st-maria-goretti-heres-why; Claire Fallon, "All the Murdered Virgin Saints and Me." *Huffpost*, November 21, 2018, https://www.huffpost.com/entry/virgin-martyr-saints-catholic rape_n_5bdb3250e4b01abe6a1c47c4.

46. Carole R. Bohn, "Dominion to Rule: The Roots and Consequences of a Theology of Ownership," in *Christianity, Patriarchy, and Abuse: A Feminist Critique*, ed. Joanne Carlson Brown and Carole R. Bohn (New York: The Pilgrim Press, 1989), 105–116.

47. Collins, O'Neill-Arana, Fontes, and Ossege, "Catholicism and Childhood Sexual Abuse," 519.

48. Katherine Fohn Cobb, "Understanding Scrupulosity: Psychopathological and Catholic Perspectives" (master's thesis, University of Iowa, 2014), https://doi.org/10.17077/etd.8xo0809.

49. A. Caspi, T. Vishne, Y. Sasson, et al., "Abstract: Relationship between Childhood Sexual Abuse and Obsessive Compulsive Disorder: Case Control Study." *The Israel Journal of Psychiatry and Related Sciences* 45, no. 3, https://www.ncbi.nlm.nih.gov/pubmed/19398821.

50. The Redemptorists are a Catholic religious order of priests and brothers, also called the Congregation of the Holy Redeemer. Their online newsletter is called *Scrupulous Anonymous*: https://scrupulousanonymous.org/

51. William Van Ornum, *A Thousand Frightening Fantasies: Understanding and Healing Scrupulosity and Obsessive Compulsive Disorder* (Eugene, OR: Wipf and Stock Publishers, 1997), 18.

52. Ornum, *A Thousand Frightening Fantasies*, xi.

53. Cobb, "Understanding Scrupulosity: Psychopathological and Catholic Perspectives"; Brett Deacon and Elizabeth A. Nelson, "On the Nature and Treatment of Scrupulosity." *Pragmatic Case Studies in Psychotherapy* 4, module 2, article 2, May 12, 2008.

54. Catholic devotional objects are physical items intended to aid with prayer and meditation. Church teaching refers to these as sacramental as they are often blessed by a priest and used to increase devotion to God through the sacraments. Rosaries are Catholic prayer beads; holy cards are small cards imprinted with images of Jesus, the Virgin Mary, or the saints; holy water is water blessed for use before or during mass, or in the home, during prayer or for making the sign of the cross.

55. Margery Kempe, *The Book of Margery Kempe*, trans. Barry Windeatt (London: Penguin, 2004), 41.

56. Kempe, *The Book of Margery Kempe*, 42.

57. Ibid., 42.

58. Chesler, 19.

59. Mary Daly, *The Church and the Second Sex* (1968); Gloria Anzaldua, *Borderlands/La Frontera: the New Mestiza* (1987); Angela Bonavoglia, *Good Catholic Girls* (2010); Roxane Gay, *Hunger: A Memoir of My Body* (2017); Chimamanda Ngozi Adichie, *Purple Hibiscus* (2003)

60. Kevin Kukla, "What Is the Marital Duty Husbands and Wives Have to Each Other?" *Prolife365*, July 14, 2015, http://prolife365.com/marital-duty.

61. Redmond, "Christian 'Virtues' and Recovery from Child Sexual Abuse," 70.

62. Ibid., 73–79.

63. Jordan, "Reconciling Women," 303.

64. Ibid., 305.

65. Redmond, "Christian 'Virtues' and Recovery from Child Sexual Abuse," 76.

66. Ibid., 77.

67. Polly Young-Eisendrath and Demaris Wehr, "The Fallacy of Individualism and Reasonable Violence against Women," in *Christianity, Patriarchy, and Abuse: A Feminist Critique*, ed. Joanne Carlson Brown and Carole R. Bohn (New York: The Pilgrim Press, 1989), 128.

68. Rita Nakashima Brock, "And a Little Child Will Lead Us: Christology and Child Abuse," in *Christianity, Patriarchy, and Abuse: A Feminist Critique*, ed. Joanne Carlson Brown and Carole R. Bohn (New York: The Pilgrim Press, 1989), 53.

69. Harriet Coldher Lerner, quoted in Brock, "And a Little Child Will Lead Us," 47.

70. Brock, "And a Little Child Will Lead Us," 46.

71. Young-Eisendrath and Wehr, "The Fallacy of Individualism and Reasonable Violence against Women," 128.

72. Jordan, "Reconciling Women," 309.

73. Collins, O'Neill-Arana, Fontes, and Ossege, "Catholicism and Childhood Sexual Abuse," 520.

74. Alice Miller, *Prisoners of Childhood*, trans. Ruth Ward (New York: Basic Books, 1981), 21.

75. Roland Summit, "The Child Sexual Abuse Accommodation Syndrome." *Child Abuse and Neglect*, n.d., 1983, 188.

76. Phyllis Chelser, *Women and Madness* (Chicago: Lawrence Hill Press, 2018), 22.

77. Ibid., 22.

78. Lebowitz and Roth, "'I Felt Like a Slut,'"376.

79. Kiara Minto, Matthew J. Hornse, Nicole Gillespie, et al., "A Social Identity Approach to Understanding Responses to Child Sexual Abuse Allegations." *PLoS One* 11, no. 4, DOI: 10.1371/journal.pone.015325, 1.

80. Brett Kavenaugh was nominated to the U.S. Supreme Court by President Donald Trump in July 2018. He was confirmed by the Senate following a series of hearings related to alleged sexual assault against Christine Blasey Ford more than three decades earlier, when Kavenaugh was a Catholic student at Georgetown Preparatory School, a Jesuit boys college prep school.

81. Barbara Bradley Hagerty, "An Epidemic of Disbelief." *The Atlantic* (August 2019), 72–84.

82. Lebowitz and Roth, "'I Felt Like a Slut,'" 385.
83. Miller, *Prisoners of Childhood* 5.
84. Brock, "And a Little Child Will Lead Us," 54.
85. Ibid., 55.
86. Jordan, "Reconciling Women," 309.

BIBLIOGRAPHY

Bernanos, Georges. *The Diary of a Country Priest.* New York: DaCapo Press, 2001 [1937].

Bohn, Carole R. "Dominion to Rule: The Roots and Consequences of a Theology of Ownership." In *Christianity, Patriarchy, and Abuse: A Feminist Critique,* edited by Joanne Carlson Brown and Carole R. Bohn, 105–116. New York: The Pilgrim Press, 1989.

Brock, Rita Nakashima. "And a Little Child Will Lead Us: Christology and Child Abuse." In *Christianity, Patriarchy, and Abuse: A Feminist Critique,* edited by Joanne Carlson Brown and Carole R. Bohn, 42–61. New York: The Pilgrim Press, 1989.

Brown, Janelle C. "Child-on-Child Sexual Abuse: An Investigation of Behavioral and Emotional Sequelae." PhD diss. abstract, University of Pennsylvania, 2004. https://repository.upenn.edu/dissertations/AAI3125791/

Butki, Scott. "Before the Violence, and After." *Cultural Weekly*, May 1, 2019. https://www.culturalweekly.com/jo-scott-coe-violence/

Caspi, A., T. Vishne, Y. Sasson, et al. "Abstract: Relationship Between Childhood Sexual Abuse and Obsessive Compulsive Disorder: Case Control Study." *The Israel Journal of Psychiatry and Related Sciences* 45, no. 3 (2008): 177–182. https://www.ncbi.nlm.nih.gov/pubmed/19398821

Chelser, Phyllis. *Women and Madness.* Chicago: Lawrence Hill Press, 2018 [1970].

Cobb, Katherine Fohn. "Understanding Scrupulosity: Psychopathological and Catholic Perspectives." Master's thesis, University of Iowa, 2014. https://doi.org/10.17077/etd.8xo0809

Collins, Christi M., Margarita R. O'Neill-Arana, Lisa Aronson Fontes, and Jennifer M. Ossege. "Catholicism and Childhood Sexual Abuse: Women's Coping and Psychotherapy." *Journal of Child Sexual Abuse* 23 (2014): 519–537. DOI: 10.1080/10538712.2014.918071.

Cornwell, John. *The Dark Box: A Secret History of Confession.* New York: Basic Books, 2014.

Deacon, Brett and Elizabeth A. Nelson. "On the Nature and Treatment of Scrupulosity." *Pragmatic Case Studies in Psychotherapy* 4, module 2, article 2 (May 12, 2008): 39–53.

Dickinson, E. J. "3 Million Women Say Their First Sexual Encounter Was Rape—But that Number Is Most Likely Higher." *Rolling Stone* September 17, 2019. https://www.rollingstone.com/culture/culture-news/rape-first-time-sex-885874/

Doyle, Thomas P., A. W. R. Sipe, and Patrick J. Wall. *Sex, Priests, and Secret Codes: The Catholic Church's 2,000-year Paper Trail of Sexual Abuse*. Los Angeles: Volt Press, 2006.

Engel, Beverly. "Why Adult Victims of Childhood Sexual Abuse Don't Disclose." *Psychology Today,* March 6, 2019. https://www.psychologytoday.com/us/blog/the-compassion-chronicles/201903/why-adult-victims-childhood-sexual-abuse-dont-disclose

Fallon, Claire. "All the Murdered Virgin Saints and Me." *Huffpost,* November 21, 2018. https://www.huffpost.com/entry/virgin-martyr-saints-catholic-rape_n_5bdb3250e4b01abe6a1c47c4

Hagerty, Barbara Bradley. "An Epidemic of Disbelief." *The Atlantic,* August 2019: 72–84.

Hamilton, Rebecca. "Many Rape Victims Have a Problem with Maria Goretti: Here's Why." *Patheos: Public Catholic*, July 7, 2015. https://www.patheos.com/blogs/publiccatholic/2015/07/many-rape-victims-have-a-bit-of-trouble-with-st-maria-goretti-heres-why/

Jordan, Elizabeth. "Reconciling Women: A Feminist Reading of the History of Confession in the Roman Catholic Tradition." *Australian Feminist Studies* 14, no. 30 (1989).

Kealy, David, Alicia Spidel, and John S. Ogrodniczuk. "Self-Conscious Emotions and Suicidal Ideation among Women with and without a History of Childhood Sexual Abuse." *Counselling and Psychotherapy Research* (December 2017): 269–275.

Keenan, Marie. *Child Sexual Abuse & the Catholic Church: Gender, Power, and Organizational Culture.* Oxford: Oxford University Press, 2012.

Kelley, Bennet, C. P. *The New St. Joseph Baltimore Catechism.* Totowa, NJ: Catholic Book Publishing Corporation, 1962.

Kelly, Gerald, S. J. *Modern Youth and Chastity*. St Louis, The Queen's Work, 1941.

Kempe, Margery. *The Book of Margery Kempe*, translated and with an introduction by Barry Windeatt. London: Penguin, 2004.

Kincaid, James. *Erotic Innocence: The Culture of Child Molesting*. Durham: Duke University Press, 1998.

Kukla, Kevin. "What Is the Marital Duty Husbands and Wives Have to Each Other?" *Prolife365* (July 14, 2015). http://prolife365.com/marital-duty/

Lebowitz, Leslie and Susan Roth. "'I Felt Like a Slut': The Cultural Context and Women's Response to Being Raped." *Journal of Traumatic Stress* 7, no. 3 (1994): 363–390.

Mayblin, Maya. "The Lapsed and the Laity: Discipline and Lenience in the Study of Religion." *Journal of the Royal Anthropological Institute* 23 (2017): 503–522.

Miller, Alice. *Prisoners of Childhood,* translated from the German by Ruth Ward. New York: Basic Books, 1981.

Minto, Kiara, Matthew J. Hornse, Nicole Gillespie, et al. "A Social Identity Approach to Understanding Responses to Child Sexual Abuse Allegations." *PLoS One* 11, no. 4 (2016). DOI: 10.1371/journal.pone.015325

Orloff, Leslye E. and Paige Feldman. "Domestic Violence and Sexual Assault Public Policy Timeline." American University, Washington College of Law. February 12, 2017. http://library.niwap.org/wp-content/uploads/Herstory-2016.pdf

Petoukov, Konstantin. "Violence, Compensation, and Settler Colonialism: Adjudicating Claims of Indian Residential Abuse through the Independent Assessment." PhD diss., Carleton University, 2018. https://curve.carleton.ca/system/files/etd/fd2669b8-3bd5-45ec-a2f0-a15d20681fb4/etd_pdf/a95af26bb69fb27c009156bac8e78bdb/petoukhov-violencecompensationandsettlercolonialism.pdf

Redmond, Sheila A. "Christian 'Virtues' and Recovery from Child Sexual Abuse." In *Christianity, Patriarchy, and Abuse: A Feminist Critique,* edited by Joanne Carlson Brown and Carole R. Bohn, 70–88. New York: The Pilgrim Press, 1989.

Schmidt, Samantha. "In 1960, She Went to Confession and Vanished. Now We Know the Priest Who Murdered Her." *The Washington Post*, December 8, 2017.
https://www.washingtonpost.com/news/morning-mix/wp/2017/12/08/in-1960-she-went-to-confession-and-vanished-now-we-know-the-priest-murdered-her/

Scott-Coe, Jo. "But What Would She Say? Reframing 'Domestic Terror' in the 1966 UT Austin Shooting." *Pacific Coast Philology* 52, issue 2 (2017): 294–313.

———. "Invisible Women, Fairy Tale Death: How Stories of Public Murder Minimize Terror at Home." *American Studies Journal* no. 26 (2017). DOI 10.18422/62-05

———. *MASS: A Sniper, a Father, and a Priest.* Claremont: Pelekinesis, 201.

———. "More Than the Sniper's Wife: Kathy Leissner Whitman and the Mad Men Milieu." In *Critical Perspectives on Wives: Roles, Representations, Identities, and Work,* edited by Lynn O'Brien Hallstein and Rebecca Jaremko Bromwich, 219–244. Ontario, Canada: Demeter Press, 2019.

———. "Priest Named on Molestation List was Texas Sniper's Scoutmaster, Friend, and Confidant." *The Press-Enterprise* February 16, 2019. https://www.pe.com/2019/02/16/priest-named-on-molestation-list-was-texas-snipers-scoutmaster-friend-and-confidant/

Summit, Roland. "The Child Sexual Abuse Accommodation Syndrome." *Child Abuse and Neglect* (1983): 177–193.

Tabachnick, Joan. *Do Children Sexually Abuse Other Children? Preventing Sexual Abuse among Children and Youth.* Stop it Now!, 2016. https://www.stopitnow.org/sites/default/files/documents/files/do_children_sexually_abuse_other_children_0.pdf

Van Ornum, William. *A Thousand Frightening Fantasies: Understanding and Healing Scrupulosity and Obsessive Compulsive Disorder.* Eugene: Wipf and Stock Publishers, 1997.

Winfield, Nicole. "Top US Cardinal Accused of Mishandling Aide's Sex Abuse Case." *Associated Press*, June 5, 2019. https://www.apnews.com/8a80c0c1276f4cc485e0599e922759c2

Winokur, Kristin Parsons, Lindsey N. Devers, Gregory A. Hand, and Julia L. Blankenship. "Child on Child Sexual Abuse Needs Assessment." Florida Department of Children and Families, Justice Research Center, Inc. February 2010. http://thejrc.com/docs/Child%20on%20Child%20Sexual%20Abuse%20Needs%20Assessment%20-%20White%20Paper.pdf

The World Health Organization (WHO). "Global Plan of Action to Strengthen the Role of the Health System within a National Multisectoral Response to Address Interpersonal Violence, in Particular against Women and Girls, and against Children." 2016. https://apps.who.int/iris/bitstream/handle/10665/252276/9789241511537-eng.pdf;jsessionid=3204109EEC16CFE563C2EB335D62C177?sequence=1

Young-Eisendrath, Polly and Demaris Wehr. "The Fallacy of Individualism and Reasonable Violence against Women." In *Christianity, Patriarchy, and Abuse: A Feminist Critique,* edited by Joanne Carlson Brown and Carole R. Bohn, 42–61. New York: The Pilgrim Press, 1989.

Chapter 9

Awareness of the Divine Feminine, Holy Sophia

Leaving behind Roman Catholic Misogyny

Mary Sue Barnett

I dreamt I have third degree burns on my face. Though the burns are severe and unsightly, I am calm and without pain. A woman walking alongside me is nervously looking for her little girl. I say to her, "your little girl's face looks like mine." She looks at me, recoils from me immediately, and rushes to find her little girl.

I begin with a dream that I had while writing this chapter. Attending to dreams is a way of honoring contact with the unconscious. It is devotion to personal wholeness through the integration of the inner and outer life. Careful attention to the content of the unconscious that comes in dreams is active commitment to one's inner mystery and demand and to authenticity of self which in turn offers healing to the world. In this dream I see that patriarchy and misogyny disfigure female lives. Wakefulness to the trauma and destruction, though deeply jarring, will open the doors to healing and transformation. Though teaching this wakefulness can often render a woman stigmatized and vulnerable, it is a necessary risk to take in order to release the feminine from of the death grip of religious misogyny.

The misogyny of the Roman Catholic Church is a disfigured spirituality that dispenses misery upon millions throughout the world. Understanding the religious misogyny of the Roman Catholic institution and its all-male clergy is to gain critical knowledge for one's own personal, spiritual empowerment and transformation. Nothing less than a new consciousness will provide healing and transformation to disparaged women and girls around the world.

The term misogyny is derived from the ancient Greek word *misogynia* which means hatred toward women or woman hater. In *Down Girl: The Logic of Misogyny,* philosopher Kate Manne argues that misogyny violates the autonomy, a central feature of personhood, by rendering a female as a sexual object by disrupting her peace of mind, "getting inside her head," causing her to suffer, or violating her bodily integrity.[1] Misogyny functions as enforcer of the patriarchal order in which men are power-holders and decision-makers. Misogyny emerges as punishment for women who challenge male-domination. In a *Vox* interview with Sean Illing, Manne states, "misogynists often think they're taking the moral high ground by preserving a status quo that feels right to them. They want to be socially and morally superior to the women they target."[2] And misogyny nearly always leads to violence.

The World Health Organization (WHO) reports that violence is a leading cause of injury and disability for women globally. The United Nations defines violence against women as "any act of gender-based violence that results in, or is likely to result in, physical, sexual, and mental harm or suffering to women, including threats of such acts, coercion or arbitrary deprivation of liberty, whether occurring in public or private life."[3] The term "gender-based violence" highlights that violence perpetrated by men against women is rooted in gender inequality. Globally, the most common forms of violence include intimate partner violence, family violence, sexual violence, female genital mutilation, femicide, sex trafficking, and forced prostitution. Health consequences of violence against women include physical injuries, disabilities, depression, anxiety, posttraumatic stress disorder, self-harm, and chronic pain disorders. The widespread social norm that supports violence against women is that men have a right to assert power and control over females.

The Office of the High Commissioner on Human Rights at the United Nations holds that gender stereotypes and gender stereotyping, the belief and practice of ascribing specific attributes to women and men, often result in the violation of women's human rights and fundamental freedoms. Typical global stereotypes for males/masculine are dominance, power, visibility, and decisiveness. Typical stereotypes for females/feminine are subordinance, weakness, marginality, and compliance. Article 5 of the United Nations Convention on the Elimination of all forms of Discrimination Against Women (CEDAW) calls for the transformation of harmful gender stereotypes and the elimination of wrongful gender stereotyping.[4] Phumzile Mlambo Ngucka, Executive Director of UN Women, insists that dismantling the foundations of gender inequality and discrimination is crucial to ending violence against women. UN Women is at the forefront in global efforts to dismantle foundations of inequality and violence. United Nations Special Rapporteur Karima Bennoune told the UN General Assembly in New York in 2017 that the world must resist a rising fundamentalism and extremism that threatens women's human rights. She warns, "What world will your daughters inherit? This is a wake-up call for our times. We face a multidirectional global avalanche of misogyny, motivated by diverse fundamentalist and extremist ideologies.

For the sake of the daughters around the world, let us come together and take an unequivocal stand for women's equal cultural rights, to reverse this worrying trend."[5]

The Roman Catholic hierarchy is a force in this global avalanche of misogyny. One of the manipulative tactics of the Vatican is to cloak its hatred of the feminine in the language of transcendence. For instance, in the 1976 Vatican declaration solidifying its position against the ordination of women (*Inter Insigniores*[6]), they use the word mystery twelve times. The word mystery juxtaposes with Christ, Church, God, and Covenant to paint a picture of divine mystery sanctioning the exclusion and silence of women. The all-male Roman Catholic hierarchy issued *Inter Insigniores* to suppress the feminine as other Christian denominations began ordaining women in the 1970s and in the wake of the founding in 1975 of the Catholic Women's Ordination Conference.

Inter Insigniores argues that prohibition against the ordination of women is absolute based upon the constant tradition of the Roman Catholic Church, Christ's calling of only male apostles, the apostles' exclusion of women as ministers and elders, the permanent nature of Christ's and the apostles' practices, the necessity of male representation in conducting the Eucharist, and the inappropriateness of considering priesthood as an individual's choice or right. Though each of these arguments is a pernicious undermining of females, I address specifically the Vatican argument of male representation in this chapter as it involves overt misogynistic violation of female bodily and spiritual integrity.

In their essay, "Power, Ideology, and Women's Ordination, Discursive Strategies in Three Roman Catholic Documents," Eun-Young Julia Kim and Beverly J. Matiko argue that *Inter Insigniores* uses value-laden words such as "better," "safeguard," "whole," and "official," to describe men's ministry carrying the notion of female inadequacy thus "connoting that women's work is comparatively inferior, unsafe, incomplete, and invalid."[7] The authors refer to the systemic denial of women's ministries outlined in *Inter Insigniores* as an institutional form of gaslighting—manipulation causing someone to second-guess their feelings and instincts. Kim and Matiko point out that behavioral psychologists use this term to describe abusive, manipulative behaviors in interpersonal relationships.

Inter Insigniores states that the maleness of Christ is ontologically significant, that Christ's maleness is at the core of his being, and therefore all males are ontologically superior as they share maleness with Christ. Thus, Christ is male, and maleness represents Christ. Accordingly, females who are female at the core of their being and unlike Christ at the core of his being are ontologically inferior beings. *Inter Insigniores* is fundamentally a document that devalues all females.

With their minds and spirits configured to *Inter Insigniores,* Roman Catholic clergymen see all females as "otherness." *God is male. Christ is male. I am male. I image Christ. God is not female. Christ is not female. You are female. You do not image Christ.* Each day, in all-male pulpits and all-male altars where females worldwide are forbidden to stand, to preach, and to bless, Roman Catholic clergymen embody *Inter Insigniores.* The misogyny of *Inter Insigniores* is the very substance of Roman Catholic male clerical identity in the world today. Roman Catholic male clergy identity is formed in the subjugation of the feminine. Disparagement of females is the spiritual disfigurement at the heart of Roman Catholic male clergy.

Roman Catholicism, the largest Christian denomination in the world, structures its all-male global leadership in opposition to female humanity. This theological violence casts an unrelenting, penetrating shadow of devaluation and degradation in the lives of women and girls all over the world, sowing seeds of male physical and sexual violence against them. For all clerics, *Inter Insigniores* operates at the center of his being, his ontological superiority and male supremacy dictating the character of his ministry. Even when individual clerics experience self-awareness and insight into their spiritual male dominance, Roman Catholic clergymen routinely choose misogyny as their identity, lacking moral courage to speak out publicly against *Inter Insigniores.*

In her book *Sexism and God-Talk: Toward a Feminist Theology,* theologian Rosemary Radford Ruether points out that although Christian tradition has affirmed the equivalence of maleness and femaleness in the image of God, this has been obscured by the tendency to correlate the lower part of human nature with femaleness, linking femaleness with the aspect of self that is prone to sin. She calls this a "case of projection," in which "males, as the monopolizers of theological self-definition, project onto women their own rejection of their 'lower selves.'"[8] For Ruether, Augustine is the source of the patriarchal anthropology which heavily influences Catholic orthodoxy. Augustine regarded females as inherently inferior making them prone to sin. Thus, females could not participate fully in the image of God.

In Ruether's discussion on feminist Christology, she unequivocally asserts that Jesus's maleness has no ultimate significance. Jesus's ability to speak as liberator did not reside in his maleness. Though his maleness does not have ultimate theological significance, it has social symbolic significance in patriarchal culture. "In this sense, Jesus as the Christ, the representative of liberated humanity and the liberating Word of God, manifests the *kenosis of patriarchy,* the announcement of the new humanity through a lifestyle that discards hierarchical caste privilege and speaks on behalf of the lowly."[9] Christ, the Word of God, is not to be encapsulated in the historical Jesus. The Christian community carries forward the work of liberation. Christ, encountered *in the form of our sister*, observes Ruether, is a dimension of liberated humanity calling the community to redemption.[10] Christ, encountered *in the form of our sister*, in diverse women and girls around the world, leads the way in the work of emptying ourselves of patriarchy and misogyny.

Groups working toward this end include UN Women and the Commission on the Status of Women (CSW) dedicated to gender equality and empowerment of women utilizing international agreements such as CEDAW (Convention on the Elimination of all Forms of Discrimination Against Women). In particular, the General Recommendations 12, 19, and 34 and the 1993 UN Declaration on the Elimination of Violence Against Women are global champions in support of the full humanity of women and girls. These women's human rights entities and their instruments demonstrate the global consciousness that all human beings are born free and equal in dignity and rights and that discrimination against women violates the principles of equality of rights and respect for human dignity. CEDAW, also known as the women's treaty, which has been ratified by 189 countries, has not been signed or ratified by the Holy See which has permanent observer status to the United Nations.

The Women's Ordination Conference (WOC) report on their 2019 United Nations 63rd CSW participatory event titled, "Catholics for Human Rights: Challenging the Holy See at the United Nations," states that the Vatican's gender ideology of complementarity relegates women to "roles of service, nurturing, and adoration," and that not surprisingly, "men are always awarded power, authority, and dominance" over women.[11] The doctrine of complementarity, in which male and female are assigned roles and destinies based solely on biological differences—a doctrine explicit with harmful gender stereotypes that women's advocates at the UN seek to dismantle worldwide—forms the foundation of the Vatican's theological anthropology. A recent invention of modern popes, complementarity has been mobilized by the Vatican in attempts to influence secular law in various settings including the United Nations' 1995 Beijing World Conference on Women.

With this Vatican strategy persisting over the decades, the WOC filed an official complaint with the United Nations at the 63rd CSW as to why the Holy See, which does not practice gender equality, is allowed a place at an event that works explicitly for the equality and empowerment of women and girls. The WOC website reads, "While many Catholics may not be aware of the privileged status the Vatican enjoys at the United Nations, nor the ironic obsession with gender and women's rights, we at WOC know this is not a harmless quirk of history."[12] WOC also asserts in its 2019 UN CSW 63 report that the Vatican's doctrine on gender complementarity reinforces and exacerbates the abuse, violence, and discrimination women experience around the world. Its doctrine, "dictates its positions in the UN system, and reveals a fundamental incompatibility with human rights provisions of CEDAW," and "partners with governments that are generally known as most repressive in terms of rights of women."[13] The report explicitly recommends that the United Nations remove the Holy See from participation in the annual CSW because "such a male-dominated and misogynist power structure should not be given power to influence policies with massive impacts on the health, safety, and well-being of women, children, and families."[14]

The Roman Catholic hierarchy, with its claim of divine-sanctioned male supremacy, imposes on the world its misogyny and stands in direct opposition to the UN's global stance that females are born free and equal in human dignity. Consequently, Roman Catholic clergymen are directly, institutionally opposed to global efforts to eradicate masculine violence against women and girls. Essentially, Roman Catholic clergymen are a spiritual gateway to masculine violence perpetrated against women and girls worldwide.

Inter Insigniores' theological violence undermines women and girls at the core of their being in relation to themselves and to the divine. Viewed daily through the misogynistic prism of ontological inferiority, females are rendered vulnerable to chronic spiritual wounding by Roman Catholic clergymen. Women's detachment from the Roman Catholic clergy's influence and women's ejection of Roman Catholic theological misogyny are crucial for their discovery of new spaces where they can heal, grow, and share solidarity with other females. Toward this end, I will include cameos throughout this chapter to demonstrate the suffering inflicted on women and girls by Roman Catholic misogyny. Each cameo concludes with a reminder (in italics) of the cameo's connection to the Church's misogynistic theology. The chapter will also embrace poetry and dreams to illustrate that symbols and images of the unconscious can be sources of personal autonomy and authority. Attending to and respecting the rich symbols and images of the inner self, of one's own self and of others, can reveal immanent divine presence with power to release a liberating, life-changing consciousness.

CAMEO ONE: HER SOUL GROANS

Ludmilla Javarova was ordained a Catholic priest in the underground church of Communist Czechoslovakia in 1970 where her identity was protected, a guarded secret even among many in the clandestine church itself. She understood that she did not become a priest on the day of her ordination. Rather, she would have to accept a ministry and work to develop the gift inherent in the call. "What changed from the day of my ordination is this: I started every evening by blessing the whole world. And I was aware of the fact that it was the blessing of a priest."[15] She found herself ministering to people who sought her out for help. She listened to their troubles with compassion. Though she could not reveal her priesthood to those for whom she cared, she knew that

God was sending them to her. Women unable to share their deep inner selves with a male priest would bare their souls to Ludmilla. She was glad to be available to women, for their spiritual care, especially women who had been brutalized by their husbands.

Word of Ludmilla's identity as a priest was revealed without her knowledge and she describes the suffering experienced in her soul caused by the cruel interrogation of a male cleric. "He began to chastise me. He was very angry. I knelt there silent and rigid, as if I had turned to stone. . . . I was in such an agonized state after leaving the church that evening that I walked through the narrow, deserted streets groaning out loud. The sounds came from deep within with a piercing intensity. I had been so serious about my spiritual life. I had done everything conscientiously. At that moment my spirit recoiled. I was filled with desolation."[16]

His eyes redden, God is male. Christ is male.

CAMEO TWO: HER DISTRESS

Elizabeth Johnson, a Catholic feminist theologian, was up for a tenure-track position in 1987 at the Catholic University of America in Washington DC. Cardinal Ratzinger called every Catholic cardinal in the United States to go to Washington to interrogate her focused on an article she had written in which she challenged the overly passive and obedient characterization of Mary by the Church.

Johnson had been in Cape Town, South Africa not long before having to return to the United States to face the cardinals' interrogation. Reflecting on her time in South Africa, she remembered walking past a pastel-colored building that had been vandalized with dark paint reading, "Hang Mandela." She noticed that someone had taken a pencil and added a preposition, transforming the message to read, "Hang On Mandela." In a time of great darkness, someone changed the message. The message spoke to her as well.

The only woman in a room filled with men, Johnson describes the interrogation. "There were these men and they had all the power. I was vulnerable and at their mercy. There was patriarchy using its power against me, to deprive me of what, in fairness, I should have been given. I kept thinking that in another century, they would be lighting the fires outside" to burn the witch.[17] Boston's Cardinal Bernard Law slammed shut the binder of Johnson's writings and pushed them away, "You mostly teach Christology. You're not going to do anymore of this feminist stuff."[18] The message was very clear.

His eyes burn, I am male. I image Christ.

CAMEO THREE: HER AGONY

Carolyn Fortney recalled that as a little girl she was regularly chosen by the parish priest to carry the baby Jesus down the aisle at Christmas indicating how special she was to him. He also gave her toys and candy and was a regular guest in her family's household. This was the Catholic priest who sexually abused her from the time she was eighteen months until she turned twelve. Carolyn was the youngest of five sisters whom he sexually abused. He kissed them, fondled them, took pornographic nude pictures of them, and was obsessed with collecting urine, pubic hair, and menstrual blood from them as they used the toilet. She cried in the arms of one of her sisters as the Pennsylvania Attorney General spoke at a press conference in August 2018 on the grand jury report about male Catholic clergy sexual abuse of children. Experiencing years of agony and wanting "to take all the pain away from that little girl,"[19] she once attempted suicide, feeling at the time as if she were two people—"herself in that moment and as a child in the grip"[20] of the priest's abuse. Carolyn lamented, "It's very lonely. Especially when it's your word against *God's*."[21] She has felt that her whole life has been a lie. "The word 'god' makes me think of him," she said.[22]

His eyes blaze, God is not female. Christ is not female.

CAMEO FOUR: HER DISQUIETUDE

In the early 1990s, I was a theology teacher in a girls' Catholic High School, an adjunct theology instructor at a Catholic University, and a volunteer advocate at a rape crisis center. I served also as chairwoman of a women's issues committee at a Catholic parish where a small group of parishioners had begun to take a close look at the issue of violence against women. Emerging from the efforts of this small group, in the winter of 1991 I had the opportunity to preach about the reality of domestic violence and sexual assault perpetrated by men against women and girls. After two months of study, prayer, and input from my mentors, my homily was complete, and I was ready to preach at three Masses. I was under the impression that I had full support of the pastoral staff, however on the eve of the preaching weekend, the parish priest stood in front of me with a pen and my manuscript in his hand. He began marking out whole paragraphs, drawing arrows to relocate sentences, and writing his words in place of mine. Next to him, a layman also on the church's pastoral staff, palpably tense, added that a homily this particular weekend should be about the Gulf War.

That evening at home I felt as though I were a stripped down version of myself as disquietude settled in. My homily, composed with specialized knowledge in the area of women's spirituality and advocacy, was undermined by competitive men in a sudden fit of severe, misogynistic dominance. The disorientation was painful. Why was I under personal siege for my commitment to the safety of women and girls in my church? How would I recover my strength in time enough to preach?

As a phoenix rises, I regained myself. My original manuscript in front of me, I looked out on my community with compassion, breaking silence and speaking hope from the pulpit. I was likely the only Catholic laywoman in my city or state preaching at Catholic masses that weekend or even that year about masculine violence against women and girls. What about Catholic churches in the country or around the world? Somewhere, yes. Wherever an individual woman may be doing so, she too stands in the pulpit very much alone. Her solitary body, soul, and voice stand not only against the misogyny in her midst, but with awareness of millennia of male, violent erasure of female bodies, souls, and voices.

The only feedback the priest gave me after I preached that weekend was negative. It was about my body posture in the pulpit. I had to pause and wonder what he was talking about. It then dawned on me that I had temporarily rested my weight on my right hip to calm the trembling in my legs. My body felt the magnitude of what I was doing publicly in the sanctuary and was expressing the vulnerability and power of my existential act of resistance. Sensitive and wise indeed was my body in those moments. I gently stilled the trembling by adjusting my body posture for a few seconds. The eye of the parish priest fixated on this fleeting detail of my body. He disapprovingly focused on my awkward stance—an inexcusable trivialization of my work at hand.

Two days later the parish priest phoned me at home saying that a parishioner called and confided in him that her husband would hold a gun to her a head. He wondered if I could talk with her. After agreeing to do so, he warned me that she can really push her husband's buttons. His words shocked me. A woman who is terrorized by her husband with a firearm, at high risk for domestic homicide, is blamed for her husband's behavior by the parish priest. I myself traversed significant misogynistic obstacles to preach and to be accessible to a Catholic woman whom I had never met, whose husband and priest were a threat to her existence. I preached from the pulpit and she emerged from the silent shadows of the pews with a call for help. How many more were too afraid to step forward?

His eyes scoff, Christ is male. I am male.

CAMEO FIVE: HER TERROR

A Catholic nun was raped by her bishop in the room of a small convent at the end of a one-lane road in rural Kerala, India. He raped her thirteen times from 2014 to 2016. "No sooner than I reached the room than he pulled me toward him. I was numbed and terrified by his act. I took all efforts to get out, but in vain. He raped me brutally."[23]

The few nuns who have surrounded her with support and who have protested publicly against the predator bishop and the church's pressure to silence them have become pariahs. In their commitment to the truth, they have received hate mail, have been accused of worshipping Satan, and of working against the church.

His eyes rage, You are female. You do not image Christ.

As demonstrated in our cameos, theologian Wendy Farley describes masculine violence against females as that which creates the excruciating transformation when a human being created in the divine image is treated as if she were a stone. She writes, "The effect of violence is privation: it is privation of personhood, of spirit. It is an obscuration of the image of God; and this violence is, above all else, evil."[24] The evil of violence not only causes pain, but it has power to deface the human spirit. Furthermore, Farley states though the evil dwells in the heart of the criminal, it is not felt there. Rather it is felt in the heart of the woman as humiliation and self-loathing.

Each day in Roman Catholic churches and chapels the world over, clergymen physically occupy the male-dominant spaces of pulpit and altar, speaking and praying Christian symbols as a system of domination. From these elevations, they look out upon the females. All women and girls present lookup at the ordained men and listen to their words with the unspoken expectation to internalize what is heard from the men as God's truth, the church's truth, and their own truth. Psychotherapist Anne Wilson Schaff likens living in this type of patriarchy to living in pollution. "When you are in the middle of pollution, you are usually unaware of it. You eat in it, sleep in it, work in it and sooner or later start believing that this is just the way air is."[25] Similarly, Ruether writes that "we are socialized from infancy to conform to systems of domination as if they were normal, natural, and the will of God."[26] Every day of every month of every year of every decade of every century for two millennia, the world over, women and girls have looked up at and listened to ordained men as the central figures and voices of Roman Catholic cathedrals, churches, and chapels. Today, millions of women and girls around the world sit silently in pews looking up at and listening to elevated, centralized Roman Catholic clergymen while internalizing their own worthlessness.

Soraya Chemaly asserts that girls learn that God is mediated only through men stating, "When girls go to churches where there are no women priests, they learn to be quiet. They are taught, through thousands of small interactions, language and rules, that their words cannot and do not have power."[27] From a very early age, girls who attend Roman Catholic liturgies learn to suppress their deep spiritual knowing as females while fueling their own self-loathing.

Luce Irigaray holds that in male-dominant discourse, women are confined to the function of a mirror, reflecting back to a man his masculinity, helping him to establish a relationship with his own masculinity. Females are obscured and masked in this male-dominant masquerade that does not contain them.[28] Female obedience and docility are normalized in Roman Catholic pews every day the world over. In sum, systems of domination foster violence and unhealthy environments that alienate human beings from one another.

Beatrice Bruteau argues that masculine consciousness is domination consciousness and a domination paradigm determines "who is dominant and who is submissive, who decides and who obeys, who is to be deferred to and who may be ridiculed."[29] She adds, "the refusal of the female, the emblem of all submission, to accept this identification and to play this role, presages a profound shift in *all* our social relations and in all our perceptions of the way being is ordered."[30] Bruteau insists that nothing new comes from domination consciousness. To preach against injustice and to preach that we love our neighbors as ourselves while human lives continue to be arranged in the order of domination/submission is insufficient, as it will be "psychologically impossible for us to desist from the practice of injustice."[31]

Untold numbers of women and girls around the world who walk through the doors of Roman Catholic churches carry with them the trauma of domestic violence, sexual assault, rape, stalking, and harassment, whether living in terror in the present moment or bearing unhealed suffering from past violations. Whether she is conscious of it or not, though it be her spiritual home, she is on inhospitable, even hostile ground, as a victim of gender-based violence. Even while sitting next to her abuser in the pew, her fear and degradation are routinely unnoticed, overlooked, and dismissed by clergymen. Tragically, too many Catholic women and girls internalize his consciousness as their own, are rendered alien to their own deepest selves, and are robbed of the depths of divine and communal care possible. In her soul, where she groans, weeps, and cries out, the shadows of misogyny fill sanctuaries like dense incense, blocking divine light, confusing and silencing her. Her church is not her sanctuary.

In his book *Pedagogy of the Oppressed,* Paulo Freire warns that oppressed people at some time in their existence will adopt an adhesion to the oppressor which distorts their perception of themselves. For Catholic women and girls, this adhesion occurs with their Catholic clergymen. Female soul-adhesion to these men is a tragically deep self-negation. She does not internalize a Christ image, rather she internalizes an enemy to her own deepest being. In her deference to him, it is he that indwells her, not Christ.

Freire states that oppressed people suffer from a duality that is established in one's innermost being. "They are at one and the same time themselves and the oppressor whose consciousness they have internalized."[32] Internalized also are the oppressor's guidelines which causes oppressed people to live in fear of freedom. Freire holds that "One of the greatest obstacles to the achievement of liberation is that oppressive reality absorbs those within it and thereby acts to submerge human beings' consciousness."[33] Freedom requires oppressed people to eject the internalized image of the oppressor and to replace that with autonomy. He urges that to no longer be prey to the oppressor's consciousness, one must "emerge from it and turn upon it."[34] That emergence requires an openness to feminist consciousness.

Ruether explains that openness to feminist consciousness calls for women to question all they have been taught about feminine virtue. "All the ways that women have been taught to be 'pleasing' and 'acceptable' to men are critically reviewed as possible tools of false consciousness and seduction, preventing women from asking who they are as persons."[35] It is painful, even traumatic to lead a quest for one's own personhood. Ruether writes that women are conditioned to think that rebellious thoughts and self-affirmation are the sins of Eve and that self-negation and suffering are Christlike. A woman's journey out of patriarchal consciousness is a murky, intrepid path as not only her church but also her inner self can be a forbidden territory for a profound welcoming of the authentic feminine in her soul. A woman's journey out of patriarchal consciousness is difficult at best.

In her memoir, *The Dance of the Dissident Daughter,* Sue Monk Kidd recounts her experience of a recurring dream in which the masculine, dressed in bishop's garb and representing oppression, tries to keep her in line and quiet. Each time the bishop appears in a dream, she tries to bring it to consciousness and "depotentiate his power."[36] After months of this process, she had a particularly impactful dream.

> *I am shut up in the Bishop's house and feeling terribly ill. I have a desperate need to vomit, and I beg the Bishop for a trash can so I can throw up. He adamantly refuses. I feel that if I don't vomit I will die, and I keep pleading with him, but he is determined to keep me from vomiting.*[37]

The dream left her nauseated and depressed, feeling as though her feminine soul was at stake for all the patriarchal content she had swallowed in her life. Her analyst encouraged her to reenter her dream where it left off by closing her eyes and allowing her imagination to choreograph. As she was back in her dream pleading for a trash can so that she could vomit, her imagination supplied her with a magnificent pair of antlers that she used to heave the bishop into the air causing his house to fall on his head. "Outside in a nearby woods … I finally threw up. I relieved myself of all the stuff that had poisoned my insides."[38] Nearly instantly, she was relieved of doubt and depression. Her imagination gifted her with enormous healing power. The bishop began to disappear from her dreams and she worked to integrate her inner knowing with her daily living. Faithful to her inner life, Kidd was able to experience necessary self-emptying of internalized patriarchy. This deepened her feminist consciousness.

As one writer states, "We are building a revolution of the psyche as well as of society."[39] A little later in the memoir, Kidd describes an experience in which her young daughter asks her what she is reading. Telling her that she is reading about biblical Sophia, her daughter draws close and settles next to her, asking to hear everything about Her. "And I could almost see in her face the way it affected her sense of her female self."[40] A woman who devotes herself to the strenuous inner work of healing internalized misogyny will cast her light of wakefulness in the world.

Divine Feminine, Holy Sophia
Holy Sophia and Her Child
My darling, girl Leap!
from the church cornerstone
that freezes you,
from the artifact that conceals you.
My darling, girl Spring!
into the arms
of Mother Wisdom.
My darling, girl Shimmy!
through My canopy.
My darling, girl Feel!
our unfathomable rootedness.
My darling, girl Swing!
on my boldest branch.
My darling, girl Laugh!
and emit our fragrances.
My darling, girl Be Swathed!
in My royal green,
earth and spirit caressing your Skin!
Child of earth, Know!
bliss in My birdsongs.
Child of heaven, Share!

jewels of the Holy.
My darling
We See! as One.
We listen! as One.
We speak! as One.
Darkness will
never separate
Wisdom and
Her Child.[41]

The Greek *Sophia*—Wisdom in English—appears in later Old Testament writings and offers women a pathway to feminist consciousness. Elizabeth Johnson writes, "language about Sophia bespeaks the unfathomable mystery of the living God in female imagery."[42] Johnson highlights several Sophia descriptions from the New American Bible (NAB) Old Testament Wisdom Literature. Sophia is described as "radiant and unfading" (Wisdom, 6:12) and "a reflection of eternal light" (Wisdom, 7:26) who "is more beautiful than the sun and excels every constellation of the stars" (Wisdom, 7:29). Sophia delivered Her people from oppressors, "guiding them along a marvelous way, and became a shelter to them by day, and a starry flame through the night" (Wisdom, 10:17). When her people journeyed through wilderness and cried out to her in thirst, "water was given them out of flinty rock and from hard stone a remedy for their thirst" (Wisdom, 10:4). Importantly, Johnson reminds us that antiquity's largest church was dedicated to Christ under the title *Hagia Sophia,* Holy Wisdom and points out the imagery of a favorite Advent hymn in which Divine Sophia is longed for: "Hidden in plain sight in this hymn is a female image of God that runs like a golden thread through the whole Christian tradition."[43]

Many other scholars agree with Johnson's emphasis on Wisdom Literature as a pathway to feminist consciousness. For instance, Rabbi Rami Shapiro writes, "Wisdom desires you even more than you desire Her … She rushes to reveal Herself to you in the midst of your life."[44] Similarly, Episcopal priest Cynthia Bourgeault states, "So it *is* true after all: there has been a feminine presence, lurking all along at the root of our Jewish-Christian universe!"[45] Constance Fitzgerald explains that biblical Wisdom is a personal "I" who summons as mother, beloved, preacher, and liberator and the experience of Sophia may be above all subversive, "because it affects how we understand the very nature of God, and our understanding of God is what affects the character and quality of our human living."[46]

O come thou Wisdom from on high,
who orders all things mightily;
to us the path of knowledge show[47]

Jungian analyst Marion Woodman writes in *Leaving My Father's House: A Journey to Conscious Femininity*, given our three-thousand-year-old cultural process focused through masculine eyes in which "men have projected their image of femininity, raising it to a consciousness that left women who accepted the projection separated from their own reality," it is our immediate task to awaken and relate to the eternal feminine who is "thrusting her way into contemporary consciousness."[48] She adds, "It is an arduous task to work toward this consciousness but it opens a woman to the world's woundedness where healing can be discovered." Her task is to make an exodus from the shadow of patriarchal power by conscious participation in her inner truth which is a "dynamic, moment-by-moment discovery."[49]

Woodman holds that patriarchy disrespects and dismisses imagery and the inner world—the soul. Living conscious femininity, a woman rejects patriarchal confines and makes her intellect, spirit, body, and soul her own. She pursues the freedom of grounding herself in imagery that rises from her soul. She finds her own sacred space where she can drop deep into her "nature and connect with the divine within."[50] For a Catholic woman, it involves choosing to no longer project "golden boy" onto the clergy, to detach from his sovereignty, and to eject his religious misogyny from her inner self. Conscious femininity is the fire of transformation searing through a woman's emotional attachments that hold her captive, releasing her from patriarchal grounding in the pews. Describing feminine consciousness as rooted in the heart, Woodman writes, "The feeling comes with the thought, and as the thought is spoken, the heart opens, and feeling flows to deeper, richer levels."[51]

In this feminist consciousness, a woman surrenders herself to the flow of the unknown and courageously asks herself, "Who am I and what am I doing?" Woodman points out, as do women's human rights advocates at the United Nations, that significant misogynistic backlash against women globally occurs as they become conscious of their female strength. Woodman adds that male reprisal is being acted out increasingly against defenseless children. "To strengthen ourselves to deal with the backlash, we have to be our authentic self."[52]

CAMEO SIX: HER AWARENESS

In her book *The Star In My Heart: Discovering Inner Wisdom,* Joyce Rupp describes Sophia, Holy Wisdom, as a feminine face of the Holy who gives her comfort and happiness, nurturing her listening heart and drawing her toward truth. She writes that the book was born on a day she was watching over a two-year-old child in a fragrant, colorful rose garden.

Toddler Elizabeth Ann was playing in the garden, laughing and splashing the flowers with her watering can. "It was there that I became keenly aware of Sophia's presence. I looked at the beautiful child at play, and I remembered how Sophia (Wisdom) speaks of herself in Proverbs: *I was at God's side . . . delighting God day after day, ever at play in God's presence, at play everywhere in God's world* (Proverbs 8:30–31). There had been many moments in my life when the sudden recognition of her radiant presence had pressed tears into my eyes. . . . This kind of recognition happened when I saw Elizabeth at play."[53]

Darkness will never separate Wisdom and Her Child

Walking away from the false consciousness of Roman Catholic misogyny, leaving the abusive language of *Inter Insigniores* and turning away from the false Christ of clerics who subjugate the feminine, is like the feminine soul leading the way toward spacious new dwellings in which to find oneself. It is where one awakens, and listens with a new heart, and feels deeply, and is drawn into the complex and joyful mysteries of the Divine Feminine. My own experiences bear witness to this transformation.

In the early 1990s, I participated in creating the *Women's Homily Series* at a Catholic parish in Louisville, Kentucky. One Sunday evening a month in the sanctuary, fifty yards from the clergyman's office door, women gathered to preach and to lead woman-centered ritual for the healing of patriarchal wounds. Women preached from the pulpit, spoke aloud their theological and biblical perspectives, danced in prayer, opened hearts to the Divine Feminine, and extended their open arms in comfort to one another. Women from surrounding parishes participated. Those suffering the trauma of sexual assault, clergy sex abuse, clergy misogynist abuse, and domestic violence found a sacred oasis. The spiritually marginalized were gathered in and greeted with deep, welcoming eyes. Daughters watched and heard their mothers preach and granddaughters watched and heard their grandmothers preach. Men who attended would quietly hold the space, supporting the voice and visibility of the feminine energy.

Beverly Lanzetta, in her book, *Radical Wisdom: A Feminist Mystical Theology,* writes, "The point at which a woman confronts her liberation as 'woman' is where she also discovers the great lie about the 'feminine' and her *spiritual* suppression and marginalization as a representative of the lesser sex."[54] The *Women's Homily Series* was a brief time in which Catholic women were confronting their liberation as women. In this communal experience, a seismic shift in consciousness began to emerge. Experiencing intense flashes and manifestations of the authentic feminine, women confronted the ontological inferiority projected on them by the clergy. In this liturgical environment, the smoke of misogyny thinned a bit as women experienced space to see each other through newly awakening eyes. The disfigured skin of *Inter Insigniores* loosened a bit, for the brief glimpsing of selves shimmering with freedom, for the brief foretelling of faces alight in the Divine Feminine. The Sunday morning pews of female silence were becoming momentarily transformed by the Sunday evening dynamism of the *Women's Homily Series*. The space became a place to experience illumination, to breathe deeply, be creative, seek honesty, and be in communion with one another gently and delightfully.

The *Women's Homily Series,* a graced, hospitable place for the emerging Divine Feminine, was sustainable in a patriarchal church for only three years. In the summer of 1995, when our Sunday evening prayer took the shape of a solidarity liturgy for a Catholic woman theologian, our own falling apart began. Systematic Theology Professor, Carmel McEnroy, at St. Meinrad seminary, had signed an open letter to the pope with hundreds of other people calling for continued discussion of the ordination of women. The pope had declared in 1994 that the exclusion of women from the priesthood could not even be discussed in the church. St. Meinrad seminary administration and church officials claimed that Professor McEnroy publicly dissented from long established church teaching, disqualifying her from continuing in her faculty position. McEnroy's friend and colleague Bridget Clare McKeever, Pastoral Care Professor, resigned from her position at St. Meinrad in solidarity with her.

Ninety people attended the *Women's Homily Series* solidarity service, including some of Professor McEnroy's seminary students. Prophetic texts were proclaimed and preached on, liturgical dance embodied the passion for justice, and friends spoke their words of grief. Professor McEnroy who was out of town and unable to attend had sent a letter and photograph. She wrote that near where she lived there was a catalpa tree that had lain on the ground lifeless for years. But that spring it had begun to sprout new branches. She wrote that the once dead tree was alive again and growing in a new direction which gave her comfort and hope. Her enclosed picture revealed a tree adorned with foliage of scintillating, new greenery. On that summer evening in 1995, Carmel McEnroy's hope was shared with courage among friends.

Inside the clergyman's door fifty yards away was an angry man who saw all of this as an embodiment of the enemy. In his patriarchal authority and his misogynist orientation, he undermined this communal effort to bring to birth the authentic feminine. It soon became too hostile to women's souls to continue this work in the household of the abusive father.

On a dark and cold February evening three years prior, the opening evening of the *Women's Homily Series,* a ritual foretold the way out of the grip of Roman Catholic misogyny and into profound transformation. On that evening, dim lights and stillness surrounded everyone. On a small table for all to see was a large glass bowl of water and placed in the center of the bowl was a tall, lighted candle. A woman went to the candle and put a slip of paper into the flame. She said aloud the message she had written on the paper: "I never again want to hear that I can't do something because I am a woman." The paper burned and the ashes fell into the water. Heads bowed and some tears fell.

I never want to hear again
She said aloud
Paper into the flame
Paper burned
Ashes fell
Tears fell
She lamented
I never want to hear again
Because I am a woman.

These words of lament, cries of pain and protest, familiar throughout the biblical prophets and Psalms, when spoken by one woman in the bosom of intimate, supportive community, had enormous power. The rising of lament from her depths and her conscious action of putting the lament to the consuming flames is a herald of individual and communal transformation. It is a spiritual event hollowing out internal and external space for a new and deeper path. Her soul's recognition of the oppression, her courage to articulate the pain, her strength to embody the resistance in a ritual action, and her trust in the circle of support during those dim and quiet minutes blaze a horizon that transcends the particular evening. Her lament dares to expand consciousness, to explore what is true and what is false. Her lament is preparation for a vision of wholeness. This one woman, this one ritual, this one small community, and the vision issuing forth from their intimate, winter ritual exude mystical sensibilities.

In her book *The Silent Cry: Mysticism and Resistance,* Dorothee Soelle uncovers aspects of the mystical path as she describes human experiences of deep inwardness, nakedness before the Holy, unmediated nearness to the Holy, a sacred summoning to one's inner homeland, "an immanence that opens itself to transcendence and takes part in it," and the breaking open of one's secluded self.[55] To open one's imagination to the intimate and to internalize the very words that describe human, mystical experience, is to be drawn into deep integrity of self in relation to the Holy. This language and what it promotes is the antithesis of patriarchal domination language that disparages the feminine.

Similarly, theologian Beverly Lanzetta writes of a mystical path particular to those whose awareness is being raised about patriarchal consciousness and misogynistic violence. She calls this path the via feminina and describes it as a process or quality of consciousness that is revelatory of the Divine Feminine breaking into history. It transforms the historical denigration of women as it "heals the ancient fracture of consciousness" that distorts the female and the feminine.[56] When someone walks the path of the via feminina, one experiences the Divine Feminine doing healing work at the very foundation of one's being. It involves a painful undoing—eradicating patriarchal content and wounds as well as cleansing one's self of false teachings, false gods, and misogynist projections. It is an inner journey of unsaying, undoing, and negating that which has oppressed her authentic selfhood. The via feminina is a pathway into the fires of transformation where there is a fusion of love between the Divine and one's soul, between the female Self with Holy Sophia. It is a path of radical authenticity and freedom. It births an honesty and boldness in her soul that she lives on behalf of herself and the lives of other women and girls. This birth is not possible in the Roman Catholic patriarchal Church of *Inter Insigniores* illustrated in the dream sequence that we began this journey with.

> *I dreamt that young Christa and I are in a spacious place preparing to teach a large gathering about ending violence against women. I hear a few men in the audience speaking words of great distress, "My life is meaningless. I have so much pain. My life should be over." Feeling concern and empathy for these men, I ask them to leave and go find help, for Christa and I have much work to do.*

In this final dream, the feminine is no longer disfigured. The burning destructiveness of misogyny has been replaced with the alchemical fires of transformation that have released her and changed her into Christa—Christ in female form. In giving herself to the healing of violence against women, she gives bread for the world.

NOTES

1. Kate Manne, *Down Girl* (New York: Oxford University Press, 2018), 85.
2. Sean Illing, "What We Get Wrong about Misogyny," Updated February 7, 2018. vox.com.
3. UN General Assembly, *Declaration on the Elimination of Violence Against Women,* December 20, 1993, A/RES/48/104, https://www.refworld.org/docid/3b00f25d2c.html [Accessed November 10, 2019].

4. UN General Assembly, *Convention on the Elimination of All Forms of Discrimination Against Women,* December 18, 1979, United Nations Treaty Series, vol. 1249, p. 13, https://refworld.org/docid/3ae6b3970.html [Accessed November 10, 2019].

5. UN, "Time to Fight the Global Avalanche of Misogyny Caused by Fundamentalism and Extremism," United Nations Human Rights Office of the High Commissioner, October 25, 2017.

6. Vatican. 1976. "Declaration Inter Insigniores: On the Question of Admission of Women to the Ministerial Priesthood." http://www.vatican.va/roman_curia/congregations/cfaith/documents/rc_concfaith_19761015_inter-insigniores_en.html. [Accessed November 10, 2019]

7. Eun-Young, Julia Kim, and Beverly J. Matiko, "Power, Ideology, and Women's Ordination: Discursive Strategies in Three Roman Catholic Documents," Critical Research on Religion, September 18, 2019, https://doi.org/10.1177/2050303219874375.

8. Rosemary Radford Ruether, *Sexism and God-Talk: Toward a Feminist Theology* (Boston: Beacon Press, 1983), 95.

9. Ruether, *Sexism and God-Talk*, 137.

10. Ibid., 138.

11. Women's Ordination Conference, "Report on the Holy See at the United Nations," Catholics for Human Rights: Challenging the Holy See at the United Nations, UN CSW 63 Parallel Event, March 14, 2019, p. 17, womensordination.org.

12. Women's Ordination Conference "Catholics for Human Rights," womensordination.org.

13. Women's Ordination Conference Report, 17.

14. Women's Ordination Conference Report, 18.

15. Miriam Therese Winter, *Out of the Depths: The Story of Ludmilla Javorova Ordained Roman Catholic Priest* (New York: The Crossroad Publishing Company, 2001), 141.

16. Winter, *Out of the Depths*, 170.

17. Jamie L. Manson, "Feminism in Faith: Sister Elizabeth Johnson's Challenge to the Vatican," March 7, 2014. BuzzFeed.com.

18. Manson, "Feminism in Faith," 2014.

19. Tricia L. Nadolny, "Five Sisters, Abused By One Priest, Tell their Stories," Philly.com, September 21, 2018.

20. Nadolny, "Five Sisters, Abused By One Priest, Tell their Stories," September 2018.

21. Tricia L. Nadolny, "Victim of Priest Abuse: 'It's Your Word against God's,'" Inquirer.com, August 14, 2018.

22. Democracy Now "Catholic Church Cover-Up: 300 Priests Sexually Abused 1,000 Children in Pennsylvania," democracynow.org, August 16, 2018.

23. Suhasini Raj and Kai Schultz, "Bishop in India Charged With Raping Nun Over a 2-Year Period," *New York Times*, April 9, 2019. nytimes.com.

24. Wendy Farley, "Evil, Violence, and the Practice of Theodicy," in *Telling The Truth: Preaching About Sexual and Domestic Violence,* ed. John S. McClure and Nancy J. Ramsay (Cleveland: United Church Press, 1998), 13.

25. Anne Wilson Schaef, *Women's Reality: An Emerging Female System in a White Male Society* (San Francisco: Harper & Row, 1981), 27.

26. Rosemary Radford Ruether, "Feminist Metanoia and Soul-Making," in *Introducing Redemption in Christian Feminism* (Sheffield: Sheffield Academic Press, 1998), 70.

27. Soraya Chemaly, "Every Altar Girl the Catholic Church Turns Away is a Gift to the Rest of the World," in *Whatever Works: Feminists of Faith Speak A Girl God Anthology,* ed. Trista Hendren and Pat Daly (Scotts Valley: CreateSpace Independent Publishing Platform, 2015), Kindle edition.

28. Ann-Marie Priest, "Woman as God, God as Woman: Mysticism, Negative Theology, and Luce Irigaray," *The Journal of Religion* 83, no. 1 (January 2003): 7, 13, https://www.jstor.org/stable/1205434.

29. Beatrice Bruteau, *The Grand Option: Personal Transformation and a New Creation* (Notre Dame: University of Notre Dame Press, 2001), 26–27.

30. Bruteau, *The Grand Option*, 26.

31. Ibid., 27.

32. Paulo Freire, *Pedagogy of the Oppressed* (New York: Continuum, 1970), 30.

33. Freire, *Pedagogy of the Oppressed*, 33.

34. Ibid., 33.

35. Ruether, "Feminist Metanoia," 76.

36. Sue Monk Kidd, *The Dance of the Dissident Daughter: A Woman's Journey from Christian Tradition to the Sacred Feminine* (New York: HarperCollins, 2002), 117.

37. Kidd, *The Dance of the Dissident Daughter,* 118.

38. Ibid.

39. Charlene Spretnak, "The Unity of Politics and Spirituality," in *The Politics of Spirituality* ed. Charlene Spretnak (Garden City, NY: Anchor Books, 1982), 351.

40. Kidd, *The Dance of the Dissident Daughter*, 150.

41. Mary Sue Barnett, "Holy Sophia and Her Child." *The Feminist Voice* 1, no. 1 (2019): 1. [Printed with permission from the copyright holder.]

42. Elizabeth A. Johnson, "God Acting Womanish," in *Quest for the Living God: Mapping Frontiers in the Theology of God* (London: Bloomsbury, 2007), 105.

43. Johnson, "God Acting Womanish," 104.

44. Rabbi Rami Shapiro, *The Divine Feminine in Biblical Literature: Selections Annotated and Explained* (Woodstock: Skylight Paths, 2010), 64.

45. Shapiro, *The Divine Feminine in Biblical Literature*, ix.

46. Constance Fitzgerald, "Transformation in Wisdom: The Subversive Character and Educative Power of Sophia in Contemplation," in *Carmel and Contemplation: Transforming Human Consciousness,* ed. Kevin Culligan and Regis Jordan (Washington: ICS Publications, 2000), 283–284.

47. Johnson, "God Acting Womanish," 104.

48. Marion Woodman, *Leaving My Father's House: A Journey to Conscious Femininity,* (Boston: Shambhala, 1992), 1–2.

49. Woodman, *Leaving My Father's House*, 1.

50. Ibid., 18.

51. Ibid., 116.
52. Ibid., 31.
53. Joyce Rupp, *The Star in my Heart: Discovering Inner Wisdom* (Notre Dame: Sorin Books, 2004), Kindle Edition.
54. Beverly J. Lanzetta, *Radical Wisdom: A Feminist Mystical Theology* (Minneapolis: Fortress Press, 2005), 17.
55. Dorothee Soelle, *The Silent Cry: Mysticism and Resistance* (Minneapolis: Fortress Press, 2001), 29.
56. Lanzetta, *Radical Wisdom*, 13.

BIBLIOGRAPHY

Barnett, Mary Sue. "Holy Sophia and Her Child." *The Feminist Voice,* 1, no. 1 (2019): 1.

Bruteau, Beatrice. *The Grand Option: Personal Transformation and a New Creation.* Notre Dame: University of Notre Dame Press, 2001.

Chemaly, Soraya. "Every Altar Girl the Catholic Church Turns Away is a Gift to the Rest of the World." In *Whatever Works: Feminists of Faith Speak,* edited by Trista Hendren and Pat Daly, Kindle edition. Scotts Valley: CreateSpace Independent Publishing Platform, 2015.

Farley, Wendy. "Evil, Violence, and the Practice of Theodicy." In *Telling the Truth: Preaching about Sexual and Domestic Violence,* edited by John McClure and Nancy J. Ramsay, 11–20. Cleveland: United Church Press, 1998.

FitzGerald, Constance. "Transformation in Wisdom: The Subversive Character and Educative Power of Sophia in Contemplation." In *Carmel and Contemplation: Transforming Human Consciousness,* edited by Kevin and Regis Jordan, 281–358. Washington: ICS Publications, 2000.

Freire, Paulo. *Pedagogy of the Oppressed.* New York: Continuum, 1999.

Johnson, Elizabeth A. *Quest for the Living God: Mapping Frontiers in the Theology of God.* New York: Bloomsbury, 2007.

Kidd, Sue Monk. *The Dance of the Dissident Daughter: A Woman's Journey from Christian Tradition to the Sacred Feminine.* New York: Harper Collins, 1996.

———. *The Secret Life of Bees.* New York: Penguin Books, 2002.

Kim, Eun-Young Julia and Beverly Matiko. "Power, Ideology, and Women's Ordination: Discursive Strategies in Three Roman Catholic Documents." *Critical Research on Religion* (September 2019). https://doi.org/10.1177/2050302119874375

Lanzetta, Beverly J. *Radical Wisdom: A Feminist Mystical Theology.* Minneapolis: Fortress Press, 2005.

Manne, Kate. *Down Girl: The Logic of Misogyny.* New York: Oxford University Press, 2018.

Ruether, Rosemary Radford. *Introducing Redemption in Christian Feminism.* Sheffield: Sheffield Academic Press, 1998.

———. *Sexism and God-Talk.* Boston: Beacon Press, 1983.

Rupp, Joyce. *The Star in My Heart: Discovering Inner Wisdom.* Notre Dame: Sorin Books, 2004.

Schaef, Anne Wilson. *Women's Reality: An Emerging Female System in a White Male Society.* San Francisco: Harper & Row, 1981.

Shapiro, Rabbi Rami. *The Divine Feminine in Biblical Wisdom Literature.* Woodstock: Skylight Paths, 2010.

Soelle, Dorothee. *The Silent Cry: Mysticism and Resistance.* Minneapolis: Fortress Press, 2001.

Spretnak, Charlene. "The Unity of Politics and Spirituality." In *The Politics of Spirituality,* edited by Charlene Spretnak. Garden City, NY: Anchor Books, 1982.

Winter, Miriam Therese. *Out of the Depths: The Story of Ludmilla Javorova Ordained Roman Catholic Priest.* New York: The Crossroad Publishing Company, 2001.

Woodman, Marion. *Leaving My Father's House: A Journey to Conscious Femininity.* Boston: Shambhala, 1992.

Chapter 10

"I Am Heartily Sorry"

The Roman Catholic Church and Domestic Abuse

Debra Meyers

The American Roman Catholic Church's emphasis on sin, shame, guilt, and punishment costs individuals their childhood, but it cost society a great deal more. Heavily influenced by the flawed theology of Jansenism,[1] the mid-twentieth-century American church led nuns and priests to avoid offering real assistance—both temporal and spiritual—to the laity. In fact, these holy people and their emphasis on sin and punishment accentuated the pervasive problem of domestic abuse that would traumatize children with lifelong consequences.[2] The church hierarchy created the environment that led to the abuse of millions of women and children. Indeed, the church actually empowered domestic abusers.[3]

A recent United Nations report boldly states that domestic violence around the world is the most common killer of women. In 2017 alone, an estimated 45,000 women were killed by intimate partners or family members.[4] For American Roman Catholic families, "one in four women sitting in the pews will have experienced severe physical violence in their own homes from their spouses or partners—including burns, choking, beating, or the use of a weapon against them."[5] Church reformer Charles Dahm acknowledged that the "Church has been complicit in" the abuse of women for decades.[6] Only recently has the church decided that this problem should be addressed by offering domestic violence resources to parishes. Yet, the church has not taken ownership of its responsibility for producing this crisis.

For decades, maybe even centuries, the church embraced domestic violence perpetrators while telling victims that it is their cross to bear and that they must reflect on their own culpability for their abuse.[7] After promising to love and forgive until death, a woman's marriage vows imprisoned her as some horrible punishment from God unleashed by her own evilness. Clerics told her that it was God's will. Her Catholic upbringing obligated her to forgive the perpetrator and then ask forgiveness for her own sins while continuing to endure the abuse that she so righteously deserved. She promised to love her husband "for better or for worse" and since his behavior was her own punishment from God, she in essence became a prisoner guarded by the Catholic clergy.

To add to the indignity of the situation for victims, abusers often justified intimate partner violence using biblical text, such as Ephesians 5:22–33 (NIV).[8] "Wives, submit yourselves to your own husbands as you do to the Lord. For the husband is the head of the wife as Christ is the head of the church . . . and let the wife see that she respects her husband." And Paul's letter to the Colossians demanded that "Wives, be subordinate to your husbands, as is proper in the Lord" (Colossians 3:18). Colossians is often read in pulpits today during the feast of the Holy Family in December.[9] The church's stance against divorce and remarriage only reified the grave injustice against women imprisoned in abusive marriages. "Strict teachings on divorce and remarriage, an emphasis on forgiveness at all costs and, less directly, the lack of women in its all-male hierarchy, are leading women to remain in, and blame themselves for, violent relationships."[10]

The U.S. Conference of Catholic Bishops published a statement condemning domestic violence after the Vatican issued the *Amoris Laetitia* (The Joy of Love) declaration in 2015.[11] Regardless of the church's recent assertions that Canon Law[12] does not *compel* women to stay in abusive relationships, the vast majority of people in the pews have been inculcated from infancy with the opposite idea. While few Catholics read Canon Law, they are influenced by the words and actions of the clergy, overwhelmingly leaving the impression that a woman's own guilt has caused the abuser to act against her—a message that reassures perpetrators and prevents victims from seeking justice.

When clergy do make efforts to address this continuing crisis, we find that "it is difficult for the Catholic Church to promote respectful relationships and sexual ethics when clergy are unable to be open about their own relationships" says criminologist Michael Salter.[13] Moreover, many Catholic women remain in abusive relationships "because they believe their church requires them to, or because they are adhering strictly to core teachings about forgiveness."[14] Peter Johnstone argues, "The Church's teachings certainly treat women unequally in the key area of its governance and its pastoral ministries—without a convincing scriptural basis." He adds, "I'm aware of statements from the church expressing in words its condemnation of domestic violence. However, the implicit messages in the structures and teachings of the Church, which clearly assume male superiority, are otherwise."[15] Victims also look around them and know that divorced Catholics are ostracized in the community, leading to a second victimization for believers even in the twenty-first century.

In addition to clergy, these ideas are promulgated by far-right Catholic lay groups. Since the 1980s, the infiltration into American Roman Catholic seminaries, hospitals, parishes, and universities by far-right-leaning Catholic groups—such as Opus Dei, Napa Institute, Legatus, Action Institute, Knights of Columbus, EWTN, First Things, and Legionaries of Christ—expanded the oppressive nature of the church particularly toward women, the poor, and the LGBTQ community. These conservative right-wing Catholic groups champion money, power, and control by means of unrestricted capitalism, rampant individualism, and minimal government support for marginalized people, all in stark contrast to the social teachings of the early church that emphasized compassion and care for the poor and marginalized. Stephen Schneck lamented, "I think we're in a kind of brave new world where these groups really are setting themselves up as authorities" above the bishops, cardinals, and even the pope. "They are challenging the legitimacy of existing structures of authority and trying to fill that space with their own agenda and their own people."[16] For instance, Timothy Busch and his Napa Institute and Foundation hope to take the far-right Catholic ideas into mainstream politics aiming to "affect church institutions and to shape the Catholic narrative for the wider culture by gaining influence on universities and media corporations."[17]

Most young people today, with their unwavering commitment to multiculturalism and social justice, in addition to their deep concern for climate change, pay scant attention to the politics of the far-right Catholic organizations as well as the church's anachronistic teachings on same-sex marriage, birth control, premarital sex, divorce, remarriage, reconciliation, women's "complementary roles,"[18] and other anachronistic church dogma and doctrines. When pushed to align their personal beliefs with those espoused by the church, they leave (in droves). So, there's hope that the far-right Catholic groups will not create a hate-filled world of unrestrained capitalism at the expense of the most vulnerable people. And yet we are left wondering what happened to the millions of lives that were impacted during the last century by the church's failure to address domestic violence and its role in creating the environment in which it flourished.

A case study from the 1960s illustrates the damage instigated by clerics in the church by means of their stance on divine clericalism, divorce, birth control, domestic violence, male superiority, and female subordination. The study illustrates the impact of clerical support for domestic violence perpetrators and the devastating long-term effects on their families. As depressing as it is for the millions of Catholics victimized by these clerics and their ideas, there is a progressive way forward for these survivors outlined at the end of this chapter. Our case study survivor found healing in feminist theology. Using feminist theology and the survival strategies she developed in her childhood, she would help others heal and flourish. (Note: the names in the following case study have been removed to protect domestic violence survivors).

A CASE STUDY

I never had a birthday party—no games, no balloons, no friends, no gifts, and no bakery cake with beautiful sugar flowers. No cake at all. My mother's pregnancy a few short months after my brother's birth was not a welcome surprise, especially to a woman who celebrated her twentieth birthday two months before I was born. Perhaps she hated me because I was a girl or maybe she hated me for invading her body. Either way, I would pay the price for my unwanted birth until I left home at seventeen. I wasn't the only one to suffer for being born to parents that didn't want us. My mother gave birth to six children before she turned twenty-eight. My father—largely absent from our lives—was busy dating other women and squandered his paycheck on alcohol, leaving little money to spend on food and clothing for his growing family. This state of affairs took a toll on my mother mentally and physically. It took a toll on the entire family.

Here is my story.

We moved to a house in Greece, New York—an Italian-American dominated suburb of Rochester—in the early 1960s. My classmates in school enjoyed loving families and a high standard of living. Their parents drove nice cars, the kids owned new bikes and toys, they all wore stylish clothes without holes and stains while we satisfied ourselves with thrift store toys and clothes. Their dads and moms always looked happy when they accompanied their children to school, the playground, and church. They hugged each other and spoke in affectionate terms of endearment while we never had positive experiences with parental contact. Their lives seemed so different from ours including their Catholicism. Unlike the Irish-American penitential guilt-ridden Catholic experience of my youth, these families celebrated life.[19] Our Catholicism taught us that life was a burden to endure, not celebrate. More than anything, I wanted my family to be like theirs.

And yet, I knew in my heart that I wasn't good enough to share in that kind of happiness. I resigned myself to the reality that not everyone is destined to be happy. Indeed, some people, like me, must continually pay for their sinfulness. My first communion[20] was a case in point.

After months of preparation, the nuns warned us that if we arrived even a minute late for this miraculous sacred event, we would not be allowed to participate. God was watching—we had better comply or we would miss out on the most essential sacrament of our lives.

The morning of my first communion, my mother was not in a good mood. She ordered me to clean the family bathroom before I got dressed for the important ceremony. Tried as I might, I couldn't clean the bathroom to her satisfaction. With my third attempt, I knew that I wasn't going to make it to the church on time—what was the point in continuing? The nuns weren't going to let me participate in this crucial event. Everything holy rested upon this important sacrament. My life was ruined. I felt the anger well up in my throat as I picked up my brother's toothbrush and scrubbed the toilet with it one last time before my mother came in for the final inspection. Calling to mind my wicked thoughts and actions, perhaps I wasn't good enough to receive this sacrament after all.

Much to my surprise, this time the toothbrush-scrubbed bathroom passed my mother's inspection. I dressed as quickly as I could and forced the tight-fitting hand-me-down black patent leather shoes onto my feet. I raced down the stairs and stood quietly by the car until my mother took her position in the driver's seat. I started to panic a little when I recounted my actions today. Surely, my evil thoughts and deeds of this day were not included in my penance the day before. Would I rot in hell if I received this holy sacrament without renouncing all of my sins—again? I carefully recited the Act of Contrition in the hopes that I would be worthy of this blessed sacrament.

"Oh my God, I am heartily sorry for having offended Thee, and I detest all my sins because of Thy just punishments, but most of all because they offend Thee, my God, Who art all-good and deserving of all my love. I firmly resolve, with the help of Thy grace, to sin no more and to avoid the near occasions of sin," I recited. I repeated it a second time, for good measure.

My mother didn't say a word until we pulled into the church parking lot. She ordered me to meet her in front of the church when the service was over. I stared at my shoes and shook my head "yes" as I reached for the car door handle. Much to my surprise the nuns gave my mother a stern look when she dropped me off. I felt vindicated.

I was relieved that I wouldn't miss the most important day of my life. The boys and girls all stood solemnly with our hands clasped in prayer until we paraded down the church aisle to our assigned pews. It was a perfect ceremony for an imperfect girl. I silently repeated the Act of Contrition one more time for good measure.

"Oh my God, I am heartily sorry for having offended Thee, and I detest all my sins because of Thy just punishments, but most of all because they offend Thee, my God, Who art all-good and deserving of all my love. I firmly resolve, with the help of Thy grace, to sin no more and to avoid the near occasions of sin," I promised.

After Mass, we all solemnly filed out of the church in two perfect straight lines—one male and one female. On the other side of the huge wooden doors, mothers and fathers hugged their precious children and took them out of line. I walked over to the side of the church to avoid the crowd. So many smiling, happy faces racing by—I had to dodge and weave to stay out of their way. If I fell, my borrowed dress would be ruined, and my mother would kill me, literally. I stepped quickly into the parking lot to avoid most of the people hurrying home to their celebration parties and bakery cakes. When the flood of people got into their cars and drove away, I started to wonder if my mother forgot about me. My feet hurt in the tight hand-me-down patent leather shoes that were a size too small for my fat feet. I didn't dare sit down and mess up the white dress that my mother had borrowed for this momentous occasion. I shifted my stance every thirty seconds as my feet began to burn. I could feel the blisters weeping into my white socks.

A nun came out of the church on her way back to the convent. She stopped and bent down to politely ask if I was all right. I looked at her pinched face in her tight-fitting headdress. Her skin was wrinkled, but it looked as if it would be soft and smooth to the touch. She seemed nice, I thought to myself.

I hardly knew what to say. I wasn't OK. I was never OK. I lived with a mother who threatened to kill her own children every day. And we never questioned her will and means to complete her promise to kill us. But what could this nun do for me? Nothing I reasoned.

I just nodded my head and looked down at my shiny black church shoes. Satisfied with my answer, she stood up and walked briskly past without looking back. Her shoes made a strangely reassuring click, click, click as she walked along the sidewalk. I watched her disappear into the Mother House wishing that I had asked for help. But it was too late for that now.

As I fell into a deep sense of hopelessness, I saw the car enter the church parking lot. My despair quickly turned to fear. I immediately regretted not having moved back to my assigned position at the huge church doors as instructed. The car stopped in front of me and my angry mother got out to check the dress carefully for damage and dirt. Satisfied with the condition of the dress, she sternly reprimanded me for not waiting where she had instructed me to wait. I stared at my shoes and nodded my head as I thanked God for the ride home with a sigh of relief. If only I could take off these tight shoes, I thought to myself, life would be perfect.

When my mother turned down our street, she handed me a small dark green book without taking her eyes off the road. It was a new Catholic missal—a step-by-step instruction manual for every type of Catholic liturgy—in English. My first book. What a perfect gift! I would treasure this book forever. This was better than cake, I thought to myself as I gushed, "Thank you!"

When she parked the car in our driveway, I went to my room to remove the scratchy white dress and the tight black shoes. I laid the dress carefully on the bed and slowly peeled the shiny shoes off of my blistered feet. Having had to deal with these Sunday shoes many times before, I left the socks on my feet knowing that the raw bleeding blisters needed time to heal before removing their protective covers. I sank into my favorite corner of the closet and prayed for smaller feet as I began to recognize that the borrowed dress was more valuable than I was. I held my new missal close to my heart and I gave thanks to God for this sacred day. I began to study the holy book carefully in the dimly lit closet. The more that I read, the clearer my calling became. Without audible words spoken, my heart heard God calling me to the priesthood.

On most Sunday afternoons following this momentous first communion day, I gathered my younger siblings and my older brother to play church. With my new missal in hand, I served my congregation as the priest, carefully replicating all of the movements that the priests performed in the morning's service. This rehearsal for my future service as a priest would be the foundation for helping other people when I grew up, I thought.

One particular Sunday afternoon, I had to ask my mother for the tiny oyster crackers to serve as hosts in my church service—a task that my older brother always performed. I approached my mother as she was washing dishes in the kitchen. Without turning around, she demanded to know what I wanted. "Five oyster crackers for church, please" I replied innocently. In a household with scant resources, we were never allowed to take food without expressed permission. Not even an oyster cracker.

She informed me that we couldn't play church since my older brother was at Boy Scout camp for the weekend. "But I'm the priest," I said without hesitation. I knew instantly that I had made a big mistake. She turned around slowly with her dull pink rubber gloves dripping soapy bubbles onto the floor. Her eyes looked as though she was staring directly into the eyes of Satan. This was the first time, and only time, that my mother looked terrified. The look on her face let me know that I had crossed a line that could lead to my destruction and perhaps the destruction of the whole family. I was about to incur God's wrath and the wrath of His entire church. Oh God, I thought. This is really bad. Really, really, really bad.

She peeled the rubber gloves from her hands and sent me to my room with merely a hand gesture. I walked up the steps slowly trying to make sense of the situation. When I got to the top of the steps, I could hear her talking to someone on the phone in a hushed tone. I stood at the top of the steps, out of sight, until she finished her conversation and called me downstairs. Within minutes, she drove me to the priests' rectory without saying a word.

We were met at the rectory door by an old woman who led us into the great hall. After a few silent minutes, the priest emerged from a large intricately carved door and motioned my mother to enter. I was too horrified to take note of much of my surroundings, but they were familiar enough since my mother often sought spiritual counseling for her dysfunctional marriage here. On those occasions my siblings and I would stand quietly for nearly an hour marked by a chiming clock in the great hall. I imagined that a king's palace might look something like this rectory with its grandeur and opulence.

When the priest opened the door to his office again, my mother stepped out and the priest looked me straight in the eye in a menacing way while tilting his head toward the door indicating that I enter his office. No one said a word. They didn't need to. The looks on their faces told me that I had committed a monumental sin. The priest pointed at the large ornate chair in front of his desk. Obediently, I sat. I felt very small in the colossal chair. Very, very small and powerless.

He sat down in the immense chair opposite mine. The massive wooden desk reminded me of the impenetrable barrier between sinners and saints. One could see over the barrier into the sacred space, but one could not enter that space. The priest rested his chin on his hands poised in prayer. His eyes were closed. The sunlight from the window behind him made the priest glow like an angel. A very angry angel. The wall of silence was broken by the chiming of the golden mantel clock. The priest stared into my eyes for a solid minute trying to see inside my soul to find out why a young girl would commit such a scandalous sin. When he finally spoke, he explained to me that my heinous, sinful actions must never be repeated and then he told me to recite the Act of Contrition. I did so with precision.

"Oh my God, I am heartily sorry for having offended Thee, and I detest all my sins because of Thy just punishments, but most of all because they offend Thee, my God, Who art all-good and deserving of all my love. I firmly resolve, with the help of Thy grace, to sin no more and to avoid the near occasions of sin," I pledged.

The priest told me to recite this prayer every hour of every day until my next confession on Saturday when a priest would absolve me of my sins, if I promised never to commit this heinous sin again. He assured me that my mother would also pay penance this week for failing to instill proper Catholic values in me. I looked at my shoes and nodded my head.

The horror just kept coming in crashing wave after crashing wave. I would spend the next week with a mother who was being punished by God and the church for *my* sins. This would not end well for me. I wondered if I would live to see my absolution on Saturday.

It was a particularly brutal week. My mother thought that sparing the rod might have provoked my sinfulness, so she laid the long punishment baton (that felt like cement rebar) on my backside multiple times a day. I tried to disappear, I squeezed my eyes tightly closed during these painful punishments and I doubled up on the Act of Contrition prayers after each beating hoping that I would be redeemed. Additionally, my mother thought that keeping me home from school to clean, do laundry, and watch the babies would also teach me not to overstep my boundaries again. If I was kept busy, I couldn't sin she reasoned. I prayed that Saturday's confession would come quickly before I died of exhaustion.

By Friday morning I was of little use to anyone after working at home all week. So, my mother sent me to school. I was so tired, sore, and hungry that by 10 o'clock I was resting my head on my school desk feeling a little woozy. The teacher walked up to my desk and slammed her hand right next to my ear with a thunderous jolt that startled everyone in the room. I jumped up in my seat. She loudly chastised me for being lazy and stupid, demanding that I stand at attention in the back corner. I obediently took my place in the back of the room and tried to figure out what I had done wrong when my head began to spin. I couldn't see anything even though my eyes were wide opened. As I fainted, I dropped straight back onto the cement floor with a crashing thud. When I woke, the teacher gave me a glass of water and I was instructed to walk home since I wasn't smart enough to stay awake in class. I walked home slowly, not just because of the dizziness or the throbbing knot on my head, but because I knew I was going to be punished when I got home. If my mother was having a bad day, as she often did, the punishment would be brutal.

As part of my mother's penance, she began watching Bishop Fulton Sheen's television program. She bought his books and read them as if they held the answers to true happiness. Sheen, in many of his programs, argued that marriage partners were gifts from God and as such we must accept our partners as they are, bitter or sweet, faithful or unfaithful, nasty or loving. The acceptance of a cheating, alcoholic husband was merely a cross to bear. Any other way of looking at God's gift was selfish and sinful.[21] I'm not sure why these messages helped my mother, but they did. Perhaps the happiest moment that I ever witnessed was when my mother arrived home after meeting Bishop Sheen of Rochester in person. She told everyone that she had a signed copy of one of his books. She acted like she had met Jesus and he had personally anointed her. My mother's renewed holiness didn't, however, keep her from beating the hell out of me. In her mind, I represented the very essence of evil in her household rather than a gift from God.

After my penance faded in my mind a few months later, I began to rethink my calling to the priesthood. I must have misunderstood God's message. Clearly the priest and my mother knew that a girl couldn't be a priest, so why would God ask me to do this?

EMPOWERING DOMESTIC ABUSERS

Our case study demonstrates the many factors influencing the character of Catholic families in the 1960s that circumvented uniformity, namely socio-economic differences, ethnicity, and the theological incursion of Jansenism into the very fabric of some Roman Catholic families. Despite these differences between Catholic families, the church's emphasis on hierarchical power and control over the sacred rites, scripture, and access to the divine provided little room for spiritual healing and growth among congregants. In their view, complying with rules and regulations demonstrated one's faith. Total disregard for true pastoral care led to the psychosis of an entire generation and emboldened domestic abusers as well as ordained sexual predators.

This fatal error on the part of the church created the rampant toleration of pedophile priests and ensured an abuse of their power that impacted nearly every Catholic in a negative way.[22] The hierarchy believed that they were saintly intercessors to God. They did not need to abide by human norms or laws, while at the same time they made their congregations feel guilt and shame in order to control them. Some of the hierarchy's behaviors crippled people for life—some led to suicides.[23] They destroyed lives and they destroyed families. And yet, there has been little in the way of compensation or even remorse on the part of these perpetrators.

Why? Because even today, clerics still believe that they stand above the laity—closer to God. When the mother in our case study sought out several priests for spiritual healing as she dealt with a cheating husband for more than a decade, the priests were only interested in mandating compliance to the sacred sacrament of marriage for life. They told her that it was her duty to God to keep bearing children that she could not tolerate and often could not afford to clothe or feed. They told her that her husband's cheating would be dealt with by God, and that she must not judge him. Instead, clerics instructed her to look at her own sinfulness that caused God to give her this particular cross to bear.

Their advice was detrimental to everyone concerned—it protected and encouraged the guilty, while oppressing and traumatizing everyone else. The most important issue in the minds of church leaders was preserving the man-made sacrament of marriage—a sacrament that didn't even exist for hundreds of years after Christ's time on earth. When the church decided to regulate marriage, it did so to control family wealth. Controlling marriage and divorce did not encourage spiritual healing or growth. If only these ordained men knew a little of their own real history—not the lies that they were taught in seminary—Catholics might have avoided the rampant empowerment of domestic abusers and priestly predators.

Marriage as we know it today is a very modern social construct. Certainly, the church did not pay much attention to marriage until the twelfth century when men decided that it was an official sacrament. "In fact, before the eleventh century there was no such thing as a Christian wedding ceremony in the Latin church, and throughout the Middle Ages there was no single church ritual for solemnizing the marriages between Christians. It was only after the Council of Trent, because of the need to eliminate abuses in the practice of clandestine or secret marriages, that a standard Catholic wedding rite came into existence." Moreover, "parallel to the absence of any church ceremony for uniting Christians in marriage was the absence of any uniform ecclesiastical regulations regarding marriage during the early centuries of Christianity."[24] Thus, both marriage and divorce are social constructions that have changed over time. Significantly, there is no biblical mandate for any particular form, process, or procedure for either. "Today some Catholic theologians and canon lawyers are themselves asking whether it might be better to let the legal regulation of marriage revert back to civic control, without denying that church weddings are important communal celebrations or that Christian marriages are sacramental."[25]

Not only did the church hierarchy create a fraudulent sacrament of marriage based on the desire for power and authority, but they also neglected the real needs of children in these marriages. When many priests and nuns saw a visually troubled child in the case study discussed, no one did anything. One priest made the situation worse when faced with a young girl who practiced being a priest. He added to her already diminished self-worth by placing the blame of all sin on her tiny little back. This priest's culpability increases significantly when we acknowledge that he knew this family's dysfunctional history in his role as the mother's confessor. The clergy's primary concern focused on the need to control the laity as a means to bolster clerical power and authority.

The Act of Contrition is a significant example of their destructive psychological control over the minds of young people. "Oh my God, I am heartily sorry for having offended Thee, and I detest all my sins because of Thy just punishments, but most of all because they offend Thee, my God." The message sent by the priest underscored the laity's powerlessness as well as emphasizing human evilness. What kind of God would punish a child for pretending to be a priest when she felt called by God to do so? The priest's punishment *justified* and *legitimized* all of the physical and psychological assaults that the victims in this case study endured. All in the name of power—church power and authority.

The gender politics of the sacrament of reconciliation encouraged the young girl to blame herself for many sins that others had perpetrated. Taking responsibility for these very painful events and asking forgiveness from a male who held power over her and her family did not provide this young Catholic with a pathway to forgiveness and healing. Furthermore, this penance ritual of self-hatred created a misleading view of its connection to the Eucharist[26] based upon its distorted gender politics. God never intended for Catholics to take responsibility for the sins perpetrated on them before being worthy to receive the body of Christ in the Eucharist. Indeed, God is not the vengeful one looking for female humiliation and total subjugation to males with power as described earlier. The focus on a little girl's sinfulness, at best, made clerics complicit in the abuse. At worst, the church was the very source of the evil that created the abusive adults in this girl's life.

THE LITTLE GIRL GROWS UP

In response to God's call, the little girl in the case study played church until adults found out that her brother was on the receiving end of the Eucharist. Once it was made clear that girls could not be priests, the little girl began envisioning herself as a future saint. The many examples of female saints in religion classes assured her that this calling was attainable, unlike that of a priest. However, this goal drifted away when she recognized her many faults. Clerics had successfully inculcated the process of self-reflection focused on one's sinfulness in this young girl at an early age.

For our case study survivor, turbulent teens turned into many years of responsible motherhood and then professional development all within the framework of the good Catholic mother until her youngest sister died unexpectedly in 2007. Before her death, her sister attended a progressive Roman Catholic Church with a female pastoral associate. This pastoral associate assisted the family in the funeral arrangements, and she presided over the gravesite ceremony. It was this experience that reopened our case study girl's heart to God's call to the priesthood.

Returning home, our case study survivor approached her parish priest to gather more information concerning women serving the church as pastoral associates with similar duties to male deacons. The priest looked sternly at her and asked why *ANYONE* would want a female pastoral associate, rather than a real priest, officiating at a gravesite? Why indeed, she thought.

Confident in her calling now, she enrolled in the Roman Catholic seminary's lay pastoral ministry program. She took graduate courses in the Old and New Testaments, church history, moral theology, social ethics, faith formation, and the theology of the church. She also spent a good deal of time with a mentor/spiritual advisor as part of this program. The program helped this woman to recognize that her special calling had been to serve single mothers who make up the vast majority of impoverished adults in the world today. They have little hope of breaking out of the poverty cycle without marketable skills.

Yet, instructors at the seminary had little to say regarding women and minorities. Priests used pejorative terms such as "whore," "slut," and "prostitute," for women with the notable exception of the Virgin Mary. And little regard was paid to the fact that Jesus was a brown Jew when referring to Muslims, and people of color as the "other." Discouraged by the omnipresent misogyny and racism in the seminary, our survivor sought out graduate courses at a local college where the more inclusive atmosphere of a Religious Studies program energized her. Graduate courses such as Religion and Human Development, Spirituality of Leadership, Spiritual Care Ministry, and Addiction and the Spiritual Life had a significant impact on her spiritual growth. More importantly, the course on feminist theology[27] allowed her to see God's calling clearly for the first time.

Several key scholars helped open her eyes to God's plan. Mary Malone wrote "Generations of Christians have accepted the invisibility or forcible exclusion of women as an essential part of Christian really, and have associated with this with a particular organization of gender: men lead, women follow, for example. . . . Sometimes explicitly, always implicitly, the conclusion has been that there is something more divine about maleness than there is within Christianity."[28] Malone attempts to recover the important leadership roles of women in the New Testament to counter these assumptions of divine maleness in the church today.

The good news, according to Malone, is that the sacred texts—both canonical and apocryphal—*do* provide women with models for an egalitarian spirituality as well as a foundation for participating on a "perfectly equal footing" in Christian institutions beginning with Genesis 1:26–27 and Paul's letter to the Galatians (Gal 3:27–28).[29] Particularly Catholic women (since Catholics had been discouraged from reading the complex and often contradictory Bible) began to question in the 1960s and 1970s why men in power emphasized the Genesis story in which Eve sprang from Adam's rib rather than the alternative story that underscores their equality. "So, God created humankind in his image, in the image of God he created them; male and female he created them."[30] Why had Catholics been told in sermons, school, films, books, etc. that women were the root cause of all human suffering through Eve when the Bible contained other more empowering stories for women? Similarly, Paul's letter to the Galatians clearly places everyone—regardless of religious upbringing, age, ethnicity, race, *or sex*—on equal footing in Christ.[31] Malone argues that "These two texts became a kind of biblical charter for a new community of female and male disciples and continue to act as inspiration to millions of women believers."[32]

Additionally, Malone points out several other New Testament examples of equitable roles for women in the church as leading disciples of Christ including Mary, the mother of Jesus, the women from Galilee, the anointing woman, the healed women, Martha and Mary, the Samaritan woman, and Mary Magdalene. Charged with doing God's work, the Blessed Virgin Mary "was far from being a timidly submissive woman or one whose piety was repellent to others."[33] And while Marian worship has experienced several long periods of adulation, other women in the New Testament have gone largely unnoticed in their roles as disciples. Both the gospels attributed to Luke and Mark confirm that a large group of Galilean women were disciples of Christ. Luke's version begins to place these empowered female disciples into more conventional gender roles that attribute their leadership to either "grateful clients, who had been healed by Jesus, or wealthy women who 'provided for him out of their resources.'"[34] Regardless of the attempt to downplay the importance of female disciples, these women remain powerful models and suggest many important female leadership possibilities within the church.

Malone summarizes for her readers how feminist scholars have used this information to begin paving the way for a more equalitarian church. Feminist exegesis—that is to say viewing sacred text from the perspective of its original audience—and feminist hermeneutics (focused on a usable-past) have each provided us with food for thought. In other words, Malone finds value in asking both questions: should we judge people of the past through the lens of their own culture (exegesis) or should we interpret the past in order to extract greater meaning for our own society (hermeneutics)? Regardless of the methodology, Malone argues "the good news of Jesus shows no demeaning word whatever towards women" and that "the invitation to co-discipleship seemed to be always part of the intention of Jesus in his words and actions."[35] Male leaders in the church have distorted women's role in the early church in order to subjugate women and build an institutional patriarchy of the church. However, Malone and other feminist scholars offer hope that women can reclaim positive female leadership role models.

Similarly, in "Female-Friendly Pastoral Care," Carolyn Stahl Bohler illustrates just how pervasive and destructive the distortion of women's spirituality has been on the lives of women and men.[36] She writes "women family therapists began to notice gender biases in the therapy they were practicing, and these therapists began to seek to correct those biases."[37] Based upon the strategies and suggestions of these female healthcare providers, Bohler provides pastoral caregivers some useful tools for identifying and overcoming gender bias as a means to provide peace and justice to all.

According to our case study female, one of the most important suggestions that she has come to appreciate in her own work as an adult is the art of listening—really listening—to others without imposing preconceived prejudices upon the speaker. Particularly well-educated people often begin constructing their next response after speaking rather than wait to listen to the other speaker. Bohler also reminds us to take extra care not to assume that the speaker's issues reflect cultural norms or gendered expectations of behavior. In other words, we often don't hear what females are really saying without projecting our own social expectations on what we expect them to say. Additionally, "Just as we pastors need to hear despair and pain, when that is a woman's experience, if we listen, we will hear resilience and relief expressed by women, too. In our rush not to avoid the despair, we may miss the particular woman before us, who is relieved or feeling freed and who now wants from us only a confirmation of her experience."[38] In other words, pastoral caregivers must encourage women to embrace their right and authority to speak by becoming a "truthful, accurate mirror . . . that evokes authority in the woman. I do not take authority from her, nor assume that I have it to give her. She has it. I name it."[39]

Bohler also reminds us that women are socialized to "consider others' desires and interests above their own" often to the point that women fail to recognize their own desires and wants.[40] Our job then is to assist women in identifying their desires and balance those with the desires of the people they care for. Bohler warns "She may be sorting out her orientation toward that basic internal conflict between care for self and care for others, a conflict that will never go away."[41] Similarly, pastors may be inclined to press women for their own culpability in cases of abuse or other injustices. These assumptions build on our cultural bias that assumes female responsibility for dysfunctional relationships. "Most pastors would not dream of intentionally blaming one member of a family for the whole situation within that family. However, our culture is so attached to female blaming, especially mother blaming, that it takes enormous efforts to wean ourselves from this practice."[42] Bohler encourages us to "think contextually, to consider the family, and we must also think about the larger contexts, bigger than families—churches, cultural messages, economic systems—which 'enable' the male, in this case, to continue his behavior unchecked."[43]

Bringing about a more just world, however, is difficult. Joan Chittister suggests that male inherent superiority has been established and reified in both theology and modern law often reinforced by women themselves when they embrace assertions of male domination over human property.[44] Following the dictates of law and habit, Chittister suggests "Obedience to legitimate authority constituted a cornerstone of patriarchal spirituality."[45] And since the purpose of patriarchy is to gain additional power through manipulation and charismatic charm, the ideas of equity and justice (social or environmental) are completely lost because "People with power on their minds do not have the aims of the group in mind."[46] Feminist scholars—as our case study survivor came to know—have concrete ideas for achieving equity and justice.

A PROGRESSIVE WAY FORWARD

Surely, the church has changed somewhat since the 1960s in part due to unfolding global sexual assault crimes and their subsequent massive cover up. But the fact that the church supported the terrible behavior of those in charge of minors is unconscionable. A total lack of regard for pastoral care displaced by the inculcation of dogma suggests that there were far more twentieth-century casualties than the pedophile scandal and worldwide cover-up would suggest. Regardless of any progress the institutional church has made in the last fifty years, the cancerous far-right infiltration in today's seminaries strives to return the church to the destructive, controlling methods of mid-century Catholicism. Then why, you might ask, would women, like our case study survivor, seek ordination to the priesthood?

To answer that question, most Roman Catholic women priests (many of whom grew up in the 1960s similar to our case study subject) often cite their baptism and their strong commitment to the community of people that make up the church without supporting the hierarchy's domination and oppression of the laity.[47] They embrace Vatican II's declaration that the church is the community of the baptized—not the hierarchy—and that all people are all called to be priests, prophets, and shepherds.[48] In their estimation, religion should never be a sin-management program that serves the needs of an institution at the expense of the laity. Religion should encourage spiritual healing and growth that suits the needs of individuals and encourages unconditional love for all of God's Creation. Growing closer to Creation and the divine should be the goal—not gaining and maintaining control over people.

Women priests seek to offer a Catholic alternative to the hierarchy that exists—one in which priests are equal partners in the human family intent on helping others to heal and grow spiritually without man-made rules and dogma. According to women priests, when God called women to ordination, God intended for them to show all people that the hierarchy had taken the wrong path from the beginning of its institutionalization. God intended humans to seek inclusive communities that spread the ideology of unconditional love. That's the real message—live as Christ lived, humbly and full of love for everyone. "Which is the foremost of all the commandments? Jesus replied: This is the foremost. Hear, O Israel, God, our God, is one. You must love the Most High God with all your heart, with all your soul, with all your mind and with all your strength. The second is this: You must love your neighbor as yourself. There is no commandment greater than these"

(Mark 12: 29–31). Christ had no rules other than to love everyone. This unconditional love that Christ modeled requires women priests to aid all of God's creations. People are not depraved original sin-infected humans as the pervasive Atonement Theology[49] professes. Instead, women priests teach that God loves each of us exactly as we are.

Women priests also believe that God calls us to push ourselves outside our comfort zones in order to be all that we can be—to make this world a better place. Indeed, we are called to be co-creators with God—called to assist in the continuous unfolding of the universe. We are called to a fuller life, not guilt. Their collective ministry focuses on being a source of *life* and love as they help others to be all they can be. In other words, women priests must help themselves and others to heal and grow following Jesus's life as a model. They often remind us of Jesus's words, "I came that people may have life and have it abundantly" (John 10:10).

So Roman Catholic women priests all over the world lead by example. They help the poor, the LGBTQ community, the infirm, the dying, the mentally ill, the imprisoned, the divorced, the abandoned people that the church hierarchy leaves behind in addition to tending to the needs of the environment and members of the animal family. Women priests and bishops don't stand above others. They walk alongside God's creations and listen and respond to their needs.

Women priests believe that God has invited all humans to be co-creators in this unfolding miracle of life and God has called women to lead this resurrected way of life because the male hierarchy has botched it so badly for so long. So, the next time you see or hear of the church hierarchy mandating compliance with hateful rules that vilify feminists, the LGBTQ community, and other marginalized groups, women priests want you to know that there is an alternative—the unconditional love espoused by Christ.

So, while feminist theology could do little to ameliorate the actual trauma of abused children, it could offer a path forward. Feminist theology has had a tremendously empowering and transformative impact on the lives of many women priests. Their role as spiritual caregivers centers on spiritual growth and empowerment of others rather than the dogma of organized religion that emphasized sin and punishment. Assisting others in their spiritual growth requires women priests to meet people where they are and provide them with challenging and empowering steps forward. They believe they are called "to preserve the unity of the spirit through the bond of peace: one body and one Spirit … one faith, one baptism; one God who is over all and through all and in all" (Eph 4:3–6). Similar to spiritual directors, women priests work to empower others to recognize *their* calling and achieve *their* missions. In the words of Joan Chittister, "We have a responsibility to the ongoing creation of life, and we share that with our humble God who is accompanying us—not monitoring us, not abandoning us, not setting out to 'catch us'—but a God who supports us. A summoning God who asks us to keep looking—A God who calls us to fullness."[50]

NOTES

1. Jansenism is a Calvinist-influenced theology founded on the writings of Cornelius Jansen (d. 1638) that came to dominate the theology of Irish and Irish American clergy in the nineteenth and twentieth centuries. This theology focuses on original sin and human depravity. For the impact of Jansenism on American Catholics, see Ross Douthat, "The Tragedy of Irish Catholicism," *The New York Times*, December 1, 2009, http://www.bishop-accountability.org/news2009/11_12/2009_12_01_Douthat_TheTragedy.htm.

2. See, for instance, Blake Griffin Edwards, "Alarming Effects of Children's Exposure to Domestic Violence," *Psychology Today*, February 26, 2019, https://www.psychologytoday.com/us/blog/progress-notes/201902/alarming-effects-childrens-exposure-domestic-violence and, Office of Women's Health, "Effects of Domestic Violence on Children," US Department of Health and Human Services, April 2, 2–19, https://www.womenshealth.gov/relationships-and-safety/domestic-violence/effects-domestic-violence-children.

3. See, for instance, Charles Morris, *American Catholic: The Saints and Sinners Who Built the Most Powerful Church* (Vintage, 1998) and Courtney Mares, "Pope Francis: Clericalism Linked to Fixation on Sexual Morality," *The Catholic Herald*, September 26, 2019.

4. Alanna Vagianos, "Domestic Violence Is the Most Common Killer of Women around the World," *Huffpost*, November 27, 2018, https://www.huffpost.com/entry/domestic-violence-most-common-killer-of-women-united-nations_n_5bfbf61ee4b0eb6d931142ac.

5. Catholic News Agency, "How the Church Can Better Respond to the Problem of Domestic Violence," *The Catholic World Report*, June 23, 2019, https://www.catholicnewsagency.com/news/how-the-church-can-better-respond-to-the-problem-of-domestic-violence-95314.

6. Catholic News Agency, "How the Church Can Better Respond to the Problem of Domestic Violence."

7. Hayley Gleeson and Julia Baird, "'Their cross to bear': The Catholic women told to forgive domestic violence," *ABC News*, November 4, 2017, abc.net.au/news/2017-11-04.

8. Ibid.

9. Biblical scholars are deeply divided concerning the authorship of Colossians. Only seven of the thirteen letters attributed to Paul in the New Testament are widely judged to be Paul's writings; namely, Corinthians 1&2, Galatians, Philemon, Philippians, Romans, 1 Thessalonians. See for instance: James Dunn and John Rogerson, *Eerdmans Commentary on the Bible* (Eerdmans Publishing, 2003) and David Aune, *The Blackwell Companion to the New Testament* (Blackwell Publishing, 2010).

10. Gleeson and Baird, "'Their cross to bear.'"

11. Pope Francis, *Amoris Laetitia* (in English), https://w2.vatican.va/content/dam/francesco/pdf/apost_exhortations/documents/papa-francesco_esortazione-ap_20160319_amoris-laetitia_en.pdf .

12. Canon Law in the Roman Catholic Church is established through papal pronouncements across time.

13. Gleeson and Baird, "'Their cross to bear.'"

14. Ibid.

15. Ibid.

16. Tom Roberts, "The Rise of the Catholic Right," *Sojourners* (March 2019), sojo.net/magazine/march-2019 (September 10, 2019).

17. Roberts, "The Rise of the Catholic Right." See also Joshua McElwee, "Francis Warns of Ideology 'infiltrating' Some Quarters of the U.S. Catholic Church," *National Catholic Reporter*, September 10, 2019, https://www.ncronline.org/news/vatican/francis-warns-ideology-infiltrating-some-quarters-us-catholic-church.

18. The Roman Catholic notion of Complementarianism prescribes mutually exclusive, complementary roles for males and females based upon male superiority. These roles aim to separate and subjugate women.

19. Jansenism—with its emphasis on original sin and human depravity—came to dominate Irish and Irish American Catholicism since Irish Catholic families tended to send at least one son into the priesthood.

20. First communion for Roman Catholics is a sacrament marking the first time a child earns the right to receive the holy Eucharist (bread transformed through the process of transubstantiation into the body of Christ) symbolizing one's communion with the congregation and God as a visible sign of God's grace. This can only take place after the child's first sacrament of reconciliation in which the child repents for all of their sins and is then absolved by a priest.

21. Many of Bishop Sheen's televised programs on marriage have been uploaded into YouTube by far-right Catholic groups in their efforts to reinvigorate efforts to subjugate women. See, for instance, *Sensus Fidelium*, "Marriage & Incompatibility—Archbishop Fulton Sheen" (originally broadcast in 1964), YouTube video, December 29, 2012. https://www.youtube.com/watch?v=QtMKPaG7vVA

22. See, for instance, Emma Green, "Why Does the Catholic Church Keep Failing on Sexual Abuse?" *The Atlantic*, February 14, 2019, https://www.theatlantic.com/politics/archive/2019/02/sean-omalley-pope-francis-catholic-church-sex-abuse/582658/.

23. Sarah MacDonald, "Irish Priest: Sex Abuse Victims Lost to Suicide 'could have been saved.'" *National Catholic Reporter*, September 8, 2016, https://www.ncronline.org/blogs/ncr-today/irish-priest-sex-abuse-victims-lost-suicide-could-have-been-saved.

24. Joseph Martos, *Doors to the Sacred: A Historical Introduction to the Sacraments* (Liguori, Missouri: Liguori Publications, 2001), 351.

25. Martos, *Doors to the Sacred*, 352.

26. The holy Eucharist for Catholics is the real presence of Christ after bread is transformed by a male priest (via the process of transubstantiation) into the actual body of Christ.

27. Feminist theology requires scholars to view religious traditions, practices, scripture, and theology from a feminist perspective. Rosemary Radford Ruether defined feminist theology as "the promotion of the full humanity of women." Ruether, *Sexism and God-Talk: Towards a Feminist Theology* (London, 1992), 18.

28. Mary T. Malone, *Women and Christianity: The First Thousand Years* (New York: Maryknoll, 2001), 40–41.

29. Malone, *Women and Christianity*, 18.

30. Ibid., 43.

31. Ibid., 43.

32. Ibid., 44.

33. Quote from Pope Paul VI found in Malone, 45–46.

34. Malone, *Women and Christianity*, 47.

35. Ibid., 62.

36. Carolyn Stahl Bohler, "Female-Friendly Pastoral Care," in Jeanne Moessner (ed.), *The Eyes of Understanding* (Fortress Press, 1996), 27–49.

37. Bohler, "Female-Friendly Pastoral Care," 28.

38. Ibid., 31.

39. Ibid., 39.

40. Ibid., 29.

41. Ibid., 31.

42. Ibid., 42.

43. Ibid., 34.

44. Joan Chittister, *Heart of Flesh: A Feminist Spirituality for Women and Men* (Grand Rapids, Mich.: Eerdman, 1998), 63.

45. Chittister, *Heart of Flesh*, 64.

46. Ibid., 65.

47. See, for instance, the Association of Roman Catholic Women Priests and the Roman Catholic Women Priests websites: arcwp.org, romancatholicwomen-priests.org.

48. Paul VI, *Lumen Gentium,* November 21, 1964, http://archive.wf-f.org/LumenGentium.html.

49. Atonement theology is best distilled down into the common phrase "Jesus died for our sins." The idea that human salvation rests upon the sacrifice of Christ is not biblical, but instead stems from the writings of Augustine (d. 430) and Anselm of Canterbury (d. 1109). See, for instance, Bishop John Shelby Spong, "Why Atonement Theology Will Kill Christianity," YouTube video, 2015, https://www.youtube.com/watch?v=jKNup9gEBdg.

50. Chittister, *Heart of Flesh*, 63.

BIBLIOGRAPHY

Aune, David. *The Blackwell Companion to the New Testament.* Hoboken, NJ: Blackwell Publishing, 2010.

Bohler, Carolyn Stahl. "Female-Friendly Pastoral Care." In *The Eyes of Understanding,* edited by Jeanne Moessner, 27–49. Minneapolis, MN: Fortress Press, 1996.

Catholic News Agency. "How the Church Can Better Respond to the Problem of Domestic Violence." *The Catholic World Report*, June 23, 2019, https://www.catholicnewsagency.com/news/how-the-church-can-better-respond-to-the-problem-of-domestic-violence-95314.

Chittister, Joan. *Heart of Flesh: A Feminist Spirituality for Women and Men*. Grand Rapids, MI: Eerdmans Publishing, 1998.

Douthat, Ross. "The Tragedy of Irish Catholicism." *The New York Times*, December 1, 2009, http://www.bishopaccountability.org/news2009/11_12/2009_12_01_Douthat_TheTragedy.htm.

Dunn, James and Rogerson, John. *Eerdmans Commentary on the Bible*. Grand Rapids, MI: Eerdmans Publishing, 2003.

Edwards, Blake Griffin. "Alarming Effects of Children's Exposure to Domestic Violence." *Psychology Today*, February 26, 2019, https://www.psychologytoday.com/us/blog/progress-notes/201902/alarming-effects-childrens-exposure-domestic-violence.

Francis, *Amoris Laetitia* (The Joy of Love), 2015. https://w2.vatican.va/content/dam/francesco/pdf/apost_exhortations/documents/papa-francesco_esortazione-ap_20160319_amoris-laetitia_en.pdf.

Gleeson, Hayley and Julia Baird. "'Their cross to bear': The Catholic Women Told to Forgive Domestic Violence." *ABC News*, November 4, 2017, abc.net.au/news/2017-11-04.

Green, Emma. "Why Does the Catholic Church Keep Failing on Sexual Abuse?" *The Atlantic*, February 14, 2019, https://www.theatlantic.com/politics/archive/2019/02/sean-omalley-pope-francis-catholic-church-sex-abuse/582658/.

Malone, Mary. *Women and Christianity: The First Thousand Years*. New York: Maryknoll, 2001.

Mares, Courtney. "Pope Francis: Clericalism Linked to Fixation on Sexual Morality." *The Catholic Herald*, September 26, 2019.

Martos, Joseph. *Doors to the Sacred: A Historical Introduction to the Sacraments*. Liguori, MO: Liguori Publications, 2001.

MacDonald, Sarah. "Irish Priest: Sex Abuse Victims Lost to Suicide 'could have been saved,'" *National Catholic Reporter*, September 8, 2016, https://www.ncronline.org/blogs/ncr-today/irish-priest-sex-abuse-victims-lost-suicide-could-have-been-saved.

McElwee, Joshua. "Francis Warns of Ideology 'infiltrating' Some Quarters of the US Catholic Church." *National Catholic Reporter*, September 10, 2019, https://www.ncronline.org/news/vatican/francis-warns-ideology-infiltrating-some-quarters-us-catholic-church.

Morris, Charles. *American Catholic: The Saints and Sinners Who Built the Most Powerful Church*. New York: Vintage, 1998.

Office of Women's Health. "Effects of Domestic Violence on Children." US Department of Health and Human Services, April 2, 2–19, https://www.womenshealth.gov/relationships-and-safety/domestic-violence/effects-domestic-violence-children.

Paul VI. *Lumen Gentium*. November 21, 1964, http://archive.wf-f.org/LumenGentium.html.

Roberts, Tom. "The Rise of the Catholic Right." *Sojourners*, March 2019, sojo.net/magazine/march-2019.

Ruether, Rosemary Radford. *Sexism and God-Talk: Towards a Feminist Theology*. London: Beacon Press, 1992.

Sensus Fidelium. "Marriage & Incompatibility—Archbishop Fulton Sheen" (originally broadcast in 1964). YouTube video. December 29, 2012. https://www.youtube.com/watch?v=QtMKPaG7vVA.

Spong, John Shelby. "Why Atonement Theology Will Kill Christianity." YouTube video, 2015, https://www.youtube.com/watch?v=jKNup9gEBdg.

Vagianos, Alanna. "Domestic Violence Is the Most Common Killer of Women around the World." *Huffpost*, November 27, 2018, https://www.huffpost.com/entry/domestic-violence-most-common-killer-of-women-united-nations_n_5bfbf61ee4b0eb6d931142ac.

Index

Note: Page numbers followed by 'n' refer to notes.

About the Contributors

Mary Sue Barnett is a Catholic woman priest, ordained by the Association of Roman Catholic Women Priests. She is the founder and president of the Louisville Coalition for CEDAW (Convention on the Elimination of all Forms of Discrimination Against Women), a grassroots nongovernmental organization that seeks to implement the rights and principles of this United Nations women's treaty on the local level. She also serves as a chaplain at a psychiatric hospital.

Miriam Duignan is head of communications at the Wijngaards Institute for Catholic Research, home of the academic website womenpriests.org and she is a leader of the campaign group Women's Ordination Worldwide. Born in the UK to Irish parents, Miriam's Catholic education included postgraduate studies at the Jesuit School of Theology in Berkeley, California.

Siobhan Fleming earned a PhD in Higher Education Research and Policy Analysis from the University of Oregon and an MA in Communication from Pepperdine University. She has worked as a researcher in higher education for more than fifteen years in the United States and in Ireland. She currently is Director of Research Development at the University of Texas at San Antonio. She is also a private researcher and consultant drawing on her education and experience in Catholic higher education conducting historical research on the sexual abuse crisis in the Church.

Pierre Hegy is sociology professor emeritus at Adelphi University in Garden City, New York. He taught for two years in Lima, Peru, and one year in Taipei, Taiwan. His main research interests are in the sociology of religion and church renewal. His notable publications include *L'autorité dans le* *catholicisme contemporain, Wake up, Lazarus,* and more recently, *Worship as Community Drama.*

Sylvia Hübel is a bioethicist and feminist theologian committed to advocating and promoting women's equal participation in church and society. She earned a Systematic Theology degree at the Université Catholique de Louvain with a thesis on *The Deconstruction of Male Discourse in the Theological Work of Elisabeth Schüssler-Fiorenza* and continued her work with a PhD thesis titled *Women's Lived Experiences of Reproductive Technologies* from a feminist bioethical perspective. She has held various positions as a teacher, researcher, and parliamentary adviser. Her research interests include theological ethics, medical ethics and humanities (phenomenology of illness, experiences of illness and medical care), women's reproductive health and rights, and healthcare policy.

Mary E. Hunt is co-founder and co-director of the Women's Alliance for Theology, Ethics and Ritual (WATER), Silver Spring, Maryland. She is an editor of *A Guide for Women in Religion: Making Your Way from A to Z* (2004, 2014) and co-editor with Diann L. Neu of *New Feminist Christianity: Many Voices, Many Views* (2010).

Debra Meyers received her PhD from the University of Rochester and is a full professor at Northern Kentucky University teaching a variety of courses in gender studies, history, and religious studies. Meyers has published eight books and dozens of scholarly journal articles and encyclopedia entries. She earned the esteemed Milburn Outstanding Professor award at Northern Kentucky University in 2019 for her distinguished service, exceptional scholarship, and excellence in teaching. Meyers is currently working on her next book, *Gender, Love, and Religion in the Early Chesapeake.*

Jo Scott-Coe is the author of two nonfiction books: *Teacher at Point Blank,* a memoir in essays, and *MASS: A Sniper, a Father, and a Priest,* a first-time exploration of the relationship between the University Texas at Austin mass shooter (1966) and his shadowy priest mentor, Rev. Joseph Leduc. Her work has been published widely in venues including *Salon, American Studies Journal, Pacific Coast Philology, Tahoma Literary Review, Talking Writing, Catapult, River Teeth, Ninth Letter,* and *Fourth Genre.* She is an associate professor of English at Riverside City College, where she was named 57th Distinguished Faculty Lecturer. Scott-Coe also facilitates community writing workshops for the Inlandia Institute. She is currently at work on a new book titled *First Responder,* a life-in-letters of Kathy Leissner Whitman.

Paul Tenkotte, PhD, has edited/authored fourteen books and study guides, contributed chapters and essays to eight other books, and written hundreds of articles for a wide range of publications. His works include topics in the United States, World, and Asian History, as well as a digital textbook, *The United States since 1865: Information Literacy and Critical Thinking* (2019). In addition, he has been a contributor to sixteen television documentaries and is a professor of history at Northern Kentucky University.

Tara M. Tuttle is the assistant dean for Diversity and Inclusion and Senior Lewis Lecturer in the Lewis Honors College at the University of Kentucky. She holds a doctorate in Interdisciplinary Humanities and a graduate certificate in Women's and Gender Studies from the University of Louisville. Her research examines the intersections of religious belief and female sexuality in contemporary American culture and the deployment of scriptural rhetoric to challenge bigotry and oppression.